Rx SHIKSE

A Transplacental Romance

FURTHER CONSPIRACIES?!

If you would like to read further on the New Age Conspiracy to elevate Human Consciousness on this Planet and elsewhere—don't simply ask your book dealer to order the following titles—**Demand that S/He do so!** They are:

THE FUTURE HISTORY SERIES
By Timothy Leary, Ph.D.

Info-Psychology
Neuropolitique
The Intelligence Agents
What Does WoMan Want?
Millennium Madness
The Game Of Life

THE ROBERT ANTON WILSON SERIES

The Cosmic Trigger
Sex and Drugs
Wilhelm Reich In Hell
Prometheus Rising
Coincidance—A New Anthology
The Goddess Obsession: Book of the Breast
The New Inquisition

THE FUTURE IS NOW SERIES
Undoing Yourself With Energized Meditation and Other Devices
    By Christopher S. Hyatt, Ph.D. Introduced by Israel Regardie,
    With an extensive Foreword by Robert Anton Wilson.
Undoing Yourself Too by Christopher S. Hyatt, Ph.D. and the Falconeers
A Modern Shaman's Guide to a Pregnant Universe by C.S. Hyatt, Ph.D. & Antero Alli
Breaking The GodSpell: Genetic Evolution by Neil Freer
    Introduced by Zecharia Sitchin.
The Sapiens System—The Illuminati Conspiracy: Their Objectives, Methods & Who They Are!
    By Donald Holmes, M.D.; Extensive introduction by Robert Anton Wilson.
Angel Tech: A Modern Shaman's Guide to Reality Selection by Antero Alli
    Preface by Robert Anton Wilson.
All Rites Reversed?!: Ritual Technology for Self-Initiation by Antero Alli
The Akashic Record Player: A Non-Stop Geomantic Conspiracy by Antero Alli
Zen Without Zen Masters by Camden Benares.
Monsters and Magical Sticks: There Is No Such Thing As Hypnosis?
    By Steven Heller, Ph.D. Introduced by Robert Anton Wilson
The Cybernetic Conspiracy (Mind Over Matter) by Constantin Negoita, Ph.D.
An Extraterrestrial Conspiracy by Marian Greenberg
The Shaman Warrior by Gini Graham Scott, Ph.D.
Man's Search for Meaning: Towards a Psychology of Fulfillment by Alan Garner
Power and Empowerment by Lynn Atkinson, Ph.D.
The Dream Illuminati Vimana Conspiracy by Wayne Saalman
    Introduced by Robert Anton Wilson
Mega-Babies: Baby Boomers are Booming by Timothy Leary, Ph.D., C.S. Hyatt, Ph.D.
    & Linda Miller, R.N., B.S.N.
Angelettes and Cosmic Sex by Pusser
Blue Star by Bonnie Hadley
Don't forget *THE JUNGIAN PSYCHOLOGY SERIES*
    THE GOLDEN DAWN SERIES / THE ALEISTER CROWLEY SERIES

For a free catalog of all Falcon titles contact FALCON PRESS:
1209 S. Casino Center, Suite 147, Las Vegas, NV 89104 U.S.A., 702-385-5749

Rx SHIKSE

A Transplacental Romance

by
J.R. Ephraim

1988
FALCON PRESS
LAS VEGAS, NEVADA

ISBN: 0-941404-75-7
Library of Congress Card Catalog Number: 88-81437

First Edition — 1988

Falcon Press
1209 S. Casino Center, Suite 147
Las Vegas, Nevada 89104
702-385-5749

Manufactured in the United States of America

Table of Contents

Foreword

I am a student with no friends, only acquaintances. My only satisfying relationships have been with middle-aged women, because they are the only ones who give me the kind of sympathy I need. Someone once told me that the big dilemma of manhood is finding yourself attracted to older women when you're young and younger women when you're old, but I think I'll stick to middle-aged women for the rest of my life. The mature woman is unencumbered with adolescent hangups and more willing to engage herself in intimate relationships without being possessive. She is warm, gentle and nurturing. I prefer to press my face against breasts which have weaned other toddlers as myself. Aren't all men big babies?

Society tells you, "Go hang out with women your own age!" It's another case of the double standard: sodomy, homosexuality, bestiality, troilism, sado-masochism and even pedophilia are acceptable deviations, but attraction to a woman who is thirty years older than yourself . . . ? How vulgar! How distasteful! What a waste! What are you, sick or something?

I've been interested in medicine ever since I was fifteen. My mother always wanted me to become a doctor, since it was a prestigious and lucrative profession, befitting a Jewish prince. Although I've never seriously considered working in the field, the language of medicine has always intrigued me and to this day I read medical dictionaries sheerly for entertainment. The medical nomenclature consists merely of contractions of Greek and Latin roots, which are hardly as intimidating as they sound and may be used frequently in a work of fiction. (For this reason I have provided a glossary of medical and Yiddish terminology at the end of the book for cross-reference.)

My infatuation with medicine has very little to do with the field itself. I don't profess to know anything about saving peoples' lives or making them well. However, I am fascinated by the privileges of the profession and the self-inflated mystique which leads many people to worship doctors as demi-gods. As a slavish victim of the M. Deity Syndrome, I have taken the honorary title of M.B.D. Many people think that this degree comes from a foreign medical school, but they're wrong. These initials stand for minimal brain dysfunction. The furthest I've progressed in medicine has been as a professional patient. I was also the keyboard player in Doc Benway, a medical rock and roll band.

At that time, all the musicians wore some form of medical uniform: the lead singer dressed in a surgical scrub suit and occasionally sang through gauze; the guitarist used a scalpel for a pick while connecting his amplifier to an I.V. drip; the bass player plucked his strings with crocodile forceps; and I wore a white coat with a purple insignia sewn above the pocket: University Hospital Attending Physician. Who needed to go through the hassles of medical school, internship and residence, when one could practice medicine en masse on stage? In the background we projected a light show, consisting of skeletal X-rays superimposed over a multi-colored strobe light. We even got volunteers to lie down in our operating theater. Although some music critics thought we represented an innocuous side-effect of the drug culture, the county medical society accused us of practicing medicine without a license, a misdemeanor. We were forced to disband.

Since all other medical opportunities were closed to me, my only recourse was to become the patient of an older woman doctor. I was determined to seek out a surrogate mother figure who could steer me along the proper course. This would extend childhood into young adulthood and give me a megadose of the sympathy I so desperately needed.

My parents sent me to Demarest State College with the intention of my becoming a great success, a young Jewish doctor who would marry an intelligent Jewish girl from a respectable family. Most importantly, we would give them lots of grandchildren. Little did they know that I would fulfill the opposite of their dreams, namely to court a *shikse*, a forty-seven year old, married *shikse*, Doctor doctor.

Midway through my sophomore year, I decided to transfer from Demarest to Kirk College of Agriculture, another division within the state university, only two miles away. Kirk was contiguous to Fairbanks College for Women. All the student services at Fairbanks College for Women had just been opened up to students from Kirk.

A recent court decision by the university board of governors mandated coeducation in all state colleges. Although most of the students and faculty at Fairbanks were bitter about the decision, they still looked upon us as pubescent younger brothers, obedient to their demands. As an entering student at Kirk, I was privileged to enjoy a high ratio of females to males. Since student enrollment at Kirk was only one-sixth the size of Fairbanks, we were hardly large enough to threaten their feminist bastion.

I didn't transfer from Demarest to Kirk because I was interested in farming, animal husbandry, or an agriculturally-related field. In fact, I held onto my status as an English major, even though the Liberal Arts Department at Kirk was virtually nonexistent, offering only a few courses in English Composition to incoming freshmen. My sole reason for transferring was to gain access to Hastings Health Center which provided comprehensive health care to the Fairbanks student body and the few male students from Kirk who had the nerve to use the women's infirmary.

Hastings was staffed by three full-time women doctors, in the spirit of feminist professionalism. Social psychologists at the university felt the all-female staff at Hastings set an excellent example for students at Fairbanks, especially those who aspired to careers in medicine or the allied health professions. My preference is for a woman physician from the old school. I don't care for the new crop of lady doctors who were admitted to medical school through the Equal Opportunity Program. She must have survived the restrictive quotas of the 40s and 50s, which limited the number of women who could become physicians. At Hastings I saw the opportunity for my dream to materialize.

On my first day of classes, I immediately set out to survey the Fairbanks terrain. My first stop was Hastings, where I made an appointment to see the director, Silvana G. Foster, M.D. I wanted to start at the top. Although my appointment wouldn't be due for two weeks, I was anxious to catch a glimpse of her from afar before we would meet formally in the examination room.

Hiding behind the coat rack in the waiting room, I saw Silvana Foster stride down the hallway. She was a slender, but solid beauty, about six feet tall, who held herself perfectly erect—a mother redwood for me. Every curl of her auburn hair, grey at the roots, was set perfectly in place and highlighted her peach-tone rouge. Her matronly breasts pressed the seams of a freshly starched labcoat layered over a dress. A set of simian wrinkles under her nasolabial frown lines showed that she was old enough for me.

Visiting the clinic became an obsession. The days preceding my first appointment with Dr. Foster passed by at an excruciating pace and so, to satisfy my craving, I wandered aimlessly through the halls of Hastings. The nurses saw me so frequently they wondered whether I was an ambulatory patient who resided in a private room upstairs. While tolerating my presence, they neglected to give me loving attention. I searched in vain for some kind of opening. One morning, while perusing the state university newspaper, the *Talon*, a letter concerning Hastings Health Center came to my attention.

> To the editor:
>
> This past week, when taken ill with a 102 degree fever, a sore throat and swollen glands, I sought treatment at Hastings Infirmary, which serves Fairbanks College. When I arrived at the clinic, there were two women ahead of me waiting to see the physician-on-duty. After waiting my turn for over forty-five minutes, another woman, who had just walked in, was paged to come to the doctor's office. At that time, I had not even been directed to the nurses' station. My skin felt as if it were on fire and my throat was so sore I could hardly swallow. When I protested to the receptionist, she told me to be patient. The other student was treated before me because she was the power forward of the basketball team and her time was naturally more valuable than my own. I had no choice but to walk out and be treated at an expensive private clinic. I am submitting the bill to Hastings and expect to be reimbursed for the inconvenience.
>
> There is no reason why athletes should receive preferential care over other students. Every student at Fairbanks has a pressing schedule and a heavy academic load. We have better things to do than sit around the waiting room, where we are exposed to infectious diseases and subjected to inhumane treatment. The nurses and doctors treat us like cattle. After making us wait for an hour, they shove us through the examining room and have no respect for our feelings. The doctors are even worse than the nurses. They have no compassion for those of us sitting in the waiting room with painful menstrual cramps. I suggest that the university board of governors conduct an investigation of this incident and others repeated with appalling frequency. When feeling ill in the future, I will avoid potential malpractice at Hastings and seek non-discriminatory treatment at the Demarest College Infirmary.
>
> Kathleen Porter, Junior
> Fairbanks College

As I finished the letter I spilled cereal over the newspaper in excitement. Now I had an opportunity to ingratiate myself with the staff. I wrote a brief letter of response to the *Talon* with the hope of becoming a hero to Dr. Foster before she met me for the first time.

Dear Ms. Porter:

Your letter, published recently in the *Talon*, threw some cheap shots at the Hastings Infirmary. If you were able to appreciate the dedication and devotion the staff shows to their patients, you would immediately apologize for your disrespectful accusations. It's time you did your homework before mouthing off. Many of the Hastings' nurses and physicians have volunteered their own time in the evening to treat indigent children in the ghetto to help meet the need for community health care.

Your assertion that the physicians at Hastings are prejudiced in favor of athletes is completely unfounded. The staff provides the same professional care for all students, regardless of the circumference of their biceps. In the past two weeks the staff has treated a countless number of additional students from Kirk College without receiving commensurate funds. This understaffing, mandated by the university board of governors, may account for the occasional delays in the waiting room. Hastings is awaiting a long-promised increase in their allocation. Nevertheless, the physicians and nurses continue to treat all students identically with the exceptional, comprehensive care for which they have been praised in the past.

> Jeremy Lipschitz, Sophomore
> Kirk College

My first letter was published in the *Talon* the day before my first appointment with Dr. Foster. I would get down to business immediately by requesting a prescription for sleeping pills to combat my chronic insomnia. This would only represent partial compensation for my letter of support. I would also complain of pains in the lower back, just north of my coccygeal region, in order to get a lower back rub. If there was time left over, I would compel her to massage my prostate gland in a comprehensive rectal examination.

For three days before my appointment I studied a textbook, *Clinical Biomechanics of the Spine.* By familiarizing myself with the minute connections in the lumbro-sacral region and all its anatomical anomalies, I knew I could impress Dr. Foster as a self-educated boy genius, for whom medical school was only an impending formality. Although I was only a sophomore in college, she would still think of me as Dr. Jeremy Lipschitz.

The day after my letter was published I walked into Hastings and told Mrs. Covello, the receptionist, that I had an appointment to see Dr. Foster. She was so pleased with me for writing the letter that she placed my chart at the top of the rack. I knew then that I would be Dr. Foster's first patient of the morning. I would catch her when she was fresh and alert. Feeling confident, I took a seat in the waiting room.

Dr. Foster walked out of the staff lounge and gave some instructions to the nurses while I meditated on her features. Her eyebrows were red and furry, angling in towards the bridge of her finely sculpted Roman nose. Sky-blue veins ran from her greying temples. This suggested to me that her intellectual faculties were being used to peak capacity. Her clear hazel irises and ivory white sclera expressed the confidence of a physician who had over twenty years of clinical practice under her belt. Although she was nearly forty-eight years old, she had retained much of her youthful figure and could have passed for thirty-nine to an untrained observer of middle-aged women. I was ready to glide my tongue along the delicate wrinkles of her cheeks.

Dr. Foster walked over to the counter and pulled out the first chart from the bin. I cringed in my chair behind the coat rack, hiding my face behind a year-old issue of *Reader's Digest*. I peeked up to observe her as she read my name on the chart and my heart pounded in anticipation. Her squinting eyes combed the waiting room for a male patient amidst the crowd of blank Fairbanks faces.

Sniffing the antiseptic vapors, I tried to steady myself for the crucial first encounter. Having readied myself for a long wait, I had barely enough time to prepare my presentation.

"Jeremy," she whispered unobtrusively.

I stepped forward boldly, then curtsied like a *schlemiel* and shook her hand feebly. Her soft, but firm grip was filled with affection. It was not cold nor raw, as I had expected of a physician's touch.

"I've heard such wonderful things about you," she said, squeezing my hand gently to quiet my trembling and assess my nervous tone. I held on to her hand for an extra seven seconds, far beyond the expected duration of a formal handshake. She looked at me inquisitively, perhaps sensing that I had psychological problems and tactfully released her hand from my dead-fish grip. "Would you please take a seat in Clinic C. It's at the end of the hall to your right. I'll be with you in just a moment." Pressing a caressing thumb into my shoulder, she ushered me towards her office and disappeared through the nurses' station. I shuddered when I felt her motherly hand rub the ribs of my skinny frame, but savored the scent of perfume trailing behind her.

I walked into the examining room and sat down on the swivel chair beside her desk. The pervasive scent of antiseptic made my eyes water. Posted above her desk was a calendar with an advertisement for birth control pills, the pharmaceutical company's reminder to keep her Fairbanks girls out of trouble. A worn edition of the *Physician's Desk Reference* was flanked by two prescription pads. They were embossed with Lilies of the

Valley, the emblem of Fairbanks College. The precise arrangement of her papers led me to believe she exercised the same meticulous habits in her practice. I was in good hands.

Silvana Foster received her M.D. degree from Ohio State College of Medicine at the age of twenty-four. Three years later, she completed her residency in internal medicine at New York University Medical Center and became board-certified in record time. I researched this information in *Who's Who in American Women* and the *Directory of Medical Specialists* while browsing through the reference shelves of my college library. The diplomas on the wall confirmed my expectations.

My keen olfactory receptors detected Fosterian pheromones cutting through the alcoholic mist of the sterile examining room before she even arrived. The sound of crisp footsteps aroused my attention; I had grown indifferent to the squeak of nurses' shoes.

Beyond Embarrassment

"So Jeremy," she said in a voice as smooth as cold cream, closing the door behind her. "Thank you for writing the letter. We're relieved that someone has finally taken the initiative to defend Hastings." Leaning back comfortably into her swivel chair, she immediately became aware of my low bedroom stare and pulled her long, full, pleated skirt over her knees.

"Oh well, Dr. Foster; it was my duty to rescue Hastings," I said, scratching my eyebrows pensively. "The staff deserves a little credit for their work. Nursing is often a thankless job. Besides, a little public recognition boosts staff morale. Confidentially, Dr. Foster . . ." I hesitated, losing confidence.

"Everything you tell me is strictly confidential."

"This infirmary has more to offer than the health center at Demarest. Although you have a smaller staff and fewer facilities at Hastings, I know I'll get the very best care here. When it comes to health care, it's the quality of the personnel that counts."

"It's great to hear good things about Hastings," she said cheerfully, yet at the same time scrutinizing my glassy eyes.

She opened her lips momentarily, revealing the narrow gap between her two front teeth and her glistening gums. My vision was fixed on the yellow boundary of egg film, rostral to her lower lip, that lingered from breakfast. The crows-feet wrinkles under her eyes could not betray her age. Anyone could readily tell that Silvana Foster had been a truly beautiful woman in her day. But as far as I was concerned, she was living in her prime now, as a middle-aged woman, a paragon of beauty, intelligence and virtue.

Somewhere I sensed a spreading line of dissatisfaction in her sunken dimples. Was her husband too old for her, I wondered? Was he moody and snappy? I wasn't sure, but I knew that he wasn't making her happy. She needed a new spark to flare her drooping candle wick. I could melt all the wax around her and mold her liquid paraffin form along my breastplate where she would cool off and solidify in perpetual attachment. I wanted to join myself to her in transplacental ecstasy.

She opened the manila chart on her desk and checked my medical history while my eyes traced the outline of her matronly curvatures. A sparkling emerald, the center stone of a white gold necklace, rested above an opening in her labcoat. I was relieved to see she could retain her femininity in the face of professional pressures. Her breasts were wide and full, but not overladen for a woman of forty-seven years. But best of all, she had the maturity and wisdom which I so admired. Only an older woman could offer me the companionship I needed.

"Well, Jeremy," she said, looking up from my chart, "what can I do for you?"

"Dr. Foster, I've had considerable difficulty falling asleep at night. The problem is compounded by early-waking insomnia." I spoke deliberately, cautiously observing her while she leaned forward to show her special concern for my medical problem. "I was wondering whether it would be feasible for you to prescribe something for it?" I asked in a more confident tone, licking my lips between breaths to make certain they were clean and not glossed over with dried saliva. "I'm sure that thirty milligrams of Dalmane, taken sparingly, and only as directed, will do the trick."

"One moment, Jeremy," she interrupted, her voice sounding shrill, "let's take this one step at a time. First tell me a little more about your insomnia." I gazed at her legs sheepishly without saying a word. She pretended to ignore my furtive, low stares. I was stupified by her warm, understanding bedside manner and envisioned lying down with my head on her lap.

She tapped her fingernails against the desk-top, waiting for me to say something on my own and then glanced at her watch, as if to scold me for wasting a physician's precious time.

"How many hours of sleep do you receive on a normal night?" she softened her tone, hoping I would be more responsive.

"Oh, I don't know, about three or four. That's on a good night. Sometimes I can't get to sleep at all." From the corners of my eyes, I stared at the cleavage between her breasts. Her hardened nipples pressed for recognition through her blouse and labcoat. The bump on my German Jewish nose shadowed my stealthy glance, while on another mental level I entered the netherworld within the hymenal linings of her throbbing womb.

I wanted to *shnuppel* my nose along a row of bronzed age spots, skirting the downslope of her bosom. Would she let me climb under her chemise and caress her papillary fronds, I wondered? Because that is where I would find the depths of sympathy; not in her heart, but in her breast. The frequency of my covetous stares was worsened by my lack of eye contact. She fidgeted impatiently and buttoned her labcoat, covering all flesh below her neck. Looking up at the medicine cabinet, I recognized a bottle of Demerol and thought, why not break open the glass, load up a syringe and shoot up a multiple dose intravenously. She'll be called in to resuscitate me.

For a fleeting moment I wanted to confess my weakness for middle-aged women, but was too scared. She looked down at her watch. Her appointments were getting backlogged. If she was going to see all her patients to safety and leave early enough to eat dinner with her family at six-thirty, her appointments had to end on schedule. But Jeremy, I imagined she was thinking, seems to be an interesting young man, different from the other students I see every day, who constantly whine to me about their problems and do nothing to improve their mental hygiene. I wonder what's really troubling him. Perhaps I could counsel him. It's too bad that I don't have the time for an extended consultation today. There's no dispute that Dalmane is the drug of choice for insomnia. Why not start out with a low dose on a trial basis. I'll recommend a follow-up appointment a few weeks from now.

"Jeremy," she asked in a commiserating tone, but inspected my pupils with a wary, critical eye, "do you feel constantly fatigued?"

"Yes, I'm real tired," I said in a barely audible whisper so she would move closer. "The semester has hardly begun and I'm already feeling exhausted. Wait until finals come around. By that time, I'll feel wasted."

"Many students express this complaint to me at the beginning of the semester. Insomnia is a common response to stress."

"But this semester I have the additional problem of adjusting to a new campus environment. I'm a new student at Kirk. I transferred recently from Demarest College."

"Yes, I noticed that in your chart, which leads me to ask: what is your major?"

"Molecular biology with a concentration in biochemistry."

Her eyes almost jumped out of their orbits. A hearty, contagious smile widened her mouth, showing me how impressed she was by my taking up such a difficult academic discipline as an undergraduate. "Molecular biology, hmm, is that a cross-disciplinary major?"

"Exactly, Dr. Foster," I said agreeably, "I have two advisors: Dr. Hoffman from the Department of Biochemistry and Dr. Schwann from Physics. I transferred from Demarest to Kirk after receiving the Franklin P. Krebs Memorial Fellowship in Biochemistry. The labs at Demarest were simply too crowded for me to conduct intensive research there. Besides, the dean at Kirk has given me permission to develop my own cross-disciplinary curriculum. I was exempted from most basic science courses due to my high scores on the Advanced Placement exams. In a few years I'll be going to medical school."

"That's wonderful," she cried, smiling with anticipatory delight. "Have you already chosen a subject for your thesis?"

"Yes, I've been toying with an idea. Since my current interest is applied pharmacology, I'll attempt to develop a non-narcotic substitute for methadone. My advisors have arranged for me to team up with a polymer chemist and a pharmacologist from the medical school, both of whom are tenured members of the faculty."

"That's fascinating," she cried enthusiastically, rubbing her clitoris unconsciously against the velvet seat of her swivel chair. "Chemistry was always my weakest subject." Whether or not she realized it, her knee was banging against my chair. She was obviously delighted to be sitting across from a child prodigy who was gifted in science. Little did she know that I was an English major who never had taken a science course other than Biological Issues and Man, a watered-down survey course designed specifically for students in the humanities.

"Yes, many people have trouble with the subject," I said haughtily, "but let me tell you, I approach the study of biochemistry and related disciplines from a different angle: learn to love it or die. I find physical chemistry and quantum theory to be disciplines which are nourishing for the mind. It all has to do with the polarization of light. You really have to get into visualizing the molecular configurations and chemical reactions, to see perfect symmetries within the icosahedral forms. When I stay up late at night, studying an enzymological sequence, I say to myself, 'This is what life is all about—the infinite continuum of chemical reactions, tails of long chained proteins snapped off into oblivion.' You have to submerge yourself within the ionic bonds, to witness with your own eyes the evolution of living systems. That's how I get straight A's."

She raised her eyebrows, obviously impressed by my solid command of science and metaphysics as well as my poetic flair. And yet I was not one of those common, competitive, pre-med "throats" who stayed up late on three consecutive nights to study before an exam, memorizing lists of terms and definitions without going to sleep; who couldn't understand the significance of what they were studying and had to struggle for B's. I knew that in her eyes I was a brilliant student, overqualified for the state university, a true Renaissance man, who also excelled in philosophy, mathematics, music and the history of science.

I decided then that for my next visit I would remind her of my precocious talents by carrying a textbook which was used in post-graduate medical school, such as *Clinical Psychopharmacology*, or volume four of *The Prostaglandins*, or volume thirty-six of *Advances in Enzymology*, or a classic in medicine such as *Obscure Diseases of the Brain*. I knew that I could talk to her with the confidence of a great neurosurgeon, the king of the medical hierarchy, who understood the biochemistry of every synapse in the nervous system.

"Jeremy, have you considered specializing in a particular branch of medicine?"

"After I finish my pre-clinical studies, I plan to enroll in an M.D./Ph.D. program for training medical research scientists. Academic medicine poses the greatest challenge. I never was that good with my hands, so surgery is simply out of the question and the routine of general practice can become boring," I said in a lowered tone, afraid that I had snubbed her decision to specialize in adolescent medicine late in her career.

"I assume then, Jeremy, that you will study for a joint degree?" Her beaming eyes seemed envious of my youth and talent.

"Yes, Dr. Foster, if I can survive the six year stint. I'll receive my M.D./Ph.D. in molecular biology or a related subspecialty. I heard that the College of Physicians and Surgeons at Columbia University has an excellent program. People have told me that the pressures at P. & S. are very intense and that one must weather the tensions between scholarship and romance, but then again biochemistry is almost second nature to me. It's child's play. I'm hardly worried. The most difficult part of medical school will be trudging through the first year courses such as anatomy and histology which demand a facility in memorization."

"Oh yes, there will be plenty of memorization, starting off with *Gray's Anatomy*," she warned, pointing to a stack of worn textbooks she had used as a medical student herself.

"I've heard that book is a good paperweight," I joked, my eyes cueing in on her as she laughed spontaneously. Good, she still has her original teeth, I thought. Her pink, healthy gums were free of gingival inflammation.

"Before I forget," she said gingerly, "let me give you a prescription for Dalmane. Remember, I get balky when someone asks for a refill."

"Oh yes, that would be very nice. I hope one prescription will do."

I admired her long, tapered fingers, sculpted through two decades of medical practice, as she opened the top drawer of her desk. She removed a prescription pad, along with her gold-tipped pen, a token from the staff in appreciation of her ten years of dedicated service at Hastings. I could see the outline of her bones beneath her smooth, transparent skin and wondered whether her swollen knuckles were a premonitory sign of arthritis or the usual sign of wear and tear on a physician's hands. A modest gold wedding band encircled her ring finger. Silvana seemed to be an amazing woman who had fought her way into medical school against unbelievable odds. She had risen from the generation of women doctors who had to penetrate the quotas limiting the admission of women to medical schools. Only the very brightest were admitted solely on academic merit. I knew that Silvana Foster had been a brilliant student in her day, as precocious as I could ever wish to be. Now she was an experienced physician, who possessed a wealth of wisdom, maturity and common sense. Looking up at her diplomas on the wall, I knew that I was in good hands.

A note on her bulletin board announced that she would be giving two lectures to the Associated Students of Fairbanks, one on breast self-examination, the other on contraception. I was thrilled to learn that the lectures would be held in the main student lounge. This would give me the option to drop by and provide background music on the grand piano. I remembered reading in the *Talon* that Dr. Foster had been instrumental in making birth control devices widely available at all infirmaries of the university. I hoped that her permissive attitudes in the field of human sexuality were reflections of her own liberated sexual nature.

"Jeremy, excuse me, before I can prescribe a sedative-hypnotic, I'm required to ask if you have suicidal tendencies."

"Dr. Foster," I cried indignantly, "you must be kidding. In the event that I had suicidal tendencies, I would never try to o.d. on a drug with a wide margin of safety such as Dalmane. Please respect my knowledge of pharmacology. If I ever wanted to kill myself, I would use my revolver."

"Do you have a gun permit?" she asked coolly, with the flat and unsmiling eyes of a gila monster.

"Of course not. The Belgian thirty-eight is registered in my father's name. He's a rabbi, you know."

"Oh really," she said, raising her eyebrows with a hint of patronizing curiosity. She scratched the apex of her skull, running her fingers through her wavy hair and gazed at me with a look of disbelief. I assumed that she was confused by the ethical paradox of a clergyman possessing a handgun, but also pleased to see me open up and speak to her about my family.

"Yes, but he's not a practicing rabbi, just funerals, unveilings, counseling and probate."

"Is that right?" she chuckled knowingly, leaning closer toward me with pricked ears.

"When I was a little kid he had a congregation, but our family soon got tired of the small talk and the social pressures. Everyone wanted to smell Mom's chicken soup, because it was superkosher and a family recipe. Her secret was to cook the broth with *kishkes;* entrails, you know. Not a single piece of chicken went to waste, something which is common to Jewish and Chinese culinary arts. But back to what you asked me about suicide. I tried to kill myself when I was nine by swallowing a whole bottle of Cogentin. As you know, Cogentin is prescribed to counteract the side effects induced by most major tranquilizers, especially when Parkinsonian tremors and Spasmodic Torticollis occurs. It was an act of creative rebellion, attempting to commit suicide with one of the medicines the psychiatrist had prescribed. By the time they rushed me to the emergency room, it was too late for gastric lavage and I went into a long coma. But I was sick upstairs at the time," I said with a contorted grimace, pointing to my forehead. "I'm completely better now. Besides, the physician who examined me was foreign-trained and diagnosed me as a histrionic suicidal type, especially since I had failed at my effort to kill myself."

"What made you consider that?" she asked bluntly with an unrelenting stare, to see if I was telling the truth.

"Oh, I had a little trouble at home. You know how it is during childhood and adolescence. I'm a late bloomer; I was impotent until I was seventeen and grossly underweight. I unleashed my frustrations on my parents and before long the whole guilt trip set in."

She stared at me in disbelief, wondering how an M.D. could have offered such an inane diagnosis, but backed off from encouraging a sudden confession before she had a chance to know me better.

"Jeremy, can I count on you to follow the directions of my prescription?" Her tone made me feel like a five year old laggard in toilet training.

"There's no need for you to have any reservations about prescribing Dalmane for me. Believe me, Dr. Foster, you couldn't find anyone in the entire university system more dedicated to self-preservation than myself. I've already paid my dues as a drug abuser, as a victim of iatrogenesis. Foiled suicided attempts are absolutely the worst bummer. You can rest assured that I won't abuse those sleeping pills."

She smiled but looked away impatiently, as if distracted by my rambling speech, which was hardly more than an incoherent word salad. I was afraid her rigorous schedule as staff physician and director of Hastings would give her no time to consult with me on a regular basis. The sound of the fountain pen tip, scratching the heavy bond paper, made my eyes water as she recorded the drug and dosage. Her signature was slightly illegible, as if it were encoded for the fraternity of physicians and pharmacists.

"I'm giving you fifteen milligrams of Dalmane." She spoke softly, without a trace of emotion in her voice, and handed me the prescription. "Take one or two capsules at bedtime, as needed. Also, you might make an appointment with Dr. Berman, our staff psychologist. In any event, I'd like to see you in two weeks. If your insomnia hasn't cleared up by then, I'll give you one refill. You know, one can rapidly develop a tolerance to sleeping pills. You can actually exacerbate your symptoms if you don't address the psychogenic component. That's why I suggest you see Dr. Berman."

"But I don't want to see a psychotherapist. I want to be treated by you. You're a licensed M.D. That's all that matters. As long as we work within the medical model, I'll get better."

She smiled to herself knowingly but rolled back her seat and kept her distance. "Next time we can explore natural methods of overcoming insomnia, O.K.?"

"Fine, I'll pay close attention to what you've told me, Dr. Foster."

She handed me the prescription and squirmed uneasily in her chair, perhaps at the thought that there were seven other patients who wanted to see her within a span of two hours. I knew that her appointments were normally scheduled in half hour blocks, but always ran late when patients were either talkative or needed extensive treatment. These thorough evaluations also helped improve Hastings' reputation.

"One other thing, Dr. Foster," I said meekly. "I have lower back pain." Leaning sideways, I placed my hand at the nadir of my coccyx and winced. Silvana wasn't going to get off so easily without giving me a thorough physical examination.

Hmm, I imagined she was thinking, as she tilted her head sideways and tapped her index finger pensively against her lower lip. This patient is going to take some time. If I get home late and Alex is hungry, he can always take out a T.V. dinner from the freezer.

"Jeremy, would you take off your shoes and undress, leaving your underpants on?" she asked, respecting the common male phobia of disrobing completely in the presence of a female physician.

I poured the contents of my pockets on her desk: a wallet, a fountain pen, house keys, chewing gum and an appointment card. Balancing on one foot at a time, I peeled off my tight-fitting jeans, afraid that a loose joint of marijuana would fall out. My fingers fumbled nervously through a row of stubborn buttons. I finally hung my shirt around the back of her swivel chair, and placed my undershirt on the seat where they were hidden from view. I had hoped she would appreciate my flair for being neat and exact in grooming, since it matched the meticulous habits of a scientist. Feeling playful, I spun the chair around and watched my socks and undershirt fall to the floor. I was ready for the physical. I sauntered over the cold tiles and stopped at the end of the examining table. With the exception of my undershorts, I stood naked before her. An ultraviolet sterilizing lamp glowed on the wall; her protection against the onslaught of student carriers. But I knew that she was not immune to my urgent needs and would find me irresistible in due time.

Feeling confident, I hopped up on the examining table. My boney ass landed sharply on the slack sheet of sanitary paper and tore it in half. She clicked her tongue against her upper palate disappointedly. I looked at her meekly, swinging my legs back and forth anxiously like a little boy.

"Would you stand up?"

I stood on the balls of my feet and held up my chin to compensate for her height advantage. My eyes were glued to her lovely features. Auburn curls dangled over her forehead. Her roseate complexion was perfectly clear. My shoulders were barely level with the top of her breasts. Would she be my dance partner and waltz with me through the clinic? At six foot two she's only six inches taller than me, I considered. Her husband must be some Watusi.

"Turn around, let me get a good look at your back," she commanded gently. After I failed to move around on my own, she rested her hands on my collar bone and rotated my body 180 degrees in a counterclockwise direction. A rush of pleasure raced up my spine to the nape of my neck. My toes struggled to keep up with her pivoting motion, so I planted my heels firmly and let my calloused soles rotate with the force of her twist.

"Tell me specifically where you feel the pain."

"The pain comes in spurts, emanating from the last thoracic vertebra and extending up the spinal column to the sacrovertebral articulation. In severe instances, I experience a sharp flash of referred pain which radiates down the sciatic nerve of my left leg."

I paused briefly to allow her to digest my graphic description and knew that she was tickled by my ability to describe my problem in explicit anatomical detail. No doubt most of her other patients were poorly versed in anatomy and physiology and rarely gave her a clue to the source of their pain before she had to send them off to specialists.

"But there's no reason for me to suspect that I have a dysfunction at the junction," I continued, "the pain is most likely due to a pulled muscle which developed after bicycling along Canal Road last weekend. The seat of my English racer was too low for me and I pedalled for over thirty minutes in an uncomfortably cramped position."

"Oh you poor fellow," she comforted me, committing herself to outward sympathy for the first time. She dug her fingers into my slender muscles, beginning with my neck and ending with my coccyx, her fingertips dancing up and down the length of my ticklish spine.

Her fingers dug in more deeply along a grid of responsive skin, extending from my pelvic girdle to the southern ridge of my scapula. She massaged my muscles firmly, but sensuously, as a physician was licensed to do, without fear of being accused of purposely stimulating sexual reflexes in her patient.

However, the vigorous massage excited me. Warm breath exuded from her simian nostrils. My tight double-mesh jockey shorts covered the shaft of a rising penis which was slanted at an obtrusive angle.

I melted under the warmth of her touch. She knew how to palpate and massage at the same time; a semi-automatic, bi-hemispherical skill she had developed after two decades of practice on both the backs of her patients and her husband. Only a physician had the training to determine the precise location of the pleasurable pressure points in the body and stimulate them to bring relief from pain. Her fingertips delivered a better body rush than Demerol and potentiated my insatiable desire for companionship with an older woman physician.

She grasped my wrists and tugged on my arms to check the tendon reflexes. A string of drool collected under my chin, until gravity dragged it down to my belly button. The feel of cold, wet slime alerted me to stay on guard or she would offer me a bib.

Please keep on rubbing. You make me feel so good, I commanded silently. Keep your hands on my back. Don't leave my spine shivering in the cold. Your hands make me feel five degrees warmer like your girdle makes you look five pounds thinner. Silvana, I really enjoy what you're doing. Don't stop.

I was surprised to see that she obeyed my silent instructions and pressed her warm hand along the obtuse curve of my back just above my derriere. At 118 pounds, I was more than 30 pounds underweight for a five-foot nine-inch male with a small frame. My protruding ribs were clearly visible beneath a semi-transparent layer of skin. To the trained observer, I was a beautiful anatomical specimen, free of adipose tissue, a perfect model for dissection. I knew that she was experiencing pleasure in making me feel good all over. If anyone deserved a massage, it was the fellow who wrote the supportive letter in the *Talon.*

"Now Jeremy, I'm going to take this ordinary safety pin and touch you with either the dull point or the sharp point," she whispered in my ear. "I want you to lie down on the table and tell me which end of the pin you feel."

Oh boy, a neurological examination! I though, rubbing my hands together with glee. This is great. She doesn't have to waste any time taking my pulse, blood pressure, or the usual family medicine stuff. "I don't want to sound pushy, Dr. Foster, but would you be kind enough to continue what you're doing? Massage has enormous therapeutic value. It restores the circulation to certain muscle groups. You should consider going into private practice as a masseuse." She smiled knowingly and dug her fingers more deeply into my back muscles, as if to reward me for my sense of humor. "But seriously, Doctor, your fingertips work wonders; I also think that my spine stiffness may be a cause of insomnia. Please continue."

For a moment I was afraid she was annoyed by my nagging request, but she kept at it, digging her fingertips vigorously into skinny pockets of flesh. Her firm strokes drained the tension from my back muscles. In one of my wilder visions, I dreamed of how someday she would massage the front part of my body: manually, orally and corporally. At that point, any discussion of insomnia would clearly be academic.

I felt ashamed that at twenty years of age, I was still trying to realize an adolescent fantasy. But my libidinal drive was overwhelming. Go after her, Jerry, I urged myself. Silvana will be good for you. Women doctors are hard to come by. Medical dating agencies charge a $600 placement fee and now you practically have her eating out of your hand.

Winning Silvana's love was a real challenge. In the past, I had tried to win the warmth of other middle-aged women by openly confessing my love to them, falling down on my knees, laying prostrate and kissing their feet slavishly like an Elizabethan court jester. Dr. Foster had too much professional integrity to listen quietly to a patient's passionate plea. Besides, it would be humiliating for me to kiss the feet of a physician, even if she scrubbed regularly with a foot towel. If I was going to be successful, she would have to be approached indirectly. Facing my dear doctor, I knew that experiencing sexual gratification through fear was perverse and immature. If I wanted to get into a serious relationship with her, I would have to be brave and sincere. By writing the letter in support of Hastings and by telling her about my career goals in medicine, our relationship was already headed towards erotic fruition.

"Now tell me either dull or sharp," she said. A sharp sensation tickled the sensory nerves in my shoulder. I keeled backwards against the pin. It gave me the perfect opportunity to bleed unnecessarily on her account. She tried to pull back the pin, but it had already plunged through the stratum corneum and pierced a blood vessel.

"Sharp point," I cried out mockingly, feeling a drop of blood surface to my skin.

"Oh Jeremy, you must not lean back when I test your reflexes," she cried. "Don't worry; it's nothing serious, only a slight skin prick. It will heal in a few days." I sensed that she was terribly embarrassed by her failure to take greater precautions in assessing her patient's neurological responses.

Pathos is on your side, the demonical part of me murmured in my inner ear. She already owes you a couple of favors for your letter and for injuring you with the pin. Play it right and eventually she'll have to return a sexual favor. Hang in there boy. Silvana's becoming more indebted to you every moment.

But I don't have the balls to approach her, a frightened part of me responded. What shall I do?

Sit it out for now. Give her time to recover. Make an appointment to see her soon and remember to keep on scheming. Just cool it with the morbid anatomy. At times, you sound so stilted, Lipschitz. It's O.K., Jeremy, you're doing fine, I thought, trying to cement the disconnected parts of a fragmented ego.

But it was to no avail. I already felt crippled inside in the presence of this highly intelligent and attractive woman. My stomach was filled by an immiscible blend of fear and admiration. I was mesmerized by her dulcet voice, her deliquescent lips, her magnetic charm.

It would take months before I could vocalize my need for her companionship and, by that time, she would be able to see through my deceptions, to dismiss me as a childish neurotic. Who could fall in love with such a pathetic creature as myself, I wondered?

Just then two warm hands touched down on my lonely shoulder blades. The benumbing touch anesthetized all memory of pain.

"Don't feel bad, Dr. Foster," I tried to reassure her, but my voice squeaked in a falsetto. "It was really my fault for not informing you beforehand that I have hypersensitive reflexes. I'm especially ticklish when it comes to sharp stimuli. My neuronal circuits occasionally suffer from signal failure. There's an impasse at the synapse. That's why I leaned backwards." Suddenly, I feared that she had found my medical hyperbole a bit overweening.

She walked over to the medicine cabinet, removed a ball of sterile cotton from a glass jar, and soaked it in alcohol. Then she applied the stinging compress over my wound and taped it tightly on my skin with adhesive. I was in a state of bliss when her fingers trailed affectionately along my spine. She patted me on the rump and ushered me to the examining table.

I hopped up on the paper-covered vinyl and made myself at home. Swinging my legs over the edge, I pretended I was watching the Flintstones on T.V., munching on a bowl of Lucky Charms cereal—in my most relaxed, infantalizing position.

"Very good," she said, pleased that my body was already oriented in the proper examining position.

My body lay helplessly on its side while she loomed confidently above me. Her feet were planted solidly on the ground. I savored the feeling of being vulnerable in her clutches and rolled over on my back with my underbelly exposed like an insect surrendering to its predator.

"Dull point," I grunted, feeling the flat end of the safety pin poke against the plantar arch of my left foot.

"Close your eyes, Jeremy," she commanded softly, so I could not cheat by watching the point of the safety pin. I enjoyed closing my eyes, because her presence was even more awe-inspiring in the dark.

"Sharp point," I cried raising my leg, but she had already pulled back the pin.

"Dull." The cold pinpoint stimulated my lower calf muscles, just above my Achilles heel. I waited for a sharp prick, but none followed. In my mind's eye, Silvana and I were reclining on her living room sofa. She was testing my reflexes and simultaneously fondling my testicles. Throughout the evening we played medically educational games. She exposed me to a live demonstration of unorthodox positions for performing coitus. I couldn't have received better training in the film library of the medical school.

"Jeremy," she commanded. "Sit up at the edge of the table." She tapped her fingers impatiently on the waxy paper roll until I assumed the correct posture.

The rubber hammer landed on my kneecap. My foot swung up reflexively and landed against her shins. I wanted her to come closer so I could bury my tibia between her soft flanks. On the second blow, I bolted my knee, refusing to be an obedient examinee.

"Come on Jeremy, just relax. I'm only testing your patellar reflex." She placed her warm palm over my kneecap, rubbing her strong thumb along my bowed shins. My ankles rattled in delight. After all, I'm only a cartilaginous fellow.

My knees remained bolted for eight long seconds. I was afraid that once she found me relaxing, she would withdraw her soothing hand and shoot down the rubber hammer.

When Maxwell's Silver Hammer came down, I repressed my natural reflexes and kept my leg bolted in place.

I was in awe of a physician's power to condition my reflexes and I felt all the more obstinate. A woman doctor could arouse a special fear, which started with a hollow feeling in my gut and ended with a gurgle around my groin.

"Clasp your hands together with flexed fingers and pull them apart without letting go," she said dryly, resorting to Jendrassik's maneuver to divert my attention and emphasize the patellar reflex. All third year medical students have learned this trick. Sensing her annoyance, I chose not to resist. The rubber hammer knocked on my kneecap. My leg found a home in the pleat of her grey woolen skirt. The contact with her cushiony thighs and the itchy wool was delightful.

"Dr. Foster, I didn't mean to bolt my knee. I'm just nervous. I haven't had a physical in years." She eyed me suspiciously. My heart skipped a beat. Had I been caught in the act of deceiving a physician, a sin worse than stealing candy from a child?

My eyes reflected nothing but boyish innocence. Surely Jeremy is a little tense right now, I hoped she was thinking. This is his first appointment. I have a hunch that we will become better acquainted as the school year progresses. His parents must be very proud of him, especially with the career goals he has established for himself at such a young age. He really is an exceptional child.

"Oh, one more thing. I have a pain in my prostate gland," I whimpered. "What began as radiating flashes down the sciatic nerve of my left leg has developed into a burning sensation deep within the rectal cavity."

She scratched her lip pensively and pretended to be unperturbed by my tertiary complaint. He could be a little more refined by saying "rectum" or just "opening," instead of rectal cavity, I imagined her thinking when her smile turned to a scowl. If he thinks that he can shock me with his graphic urological descriptions, he'd better go somewhere else.

I figured that what she hated most were patients who fabricated medical problems only in order to boast a knowledge of anatomy. A doctor's time was worth money and the world suffered from a scarcity of physicians. I was afraid that my status had degenerated rapidly. The gifted Krebs Fellow was now a mere hypochondriacal pest.

But I was completely mistaken. Her warm, benevolent smile gave me encouragement that she was ready to work with me. With a little personal effort, I could recover from my psychosomatic ailments. She had the magic, curative power to drain away my loneliness and depression.

"Tell me Jeremy," she whispered in her maternal, high-pitched voice, which must have been reserved for digging into a patient's most sensitive problems, "where specifically does it hurt you?"

I tried to visualize the anatomical chart of the male urogenital region I had memorized in preparation for the visit. Her sobering stare alerted me to stay on guard. Hey Jerry, Foster asked you a question: Where does it hurt? The key words are urethra, urinary duct, epididymis, scrotum . . . Get the picture?

No. I don't know my ass from my elbow.

"I'm not able to locate the specific source of pain. The spasms appear to be emanating from a general area, extending from within the anus to the testicles. I have had trouble with varicose veins for six years now," I muttered timidly, and looked down at my trembling fingertips. "These swollen vessels in my scrotum have irritated me lately."

Jeremy is almost as old as my son, I could hear her thinking as she softened her stare. Wouldn't it be wonderful if the two fellow had the chance to meet? Perhaps I'll invite Jeremy over to the house when Tim has a free weekend. The boys could have a picnic lunch, play basketball and then spend the rest of the day at the swimming pool, like two fine Eagle scouts. No, perhaps it would be too risky. I haven't had a patient over to my house in years and I must keep my professional and private lives separate. But then again, he's such a cute, curly-haired youngster, and so lonely, poor fellow. He needs warmth and compassion. That's what's bothering him. He's away from home for the first time. Just imagine the creative experiments the boys could design with Tim's chemistry set after spending a few friendly hours together. Eventually, they might apply for a youth grant from the National Science Foundation. We could broil a couple of porterhouse steaks on the barbecue and toast some marshmallows after dinner. How wholesome!

"Jeremy, have you considered wearing a suspensory?" she asked delicately without looking up, knowing that any direct eye contact might aggravate my embarrassment.

"I've tried wearing many types of supporters, Dr. Foster, but all of them are uncomfortable. Even the jock straps made from the softest fabrics irritate my inner thighs and cause a burning rash after half an hour of wear. I've tried satin-laced suspensories and even silk blends from Paris. Would you consider it presumptuous of me to say that I'm allergic to designer jock straps?" She didn't smile along. "O.K. Call it contact dermatitis. My pain comes in spurts," I stammered, before she could get a word in edgewise. "When the pain strikes, I can barely stand up. Why, one time, I even fainted."

"Hmm, I don't like that at all," she said, with an intense, probing stare.

Hey, wait a minute, Jerry, I thought. There's nothing organically wrong with you. Remember that. She can't diagnose a disease if the actual symptoms are nonexistent. That would be very unprofessional and indicative of the Procrustean sin, which so many green second year medical students fall prey to when they take their first stab at pathology.

Let's not doubt her professional skill, but remember, you're clean as a whistle. Be cool. She's in a great mood. Keep up the good work and before you know it she'll be your surrogate sexual therapist.

"Do you have a history of fainting spells?"

"No, no real history. It's totally episodic."

"Which symptoms appeared first, the syncope or the pain in you . . . "

"The pain in my prostate. It's O.K., Dr. Foster, you can be more explicit with me. Besides, it's time for a rectal examination," I said and hopped off the table.

Stretching apart my cheeks, I readied myself for the procedure. Perhaps one day we would meet as colleagues at a medical convention. No longer would I be the whining patient with endless complaints. Bending down before her, I felt like an eminent physician. Tinges of grey hair streaked my temples. I carried a specialist's grin; a thirty-four year old, board-certified neurosurgeon, an officer of the American Medical Association. A pin of the Staff of Aesculapius was stuck to my breast pocket, aside my name, Jeremy Lipschitz, M.D., Ph.D., F.A.C.S. Yes, this was the kingdom of God, to be the holy doctor, licensed to bully nurses and paraprofessionals, to build a seven figure income from the misery of others, to have patients by the balls . . .

"Ah," I shrieked. My unexpected gasp responded to a sharp pain radiating through my scrotal void.

"What is it?" she asked, her voice tinged with alarm. She stood directly in front of me and shook my shoulders. "Tell me, where does it hurt you? Let's see if you can pinpoint the location."

"I think I'd better lie down. I've lost the strength in my legs." She lifted me up with one hand, then plopped me down gently on the examining table, in one fell swoop. Boy, she sure is strong, I thought. She could probably beat me up.

Rolling over on my back, I cycled my legs in the air to loosen up before she touched my crotch. I tried to slide my legs through a pair of stirrups which were used for pelvic examinations, but I couldn't coordinate my efforts. She positioned her hands under the base of my skull and tried to get me to relax. The overhead fluorescent lights made me feel like an anatomical specimen and I closed my eyes to escape the intensity of the glare.

When I opened my eyes, she was looming over me. Now she had the definite advantage and could gouge out my entrails with her sharp talons.

She slipped her fingers under my jockey shorts and stroked my penis and testicles lightly, but firmly, as a physician was licensed to touch. Although my organ was already engorged with blood, her touch helped me to relax and respond more discretely. I fought an ecstatic shiver racing up my spine. She palpated the nooks and crannies of my scrotum. Then she lifted my tingling penis with the tip of her index finger and held it to the light. Her hand seemed so huge in comparison to my resources.

"Hmm," she muttered to herself, twisting my organ counterclockwise so she could examine the underside without turning her head. She pinched my scrotum gently, shook my testicles in her hands and palpated the tortuous and sacculated veins. I interrupted her procedure with a contemptuous cough, hoping she would fondle me more delicately.

She looked me straight in the eye, then smiled to herself when she saw that she was giving me physical pleasure. One couldn't fight reflexes for long and my penis stiffened into a broomstick. I couldn't hear anything, nor speak, nor see clearly, so I tried to smell her presence. Silvana smelled only medicinal. Her natural odor was hidden by the pervasive scent of rubbing alcohol in the room, but then I detected a subtle scent of lilac perfume.

"Except for the varicoceles, Mr. Lipschitz," she said coldly, putting my penis to rest, "there appears to be nothing wrong with your urethra or scrotum. Your genital region is normal, quite normal. Would you kindly lie on your side?"

She placed her hands on my outer left thigh and positioned my body so that my hips jutted out towards her. Turning her face to the side, she examined the narrow approach through my rectum and warned, "Now this may be a little uncomfortable."

I was forced to stare at the green institutional tiles below the window and meditate on several stray scuff marks on the wall, while she slipped on a transparent surgical glove and lubricated the finger sleeves with a healthy dab of K-Y jelly.

She plunged two fingers through the gateway of my anal goatee into my rectum. A dangling dillberry brushed against her knuckles. Dr. Foster was largely innocuous but good for tickling my *toches*.

I felt nauseous when her fingers penetrated through the streamlined funnel all the way to my descending colon. The attack intensified. She landed a flurry of short jabs, culminating the series with a right uppercut to the posterior lobe of my prostate. Her fingernails tickled me through rubber gloves. She seemed to be intrigued by the architecture of the chestnut-shaped gland and by my uninhibited contractions. I felt completely powerless while in the grasp of her two controlling fingers, but at the same time her digital massage put me in a state of bliss.

She felt the consistency of prostate secretion, the remains of a milky fluid, strikingly rich in zinc, which was discharged by excretory ducts at a time of seminal emission. Throughout this urodynamic workup she cleaned out my anal reservoir. I panted breathlessly, but her thrusts continued.

"More, mmn, more, ah! More. Oh, that's so good. I love it. Harder, deeper, wider, now you're getting it, into the intima," I whispered in unintelligible groans of ecstasy. She turned her wrist inwards and tried a backhand shove, maneuvering her fingers to cover the whole expanse of my rectum—her chance to get even with the male sex.

"Aside from a slight sensitivity of the rectal tissues, I do not detect any sign of inflammation or prostatic obstruction." She gave one final push with three fingers and held them there in place for an extra seven seconds before slipping off the glove and depositing it in the trash. "I have nothing else to tell you," she said and walked over to the sink to wash her hands.

"Dr. Foster," I managed to squeak, as soon as my breath returned to normal. "In other words, the source of my pain is largely psychosomatic, due to my anal retentive behavior."

"That's right. The discomfort is probably psychosomatic. Many patients in pain are often disappointed when a physician informs them that there is nothing physically wrong with them. Don't worry," she whispered rubbing her hand over my shoulders, "you'll be O.K. Before you leave Hastings, stop by the receptionist and make an appointment to see me in two weeks. If my schedule is tight, you can tell her that I insist she squeeze you in."

"Sure, I'll run over there as soon as I get dressed," I said buoyantly, savoring the special treatment. "Dr. Foster, I really appreciate the time you've given me in this most thorough physical examination. Most of the physicals which I get from my family doctor or the run-of-the-mill specialist are like a ten minute quickie." Paranoia gripped my belly when I realized I was talking nonsense. Quickies were for hookers, not physicians.

This boy is certainly peculiar, I imagined her thinking. I wonder if he's trying to impress me. What he says is true. I do enjoy being thorough and methodical; it's my nature as well as a result of my training. Jeremy certainly possesses enough enthusiasm to make it through medical school. I only hope that he's not tripped up by his own phobias. It would be a shame if the medical profession would lose such a gifted young mind. He has a brilliant career ahead of him. Perhaps I should spend some extra time with him. She decided then that she was going to help me recover, I chose to believe.

Gifted Child Syndrome

Although my mother is a perennial optimist, true joy always misses her. I've never seen her laugh or smile without also evincing pain. The semi-circular wrinkles in her cheeks which express her fleeting happiness are only inverted grimaces anticipating an imminent horror, perhaps a Fourth Reich. Just as she once dyed her hair red to hide her Jewish identity while working in the Dutch underground, she forces herself to smile today to protect her children from her memory of the Nazi slaughter which claimed the lives of her parents, friends and relatives. But the bitter phlegm which she swallowed crossed her placenta and became embedded in my psyche.

My father, too, lost his mother. It was in 1933, the year Hitler came to power. Dad tells me that she was a stunning beauty before she died of bacterial endocarditis, leaving three young children behind her. Ten years later she would have been saved by antibiotics, but my grandfather, a widely respected physician from Munich who treated the poor at no expense, stood helplessly at her bedside.

My mother never read Dr. Spock's *Manual on Child and Baby Care*. That's why I spent the first two years of my life in a crib, while she worked in the kitchen or taught Hebrew school and left me alone in the bedroom. The crib protected me from the outside world. No one was going to steal her baby for an experiment with tuberculin vaccines.

The crib was a convenient place to keep a hyperactive toddler, who said "no" to everything. My muscles were too weak for me to climb above the high bar and escape on my own, and, lying there, I was constantly hallucinating, watching parades of insects with sharp pincers crawl up my legs. My stubby fingers tried to squish them dead, but the bugs survived, digging in under my clammy skin, where they deposited their eggs in my baby fat to hatch into future neuroses.

My father enrolled me at the age of five in a Yeshiva because he wanted me to get the same Orthodox education he had received. We were among a handful of observant Jewish families living in a predominantly non-Jewish upper middle class suburban community. My parents arranged for me to join a van pool transporting seven Orthodox Jewish children from the neighboring communities to Bar Kochva Academy, the closest Yeshiva, located fifteen miles away. The ride took almost an hour each way. Every night my parents sent me to bed early so I could wake up at six-thirty to recite my prayers at the crack of dawn.

The mornings at Bar Kochva were filled with Hebrew lessons. The afternoons were taken up with English. Laws and Customs held the highest priority—the rituals learned by rote rather than by reason. Every Yeshiva student learned to pray to God after he washed his hands or wiped his *toches*, in that order.

I knew most of the prayers before they were taught in the class, thanks to my father's coaching. He had been a professor at a rabbinical school. His special subject was Midrash, an ancient biblical commentary. Although he had studied under Martin Buber, he didn't know the first thing about communicating with his son.

One day my third grade Hebrew teacher, Mr. Rosen, taught the class to recite the blessing over wine and rewarded a dixie cup of grape juice to anyone who could sing the entire prayer without making an error in pronunciation. I was the only kid in the class who went to recess with purple lips. I went on to win awards in speed praying, reciting the Grace After Meals in forty-seven seconds flat, five times faster than the norm. My teachers placed me on the honor roll in Hebrew, English, and Deportment, until I advanced to the fourth grade. Then things began to sour.

One morning I saw Rabbi Zimel, our principal, pull a boy by his ears into his office. The next day I saw another fellow slapped with a two week detention slip for taking off his jacket on a cool Spring day, in defiance of a student marshal's orders. I thought at the time that Rabbi Zimel was out to deny us sunshine.

On one occasion, Mrs. Atkin, my English teacher, overheard someone call her a *putz* from my corner of the classroom. She made the entire class line up against the wall and stand at attention until the guilty one among us confessed and apologized. If no one would speak up, everyone would be detained after school.

I was a model student in everyone's eyes: quiet, obedient, articulate, a *superchazen* when it came to leading the class in prayers, and the truth was that I never did call her a *putz*. But I was tired of the privileged status given to a rabbi's son as I stood against the wall at attention with my fellow classmates until Mrs. Atkin had her way. Can you imagine how long forty-five minutes is to a nine year old?

Moishe, the fat kid sitting next to me, who would often pick my mother's liverwurst and pickle sandwiches from the garbage can after finishing his own lunch, was always calling her names. Everyone was afraid to squeal on him because Moishe was known to retaliate physically. I raised my hand and waved it conspicuously until she recognized me.

"Mrs. Atkin, I was the one who called you a *putz*. I promise I'll never call you a *putz* again," I cried emphatically, so she would never forget it. My classmates looked at me as if I were crazy. Why was Jeremy shouldering the blame? Moishe looked at me curiously, sighed, and wiped the liverwurst off his mouth with the back of his hand.

Mrs. Atkin's horn-rimmed glasses fell off the crown of her long, beaked nose as she whipped back her head and glared at me incredulously. She looked bewildered, refusing to believe that the *putz* call had come from my mouth, but after I flashed a fiendish smile, a molten grimace suffused her cheeks. I followed her angry finger out the door and sat all afternoon in Rabbi Zimmel's office, copying the Ten Commandments eighteen times, the numerological equivalent of *Chai*—That's Life!

That very same day my name was scratched from the honor roll and added to the Yeshiva blacklist. My mother was asked to come over immediately to Bar Kochva for a private conference with Mrs. Atkin and Rabbi Zimel. Two hours later, I was released in her custody. She had intimated to Rabbi Zimel that I had emotional problems at home.

The following day I helped organize the first gang in the history of the academy. Our gang, the Masada-five, terrorized the obedient sissies who did everything the Rabbi told them to. We cordoned off the bathrooms and charged them a nickel for crossing our path, or a dime for a round trip. Since we were a charitable organization of orthodox extortionists, good deed doers, real *mitzvahs*, we offered a discount plan for students who wanted to purchase two-week commuting tickets for a dollar.

Rabbi Zimel's telephone wouldn't stop ringing. Angry parents called to find out who was responsible for stealing their children's lunch money. Rabbi Zimel called us individually into his office and warned that we would be punished if we were seen loitering near the bathrooms, water fountain or even the playground. During recess, all of the other children could play together without restrictions. They could skip rope, play tag, and even flip baseball cards for money, but no more than two members of the Masada-five were allowed to congregate on the premises of the Yeshiva. How were we ever going to get a *minyan*? I hated this infringement on my freedom and I didn't like his hairy ears either. Zimel was in for more trouble.

Before a Jewish boy is Bar-Mitzvahed at the age of thirteen, he is obliged to wear a *tzitzis* throughout the waking day. *Tzitzis* are those loose white fringes sewn on a prayer shawl which serve as a visible reminder of one's Jewish identity. While reciting our holiest prayers, we wound the fringes around our fingers and kissed them. Although we were only permitted to kiss them while we prayed, I used to chew on the fringes all day to break in my second set of teeth.

Not wearing *tzitzis* was an unthinkable act. One morning I didn't wear them to the Yeshiva. All the different punishments and humiliations resulting from my phantom *putz* call and gang activities upset me. Really, that's why I decided not to wear my *tzitzis* to school that morning.

Forgotten *tzitzis* always required a special trip to Rabbi Zimel's office and the necessary penance of purchasing one of the Yeshiva's own brand for sixty cents. It was drip-dry and stamped with the Star of David along with the Bar Kochva monograph—totally Kosher. Everyone knew that Rabbi Zimel made a forty percent commission on every pair of *tzitzis* he sold through his moonlighting job as regional manager of Testament Enterprises, a distributor of *mezuzas*, holy water, jade Buddhas and other religious supplies.

When I walked into Rabbi Zimel's office, I looked at him sheepishly—a real *nebische*—and told him that I didn't have the money to buy a new pair of *tzitzis*. He blessed me, laid a fresh pair on my shoulders and escorted me back to class. I had no intention of paying him back. Ignoring the debt soon became a subconscious habit and I never paid a dime. They called my folks at the end of the month and made them pay a fat bill for a dozen sets of new *tzitzis*. It was compounded by a service charge and an interest penalty.

Mr. Rosen didn't give up on me. Although I had a few behavioral problems, I was still his most resourceful student. I proved to the class what a *mitzvah* was by tutoring students with learning disabilities. He was extremely pleased the day I brought a stopwatch to class, helping me to organize relay races for our speed-praying league. First prize for the fastest team was a copy of *The Biography of Sandy Koufax*, the man who stunned the world by refusing to pitch on Yom Kippur during the World Series. Together, Mr. Rosen and I egged on the slower students to hasten their pace, as if we were all part of one big relay team and every Jew counted in the race to heaven.

Poor Mr. Rosen, who saw me do nothing wrong, learned from other teachers that I was a sneaky terror. One of the student's mothers called Rabbi Zimel to find out which naughty child had dipped her daughter's blond pigtails in a jar of red fingerpaint. All teachers were assigned to watch me closely. When Mr. Rosen found out that I was responsible in the fingerpaint affair, he dismantled my speed-praying league and in doing so poisoned my feelings towards Yehova, Lord of the Jews.

One morning, while the class was practicing the Kiddush, the blessing over wine, Mr. Rosen asked me to write the prayer on the blackboard. I broke a piece of chalk in half and squeaked the rough edge against the slate until my classmates pleaded for me to stop. Instead of writing God's name in the traditional abbreviated spelling, I dared to write his name, Yehova, in bold Hebrew letters as it was printed in the prayer book. Everyone knew that only a rabbi could write God's real name by hand.

"Yehova, Yehova," I shouted so that everyone down the hall could hear me call out God's name in vain, "come out, come out, wherever you are." A surge of fear raced up my spine. With the stage to myself, I threw my *yarmulke* on the floor, spat on the blackboard, where I had written God's name, and danced the Hora by myself in front of the class. The children couldn't believe their eyes.

All of a sudden I heard Mr. Rosen's squeaky, winged-tip shoes coming straight at me full speed ahead. Before I had time to catch my breath, he wrapped his hairy hand under my chin and held me up at eye level so close that his red face became a blur.

I shivered, my feet dangling in space. My neck muscles strained to hold up the weight of my body. He shook my mouth so hard my teeth rattled. I must have looked like I was having convulsions. I was thinking of calling on God again, only this time I needed help. At the same time, it was a beautiful feeling being the agent of another person's rage. Would he be forced to apologize to me before the class?

Before I knew what was happening, Mr. Rosen wrapped his arm under my knees and carried me out to the hall, my head trailing inches above the floor. I had never seen my classmates upside down before. He uprighted me against the wall lockers and slapped me three times in the face with the back of his hand, each blow driving my head back into the lockers. I felt like a yo-yo. Flesh-metal-flesh-metal-flesh-metal . . . A fine stream of blood, trickling out of my right nostril stopped him, and I saw his hatred replaced by fear.

"I'll sue you, I'll sue you, you, you. I hate you!" I cried, my back sliding against the locker knobs. I buried my head in my arms and kicked my legs blindly under his looming shadow, hoping that a leather heel would land on his shin. "You're not my Daddy," I screamed, clenching my fists under his wheezing nose. "You can't hit me. I hate you. Rosen, you are dead. When I get big, you're going to suffer." I knew he couldn't hit me again. I noticed the blood dripping down the side of my nose tasted salty. "Rosen, I wish blindness unto you and your blessed family before the New Year, you lousy fuck!" My voice carried down the hall. Mrs. Grossman, Rabbi Zimel's secretary, stuck her head out of the office, saw that Mr. Rosen was in charge and went back to her typing.

"Get off the floor, Lipschitz," he said. "We're going to Rabbi Zimel's office." Pulling me to my feet, he almost yanked my shoulder loose. My wrist was crushed in his hairy hand.

"Get your fucking paws off me, you creep. Oh, I'm going to get you, Rosen," I snarled, my words following my index finger up to his nose. When he let go of my wrist, my body dropped to the floor. I was amazed to spot an unmistakable fear in his eyes. Suddenly I realized that I was in command and felt a strange glow of triumph. I tried to relax by lying limply on the floor, but heard his squeaky shoes shuffle beside me. Gloating inside, I felt a bizarre mixture of self-pity and rapture in my conquest of an adult. What happened? Why did he do this to me? It had all gone by so fast. Soon, sustained and soothed, I pretended that I had fainted.

Mrs. Grossman, who was also the Yeshiva nurse, arrived and prodded my ribs with her pointed shoe. "Ouch. Hey, you're hurting me!" I screamed, getting up off the floor.

"See, Rabbi Zimel," she said, looking over her shoulder, "I told you he's only faking." Four teachers, Rabbi Zimel and Mrs. Grossman surrounded me, quarantining me from the other students.

An hour later I sat outside Rabbi Zimel's office with a plug of cotton in my nose, not knowing how long I would be detained before I was allowed to go home. It was raining hard outside. All of the other students had long since boarded their buses home. Most of the teachers had already left for the day. Mrs. Grossman covered her hair with a plastic rain hat and waited inside for the rain to abate.

As I was thumbing through my coloring book of Noah and the Ark, I wished that it would rain for forty days and forty nights. Then nobody would be able to go to Yeshiva, not even the kids who lived around the block. The sound of wet galoshes slushing down the hall startled me.

When I saw my father's angry face, I almost wet my pants. There was nothing more embarrassing than seeing my parents in school. His salt and pepper beard was soaked with rain; a few drops beaded on the most resilient bristles. He walked straight towards Rabbi Zimel's study, pretending not to notice me, then turned the door knob without knocking and slammed the door behind him. A sharp crack of thunder broke the sound barrier and the vibrations released a few drops of pee down the sides of my legs. Uh oh, I thought, I'm in for some real trouble.

"Hello, I'm Rabbi Lipschitz," I heard Dad say and saw them shake hands. "Has my boy been giving you trouble? You know, we don't tolerate this sort of behavior at home." My father was escorted into the Rabbi's study and the double-doors were closed behind him.

"Sit down Manfred. Relax. Do you mind if I smoke?" I strained to hear what Zimel was saying and edged my chair closer to the door. Mrs. Grossman flashed a reproachful stare in my direction, adjusted her raincap and finally decided to walk to her car.

"You know, it's not every day at Bar Kochva that we have such a distinguished guest."

"Well, I could have come here under better circumstances. Now tell me Seth—I want to know all of the details—what did my boy do?"

"Before we go into it, Manfred, I want you to know that I really enjoyed your last article on the Maccabean Revolt in *Jewish Frontier*. I didn't know that Midrash was your specialty until I read your by-line. How long have you been teaching at the rabbinical college?"

"Oh, on and off, seventeen years since my wife and I returned from Israel. The seminary's changed a great deal in the past few years. The neighborhood's changing too. I'm afraid to walk the streets these days."

"What I want to know, Manfred, is if the Greek language was influenced by Hebrew. This would have a tremendous impact on Hellenistic studies, if it were found to be true."

"Well, the scholars approach it in various ways. Although there are some similarities between the linguistic roots of Greek and Hebrew, the truth is that we simply do not know. Only God knows the answer. But all of this is way off the track. I want to know what Jeremy did. Why was I called out here, made to drive for twenty-five miles on Thursday afternoon? The traffic was horrible. And as it stands now, he's already spoiled my *Shabas*." A cloud of cigar smoke seeped through the door cracks and I knew that the conversation would get heavy. Rabbi Zimel cleared his throat and rolled his chair back and forth.

"He wrote the name of *Ha 'Shem* on the blackboard, spat on his *Kipah* and...

"What! Oh, I'm going to see that he gets a licking when he gets home..." I could hear Dad's leg shaking nervously through the door.

"I'm afraid, Manfred, that this is only the icing on the cake, and I'm talking about *Goyische kugle*. To be frank with you, I'll have to ... You're going to have to put Jeremy in another school. We can't handle him here at Bar Kochva any longer. I hate to do this to the son of a rabbi and a boy so bright, with such promise, such potential, he could be a doctor yet, but parents have been complaining and I've got a school to run. Have a little *rachmones* on me too, Rabbi?"

"Don't give me any of this *rachmones* crap. That's why we pay tuition. Don't ask me for sympathy. Your job is to educate our children to lead good Jewish lives. Where did you receive your training anyway?"

"That's telling him Dad," I whispered.

"Yeshiva University. Magna Cum Laude."

"Then what are you doing in a dive like this?"

"It's close to home. My brother owns a yarn factory in town. My parents live around the corner. I'm *Shomer Shabas* so it's a short walk to the temple on Saturdays. What do you want? I grew up here."

"My God, don't you know how to run a Yeshiva? When I was in a Yeshiva the teachers gave the kids a *pach* right on their *popess* and if that didn't work, they'd use a strap."

"We've tried everything, Rabbi, including corporal punishment. We can't discipline him. Your son is incorrigible. I hate to say this, Manfred, but I think his soul is spirited by a *dybbuk*."

At these words my father stormed out the door, grabbed me by the wrist and pulled me out of the office. On the way home, he gave me the silent treatment and didn't speak to me or recognize my existence in any way for four days. His silence hurt much more than the strap, but deep down I knew that he loved me and did it for my own good.

The following week, my parents enrolled me at Thomas Jefferson, the local elementary school. At first they considered sending me to another Yeshiva since there were only two other Jewish children in our school district. However, I resisted the idea of another orthodox environment and convinced them that the public school was better, even if they risked provoking an anti-Semitic backlash. Thomas Jefferson was but a hop, skip and a jump from home and I was thrilled that I didn't have to commute for two hours every day.

Sometimes I ate lunch over at a classmate's house and savored the non-Kosher foods. I would gobble down slices of soft, white bread with the crust torn off. I would get bacon, macaroni and cheese, angel food cake and other *Goyische* delights which were not available to me, either at the Yeshiva or in my parents' kosher house. The transition to public school was difficult. While I had previously been able to intimidate the feeble Jewish students at Bar Kochva, Thomas Jefferson Elementary School had bullies of its own, some of whom were already carrying switchblades. Moreover, all of the teachers were extremely strict and would tolerate no disrespectful behavior.

My new teacher was Mrs. Grace Wright, an elderly lady who had lived all her life in our town and taught for forty years at Thomas Jefferson. Although she was a tough disciplinarian, her intimidating shouts would often modulate to a maternal whisper. She had a heart of gold. Mrs. Wright was my first *Shikse* mother. I really admired her for her teaching us good Christian values, which I had never learned at Bar Kochva. One of these lessons was, "Kindness doesn't cost a penny." I remember hearing her tell us stories with tears in her eyes about kindness being rewarded many times over. Kindness would lead our fellow human beings to be kind to us in return. She said if there was only one lesson we would remember from her class, it should be to be kind to all, friends and strangers alike.

The object of this lesson was to direct our attention towards a new student in class who was a midget and whom the kids called "head." As the other appointed freak in class, I too received my share of nicknames. To balance the attack, everyone called me "curly locks." I was so frightened by my physically fit and fearless classmates that during recess I isolated myself in the playground.

One morning, Mrs. Wright overheard some four-letter words in the hallway and wanted to find out the source of this obscene language. She called us individually into the hallway and confronted us one on one. She asked me whether I had called her by any names. I answered, "Sure, fuckface. You're nothing but a Christian bitch."

Somehow I couldn't refrain from admitting guilt for acts I had never committed. Denying any accusation was more difficult for me than incriminating myself for another student's mischief. Besides, this was the only way I could become the center of attention. As the only Jewish child in class, I could be their scapegoat. Eventually, I might avenge the death of my grandparents, by stirring up an anti-Semitic backlash.

Since corporal punishment was forbidden in public schools, Mrs. Wright made sure she would have an opportunity to traumatize me psychologically, so that I wouldn't utter an obscenity again for the rest of my life. When I returned to the classroom, she humiliated me so badly that I wanted to crawl out of my skin and hide under the radiator, like a dried-out cockroach. There was no place to which I could flee.

The next minute, I was exiled from the classroom. Not even a trace of my former presence in the class would remain. Judenraus. I was forced to clean out my desk with soap and water, removing every pencil shaving and crayon bit. Shivering before the disdainful stares of my classmates, I scrubbed the old wood and wished that I was back in the Yeshiva with my fellow Jewish sissies. The whole procedure took over half an hour and was more important for the class to witness than their lesson in American history. I was eventually ushered to the principal's office and forced to hand copy twelve pages from a textbook of geography until I developed writer's cramp.

My parents were called in for a conference with the principal and Mrs. Wright. They were effusively polite and apologetic. The following day, I was referred to the school psychologist, who gave me a battery of tests measuring intellectual growth and psychomotor development. I gave all the wrong answers to insure that they would classify me as a mental defective. Eventually I was transferred to a special class for students with minimal brain dysfunction. My new teacher was so puzzled by my unresponsiveness that she thought I was autistic. As soon as I returned home I took it out on my parents.

After dinner, when my parents were trying to relax in the living room with danish and coffee, I stampeded around the house, marking up the walls with indelible ink, over-turning the furniture, even burning their hard-earned money in the fireplace. It's amazing how much damage a nine year old can do. After scaring my father half to death with a steak knife, I locked my parents out of the house. Then I opened the living room curtains, took off all my clothes and banged on the piano. I resented my father's silent treatment and enjoyed acting like I was sick in the head to punish them in return. I told my father that it was a shame that Hitler didn't finish him off before he had a son. My parents took a long walk in the county park, wondering whether Hitler's curse had lingered beyond the date of Liberation. Why were children of survivors vulnerable to post-Holocaustal psychogenic trauma?

One day Mom picked me up at school and said that she was taking me to the doctor. I felt fine physically and didn't know what she was talking about. When we got there my mother sat dejectedly in the waiting room. She hadn't even bothered to take off her coat. From time to time I could hear her mutter, "*Oy ves mir*, what is happening to my child?" Before long the double doors were opened and I was led into a spacious office. My mother stayed behind, thumbing through dated magazines.

I sat down on a plush velvet chair across from the psychiatrist's rosewood desk, listening to unfamiliar words, and grasping that decisions were being made about my future. Dr. Sheer looked like a businessman in his iridescent suit. He asked a few dozen questions, to which I only answered yes or no. I followed him around a spiral staircase leading to the playroom and crawled inside a cardboard dollhouse. While I played with the dolls, he loomed over me, chain smoking. I punched the "mother" doll in the face. Dr. Sheer quickly noted this on his yellow pad.

When the forty-five minute session was over, Dr. Sheer handed Mom a prescription and a few samples of Thorazine, without warning her about the potential side effects. The sugar-coated tablets looked like fruit-flavored vitamins.

"Thank you, Dr. Schultz," she said, handing him a check for sixty dollars, an amount which matched our family's weekly food bill at the time. "I'll make sure that Jeremy takes his medication four times a day."

"We'll see you next week, Mrs. Lipschitz. Goodbye, Jeremy."

"Jeremy, say goodbye to Dr. Schultz."

"No," I said sullenly and stamped my foot.

Sensing our mutual embarrassment, he backpedalled discretely into his office and shut the doors behind him.

"Why do I have to see this creep Schultz again Mom?" I asked, flinching away from the static electrical shock of her coat.

"Sh, the doctor can hear you. We're very lucky that he accepted you as his patient."

"You're wasting your money."

"Jeremy, now don't be fresh. Dr. Schultz only wants to make you feel good, so you can play ball every day after school with your nice friends. Remind me to stop off at the pharmacy before we go home. And if you're good, I'll pick up a couple of eclaires."

The intensive psychotherapy and daytime sedation had no effect on me. Instead my behavior grew worse. Dr. Schultz experimented with more powerful phenothiazines, Stellazine and Prolixin, which gave me agonizing side effects, causing tetanus-like convulsions in my neck muscles and Parkinsonian tremors in my fingers and toes. Stellazine gave me cotton mouth, urinary retention and induced the same visual and auditory hallucinations I had remembered as a toddler in the crib. Dr. Schultz reassured us that although these side effects were unpleasant, they also proved that the medication was working. Since I weighed under sixty-five pounds, he would consider changing to Mellaril and prescribe Cogentin to alleviate the muscle spasms.

When dinner was served, Mom dropped a little brown coated tablet of Mellaril on my plate. My father and my two sisters, Miriam and Tzipporah, watched me, but didn't say anything while I toyed with the pill and bounced it on the plate. I even cut the candied shell with a steak knife to expose the bitter white core.

"Jeremy, stop playing and take your medicine this instant," Mom shrieked as she stirred the noodles over the stove.

"Why should I have to take those pills? How would you like to be sleepy for the rest of the day?" I whined, wiping up a few flecks with a crust of buttered bread.

"Jeremy," my father screamed, his face turning as red as the borscht in his soup bowl. "Don't you know that I had to eat plaster and tulip bulbs during the war? It's a sin to waste food!"

"You call this food? The only thing this medicine ever does is make me sick."

"Dr. Schultz says you need the medication to help you control yourself," my mother barked. "Now take your medicine and eat your dinner."

"I don't need anybody to tell me how to control myself," I screamed, flinging a wooden bowl of celery and carrot sticks at my mother's head.

"Jeremy, leave the dinner table this instant," my father warned, raising his hand threateningly in the air.

"But I haven't eaten dinner yet."

"Jeremy," Tzippy shouted. She grabbed my arm firmly, but unaggressively, hoping I would obey my father's command and avoid a major confrontation.

"Get your paws off me," I warned, yanking my skinny arm from her slackening grip. "I'm sick of taking medication. From now on, I'm on strike. I'm tired of having to go to bed at nine o'clock every night while all the other kids are staying up late and watching T.V. If you took some of this stuff you'd know how I feel."

I pulverized the tablet with the back of my spoon and pinched the powder between two fingers. All eyes were on the residue of the expensive medicine. For a moment everyone was silent. Reaching across the table, I sprinkled the powder on my father's salad. The solute slid down in a stream of red vinegar along a vein in a piece of lettuce.

Dad slapped my hand and warned me with an upraised finger that I was going to get a real licking if I didn't pull myself together. But it was the worst thing he could do. I tilted the table and the salad bowl fell on his lap, soiling his new suit.

"Don't hit me," I snarled with an impish grin, my hand curling into a fist, "or I'll push over the whole table."

My father started to cry. "Dear God," he whispered, "I beseech you. Have mercy on my son. Clear up this divine excrescence and purge the *dybbuk* from Jeremy's soul. He's only a child. He's my only son. Lotte," he said in the same breath, "I'm going upstairs to change. Will you take this suit to the cleaners tomorrow morning? I don't want the stains to set in."

"Sure, Manfred, go upstairs. We'll take care of Jeremy."

Tzippy, who had decided that she would be my therapist, tried to take charge. "Jerry, if you'd like to eat here with everyone," she said sternly, "then you must behave in a civilized manner. If you're concerned about the side effects of the medication, we can talk about it later. But right now we're eating dinner." She rested her arm on my shoulder, scratched the length of my spine, and whispered in my ear, "We can play a long game of Risk after dinner and I'll even throw in a Brumpskiss, if you're good."

"Nah, I'm going to eat my dinner on the porch."

"No, Jeremy," Mom interrupted, "everyone's eating in the kitchen. If you don't want to eat now, you can go straight to bed."

"But I'm not sleepy," I laughed, brushing off the few remaining flecks of tranquilizer powder from my plate.

"Then take your Mellaril," she shrieked, and dropped a fresh tablet on my plate.

"I thought we'd already been through that," Tzippy interrupted, defending me for the first time. "Let's forget the whole thing and enjoy the nice meal mother has prepared for us." I was pleased to hear her back me up, although it sounded like she was just showing off what she had learned recently in a college sociology course.

I positioned the tablet between my cheek and upper gum and, gripping it there, I pretended to swallow it. As soon as everyone had settled down to dinner, I excused myself, ran to the bathroom and flushed it down the toilet.

Other incidents were not forgotten so easily. My family knew that I was dangerous to live with. I spent an entire day in a neurological laboratory with electrodes plastered to my scalp. The results of the EEG tests were normal and the neurologist's diagnosis was that I had a character disorder and would eventually grow out of my pre-adolescent rebellion.

The following day I locked my mother in the bathroom for three hours. My father had to come home early to call a locksmith. That evening I overheard my parents talking about me in German.

"Lotte, I really don't think we can stand these outbursts any longer. Other parents would have sent him away to an institution long ago."

"What's his status on the waiting list at Mt. Sinai?"

"I think it will be at least three months before they can accept him."

"What! Three months! Can't you influence them? You're a rabbi with connections!"

"I've been trying, but the Federation of Jewish Philanthropies is committed to accepting the Schwartzes and Puerto Ricans before they can take in a white child. Now I know how Job felt. There really is no justice in this world. So in the meantime, Lotte, we'll have to send him to the county hospital. These outbursts can't go on. We have a right to enjoy our lives too. There are other people in this house besides Jeremy. Don't worry, I love him just as much as you do. It's not the final solution. He'll only be there for a few weeks. Eventually he'll be transferred to Mt. Sinai."

"All right, Manfred, whatever you say. I know you only want the best for him.

When I heard that they were serious about their intention to send me away, I rummaged through the medicine cabinet and emptied the bottles. I flushed all of the tranquilizers down the toilet, but saved a vial of Cogentin, the potent muscle relaxant which counteracted the side effects of the tranquilizers.

O.K., Mom and Dad, you can send me down the river, I'll make it easy for you. Take me straight to the emergency room.

I woke up in Whitestone Hospital after two days in a coma. When my pupils were no longer dilated but responded to light, I was transferred to the locked ward for acute psychiatric cases and incarcerated criminals, who were either awaiting transfer to another state hospital or simply alleviating overcrowded conditions in the county jail.

My eyelids moved. My head felt like a block of cement. A film of mucus coated my tongue. I could barely swallow. My arms and legs were strapped to the bed so that they reached toward the four corners. I tried to kick my legs, but could only slide them sideways along the sweat-soaked sheets. The straps were like heavy chains, except they were worse; the tight leather didn't let my skin breathe. After struggling helplessly for a few minutes, I screamed at the top of my lungs, "Let me out of here!"

"Shut up," an old man groaned from the far side of the room.

"Let me OWOWOWOWOWOUT!" My cry echoed down the hall and evaporated into the hum of the fluorescent lamps. No one responded.

Twenty minutes later, after I was completely exhausted from kicking my legs against the restraints, a nurse came in and slipped a thermometer in my mouth, ignoring my struggles.

My parents, following the advice of Dr. Schultz, decided to let me stay at Whitestone for what would become the three longest weeks of my life. They seemed oblivious to the fact that I was lone child in a ward for the criminally insane. The county children's shelter was still under construction at the time and there were no other emergency facilities, not even an adolescent psychiatric ward, where I could be placed temporarily.

They finally unstrapped me and let me wander down the smoke-filled corridors of the day room, where most of the men hung out, playing cards or watching game shows, soap operas and the four-thirty movie on T.V.

I explored the confines of the ward, all twenty-five hundred square feet of it, but avoided the dangerous dart game under supervision by the nurses' station. "If I'm gonna survive," I thought, "I'd better behave like a man." Peering out from my lonely vigil near the guarded elevator, I watched the drugged, zombie-like patients walk around in their light blue pajamas, which were sticky and had a cardboard texture from dried drool.

On several occasions I joined in on the communal walk up and down the hall, following the endless procession to the punching bag at one end and the locked double doors at the other. There was nothing for me to do but pace along the hallway, play tic-tac-toe on the checkered floor tiles, or flip baseball cards against the walls. I recognized my face in the reflection of the linoleum tiles, but never saw my features clearly. There were no mirrors on the ward. All the windows were barricaded with two sets of steel mesh screens, so that I had blurred vision again.

When I asked the nurses why I couldn't go home and had to stay in the hospital, they told me that I had been a very, very bad boy. There was nothing I could do but sit out my punishment and miss my dessert. Because it was a maximum security ward, my parents were not allowed to visit me. My only contact with the outside world came through gifts mailed to me from friends of the family. I tried to play with my toys on the cold, waxed floor but only thought of going home.

One evening the nurses served me pork for dinner. When I explained the dietary laws of my faith, they said that they had already known about this restriction and had called my father who gave them permission to serve me non-kosher food. I knew God made provisions for those who were ill to break the commandments, but I found out afterwards that they had never consulted my father. At times I even wished I was back in the Yeshiva, remembering the secure feeling of communal prayer. I would wear my *tzitzis* every morning and be a good boy, if they would only release me from the hospital.

The following morning I heard my name broadcast on the intercom. I was told to report immediately to the shower room in my robe and slippers.

They herded me inside the shower room alongside three mean-looking men. The orderly gave each of us a fresh bar of ivory soap, pointed to the hospital towels hanging on the rack, and closed the door behind us. All of the showers were in a row, without partitions. I chose the one nearest the door and turned the cold water knob to produce a low pressure stream so I could hear what the men were saying. When I saw them stare at me below the waist, my testicles retracted back into my groin. Their hairy chests made them seem powerful and mature like my father. One of the men twitched convulsively and massaged his nipples to smooth out the tremors.

I remembered Mom telling me how her mother had perished in a shower in Auschwitz. In my mind's eye, my grandmother stood in a long line of people who were awaiting inspection by a Nazi physician. The doctor pointed in one of two directions: hard labor or the showers. The wailing chant of *Ani Maamin Bemeveat Hamashiach—I Believe in the Coming of the Messiah*, was absorbed within the walls of the chamber. After the doctor felt Oma's aging skin, she was screened to stand in line with the old, the infirm and the very young.

Ani Maamin. Ani Maamin.

Come on Oma, gouge out his eyes. Just one Nazi. Do it for your grandson. You have nothing to lose.

A Nazi guard prodded his rifle butt against her soft flanks. A Jewish laborer was ordered to open the oven door. She was only fifty-three.

Come back to me, Oma. Although I never met you, I am very close to you. Hold my hand, Oma. I don't want to go into the shower alone.

Huddling in the corner, I eased open the hot water and tested the temperature with my foot before stepping under the shower. A glob of yellow-green mucus swirled around the drain cover and floated towards me. Within a few minutes a pool of psoriasis-flaked water rose up over my ankles.

The tall, grisly-looking man had pock marked cheeks and scars all over his body. With a bass voice he sang German lieder. He slid the cold soap around his hairy chest and groin. His voice boomed against the tiles and its echoes pounded fear in my ears. Although the tunes were familiar, I couldn't recognize any of the words. There were no musical tones in his voice.

I didn't want him to catch me looking at him, so I faced the wall and pretended to adjust the hot and cold knobs. My heart started to beat wildly when I saw, from the corner of my eye, the grisly man play with his stiffening penis. The other men laughed hysterically and, following his initiative, began to play with their hardening horns. I was shocked when I saw them fondle each other and wondered whether they were doing it for my benefit.

They put their hands over each other's shoulders and danced in a circle under the steaming spray. A part of me wanted to join in the fun and dance the Hora. The man who was singing out loud walked over to me, cleared his throat of phlegm and spat the gob between my legs. The mucus choked the drain completely and the water started to spill over to the rest of the bathroom.

"Hey you," he shouted, "little pecker, what are you looking at?" The other men turned off their showers to watch the commotion.

I kept my eyes focused on the crack in the wall between the green tiles, remembering the crib. Suddenly I saw the insects again, crawling up my thighs. Huddling in the corner, I couldn't stop hallucinating. The walls crept closer, pressing me between their flanks, crushing my brittle bones into powder.

My ears were plugged up by a frightened swallow. Free me from the universe. Engulf me in your oblivious heat. I believe, I believe, *Ani Maamin*, I cried, without a sound or tears, hoping that some attentive mother, a female Yehova, would rescue me from the shower. But my voice was only a muffled cry.

"Hey, I'm talking to you. You're staring at me. What are you looking at? Huh? Come on, I'm waiting for an answer." He stepped towards me and pointed a finger threateningly under my nose. I shuddered. My lips turned blue-violet.

"Leave me alone," I cried, turning around to face my enemies with clenched fists.

"Fee, fi, fo, fum, I smell the blood of a little pecker," the grisly man bellowed, stepping closer. A wry smile came to his lips. He pointed to my genitals. "Eeny, meeny, miney, mo. Catch a pecker by the . . . huh, huh, huh, huh." He took a mock swipe at my organ, but didn't quite touch it, preferring to torment me slowly. The other men laughed more loudly and huddled around me, sealing off my exit. I was pushed backwards until I felt the cold tiles pressing against my shivering skin.

"Look at the kid get mad, fellows! Check out his goose-pimples. Bob, I want to have the first crack at him!"

The grisly man planted his feet in front of me. "I'd like to be shown a little respect, young man. Now bend down!" He stared at me with glazed eyes, then pushed the drown of his penis against my throat. His testicles brushed against my collarbone. The other men pressed closer.

"We can hold him down for you if he's slippery."

"Turn him around so you can penetrate, Bob. Looks like a tight fit."

"Kick the kid a little, so he learns to respect his elders."

"Come on, Bob, hurry up. We want a shot at him ourselves."

All cries remained sealed within the steel doors. Suddenly I felt his hand touch my penis gently. He stroked it delicately, as if it were a choice baby knockwurst. The other men were stupified by the sight of my organ and crouched down on their haunches to get a better look at what was going on. The grisly man twisted my organ into a spiral of macaroni. He rubbed his thumb over the crown of my penis.

"I am your father," he bellowed, stroking the shaft softly, "you will obey my command." His warm hand was comforting. Nobody had touched me for weeks. I felt as if I was now one of the guys. But staring into his sick swollen eyes, I remembered how Mom had told me never to talk to strangers.

My muscles were powerless. I didn't have the strength, or the room, to take a step in any direction. I bowed down to his feet. My ears were close to water level, listening to the muffled sound of the high-pressure showers spraying against the ankle-deep pool like silenced bullets. When I looked up at his face, I knew that he was disappointed by my cowardliness and wanted to see me defend myself like a man.

"And now, boys, will you hold him down, so I can have a look inside."

"Help!" I cried pathetically, my voice choking. I tried to stand up, groping blindly for the dry towel rack. The viscous water splashed in my face and burned my eyes. I lost my footing and bruised my kneecap on the hard, wet tiles. "Ouch! Hey, you hurt me!"

"Aw, does it hurt? Let me kiss it," the grisly man said, bending down to ape me. Bubbly saliva poured out the sides of his mouth. His tongue curled into a U and darted through his lips.

Breathing deeply, I suddenly felt a surge of strength. I pushed myself up from the floor, reared back my leg and lashed out, kicking him in the eye with my big toe.

"Aaaaaaah!" The piercing scream was loud enough to penetrate the doors. The other men ignored him and ran back to their showers, soaping their bodies innocently under the steaming water.

The grisly man lunged at me blindly as I ran out of the shower, but I was already halfway out the door and was too slippery for him to latch onto. I ran down the hall towards the nurses' station, leaving a trail of water behind me.

When the head nurse saw me she rushed out of her office and barked to one of the orderlies, "He's naked! Take him away and strap him down. We don't tolerate this type of behavior here. I'm going to call Dr. Grant."

I stood shivering before her. An orderly poked a needle into my behind.

"They . . . They, they, ah . . . " I collapsed on the floor and only remember waking up a day and a half later as if I were coming out of another coma.

Too Valuable to Lose

Every evening, as soon as my classes were over, I returned and found Dr. Foster resting on my mattress in her peach negligee. Silvana would come to me with her arms extended and rub my cold nose along the crevice between her breasts. She held my head against her tender cushions, assuring me that I would be hers forever. Never again would I eat alone in the attic with a box of take-out chicken. She would nourish me with home-cooked meals and add a little fat to my bones. I would be able to swim in an unheated pool without shivering.

She was lying so peacefully, beckoning me to entangle our limbs. Loyal kisses fell like rose petals on tender parts between my scrotum and coccyx. She bent down to mouth and tongue-kiss the crown of my penis, then sucked on it voraciously, as if the fluid generated from my loins was a precious nectar, the only available protein for subsistence. Sucking on it as hard as I would teeth on her nipples, she lured me into neoembryogenic foreplay, then melted into oblivion.

Ten minutes later she returned. A stethoscope hung loosely between her breasts. First she pressed the cold metal disk against my sternum, which made me shiver and recoil, but then she lunged forward with her hot nipples, oozing pheromonal secretions. She clawed my back, her nails leaving bloody crescents, half moons on my scapulae. No, she would never let me go. I was hers for the evening.

But then I realized that she would have to return to her safe, suburban haven over the bridge to shoot pool with her husband. He needed to unwind in their enormous recreation room after setting so many bones in plaster casts during the day. Why did orthopedic surgeons have to be so successful, socially and professionally? He'd put a little chalk on the cue tip and tweak it as if it were his wife's nipple, then line up his shot. After a moment of hesitation, he'd push that cue ball so tenderly that the eight ball would drop in the pocket without scratching and he'd come perfectly on target, staining the satin sheets which had been earned by soaking their patients in their misfortune.

Why didn't the Fosters have a joint practice in their home and gross $500 an hour with low overhead, a real family practice in cash medicine? Wasn't it a challenge to make a financial killing in the care of sick people? They could put their patients through the mill and soak their pocketbooks dry. With all the money they'd make in a day, they could have a cash orgy. They could wallpaper their bedroom with cash and wipe each other's genitals dry with that silver-threaded paper, until the crust obscured the serial numbers. Wasn't it wonderful to belong to the ranks of the privileged profession which guaranteed a base income of $60,000 a year, even for the most *schlemielische* M.D.'s who didn't know the first thing about billing or insurance? They'd always go on such nice vacations to the Bahamas or Guadeloupe, but never for more than two weeks, because there was always a problem with patients who were too attached to them and would go through M.D. withdrawal, an ordeal worse than kicking a heroin habit.

Silvana was my mamma maraschino, her nipples stained with red dye number four. Her subspecialty to internal medicine was human sexuality, without a psychiatrist's detachment or host's resistance. Silvana had a special magic about her, perhaps a God-given gift, the power to heal, and the strength to sustain me. But I would break the stone tablets and shine forth Moses' wrath at the golden calf. Who sanctioned this heathen idolatry: worshipping the golden calves of a *shikse*? Oh, but I loved her legs so much; they were hard and curved as bowling pins. If brought together, they could bruise my glands and leave them soft and purple as canned plums. But she would treat them ever so delicately. Ever so gently she would guide my hot rod through her cavernosum. But perhaps she would dissect my penis, this professor of anatomy, and pull apart the veins and tubules with tweezers, just as it became engorged with blood. And urological surgeons would have to be called in to stem the blood flow and to sew up a new urinary duct.

The eleven o'clock siren blared across the churchyard like a cat in heat. It was time for me to retire, but always I remained rigidly awake for four or five hours before I could get to sleep, and even then it was from sheer exhaustion. My skin was feverish with desire. Thoughts of Silvana brought on inconquerable cycles of insomnia, compounded by depression and loss of appetite. Lying supine on crusty sheets, I reached to discover Silvana's corporeal dimensions, but felt nothing other than the film of fetid perspiration covering my chest. What I imagined as Silvana's breasts were only lumps in the fiber-fill pillow. I was a sleepless rooster; my cock cried out for her.

In one of my wilder visions, I awoke at Hastings in a straight jacket with my boots chained together and my mouth gagged with a wad of medicinal cotton. The nurses wouldn't know how to handle me, afraid that if they removed the cotton, I would bite them. But I would only beg to be hospitalized with Silvana at my bedside. If I didn't see Dr. Foster real soon, I would spend the rest of my life standing on the street corner selling pencils.

One morning, after another sleepless night, I called the receptionist at Hastings. I tried to make an early appointment, but could only make one for three weeks later. She was all booked up. I was infuriated at the thought of Dr. Foster's intense popularity with the other students, especially with the pre-meds from Fairbanks who filled her schedule. One of Dr. Foster's responsibilities at the university was to steer the pre-med students along the proper course to medical school. I could just see them—little colon climbers who kissed ass every week so that in their senior year they could squeeze out a letter of recommendation from an M.D. I called every morning to see whether a slot had opened up in her schedule. After a week of relentless calls, one of the students cancelled. I was scheduled to see Dr. Foster the following morning.

I lay awake the entire night, counting the tortuous minutes remaining before my appointment. The radium-dipped hands of the alarm clock rotated in deliberate revolutions. My eyelids sagged until I looked like a rock musician at the end of a trans-Atlantic tour. Finally, the first ultra-violet rays peeked above the roof of the Demarest Student Center, signalling the crows and sparrows to screech from their perches on sagging power lines. Dawn, you've come at last! I be-bopped out of bed but refrained from eating breakfast that morning to avoid forcing a shit and to look more undernourished and withdrawn.

Stepping into the hot shower, I soaked my brillo-like hair with medicated zinc shampoo and followed it with a lilac-scented cream rinse. It took a half hour for me to wash all the crooks and crevices of my angular body—under my slippery feet, the bends in my knees, armpits, crotch—all tasting the cold amber bar of hypoallergenic soap. Would my thoroughly scrubbed skin match her sanitary standards, I wondered? With a clean pair of underwear I decided I could go to the clinic with the greatest confidence and did. Then I selected white permanent press pants and a light blue pullover sweater because the colors matched the nurses' uniforms. With only an hour to kill before my appointment, I rolled a joint, stuffed it into my shirt pocket and took the campus bus to Fairbanks.

Meandering through the foothills of Fairbanks, I wandered upon Passion Puddle, a pond which was named after the young couples who sat underneath the willow trees and necked in public in between feeding the ducks. Even at eight o'clock in the morning there were two happy teenager couples tongue-kissing by the edge of the pond. Their public exhibition was obviously meant to tease lonely passers-by. What show-offs, I thought, scratching my scrotum in envy. Before walking away, I smoked the joint and topped it off with a hit of Binaca spray.

The health center received its first customer at eight forty-five in the morning; it happened to be me. The waiting room was empty. The receptionist hadn't even arrived yet. A night shift nurse still manned the counter. She was one of the few who didn't know me by name. I could tell by her prim smile that she approved of my blue and white outfit.

I told her my name before she could ask: "Jeremy Lipschitz."

"How do you spell that?" she asked.

I assumed the fourth position of dance, my chin raised high above my Adam's apple, my hands clasped like an opera singer. Through my dried, cracked lips, I hissed, "With a 'C.' "

"Where does the letter 'C' go in a name like Lipschitz?"

Like a real American Christian, I spelled out my name clearly and slowly. I thumbed the lobes of my nose *shnipsingly*; no one could tell.

"So that's where the 'C' goes." After taking several deep breaths she asked, "Jeremy, what class are you in?"

"I have advanced standing. That's a separate category you know."

At the time I transferred to Kirk I was required to fill out a medical history form for Hastings Health Center. I refused to state the year I intended to graduate, so I would remain unclassified. I also lied about my age, telling them I was only sixteen, although I was really twenty-one. On paper, I was the youngest student in the university, admitted by special examination. If I could convince the doctors and nurses that I was truly advanced, then they would treat me as if I were advanced, just a step away from an assistant professor. Maternal instinct would compel the staff to fill in that gaping lack in me.

My boyish face softened the nurse's eyes when she looked at me across the counter and decided that I was precocious. But she had obviously never heard of a category called "advanced" so she could not decide where to look for my chart.

"Jeremy, perhaps you could save me the trouble of searching through these files. When do you plan to graduate?"

"It's hard to tell. I'm in the accelerated track," I said haughtily.

She turned her back and bent down to search through the lower file drawer. A run in her translucent pantyhose revealed a patch of her scaling thigh which she had neglected to shave in her bi-weekly overhaul. She removed my chart and rolled back the file drawer with her knee until it clicked shut. The rim of her indented nursing cap soared when she stood up to face me. I quickly recoiled my head and wandered down the hall towards the clinic.

I sat down on the bench outside Dr. Foster's office and twiddled my thumbs. Mrs. Godfrey, who headed the wart clinic, found me sitting alone and decided to keep me company for a few minutes.

"Hi Jeremy, are you still writing those nice letters about Hastings?" She tried to cover her mouth while yawning, but it was opened so wide I couldn't see anything but red. I was taken aback by the smell of eggs on her breath so I nodded without saying a word. All my thoughts were trained on Dr. Foster, who must have been caught in the rush hour traffic. If only she would make a dashing entrance and rescue me from Mrs. Godfrey, I thought.

Just then the front door opened, setting off a flurry of activity among the nurses. A mixture of pleasure and fear welled in my lower bowel. Afraid to look up, I gazed at Silvana's long, shapely legs striding down the hall in my direction. A beige tweed blazer complemented a brown cotton skirt. This conservative dresser also liked to be comfortable. I could tell by the stitching that the suit was of an expensive design. She looked fresh and energetic, eager for her first patient. Within minutes I would have her all to myself. Dr. Foster hurried past just as Mrs. Godfrey was about to shower her with the morning news, but when she recognized me sitting on the bench, she paused and looked at me closely. For a moment she was expressionless and I panicked, but then a smile cradled her lips.

"Jeremy, keep your seat," she said in a voice so soft that it made my spine shiver. "I will see you in just a few minutes." Her sleek hand, discolored by scattered age spots, turned the knob and she closed the door behind her. All the nurses returned to their stations.

I buried my head in my hands and tried to think clearly. The vibrations from my quivering thighs rattled my jaw as it hung agape. How am I going to make her grow fond of me, I wondered? A physician's time is precious. Should I impress her with my knowledge of science or rely on pathos this time? Better be pathetic and mix up the cards, I considered. And then at a weak moment I can offer to hire myself out as her butler. Servitude to Silvana would be bliss. Bring out the chains.

The door to the examining room opened. The feminine fragrance of

Sophia trailed around the corner. Her beige outfit was covered by a stiff white labcoat.

"Would you please take a seat in my office, Mr. Lipschitz?" she said in her strained professional tone.

I was angered to hear her address me by my last name and considered telling her, sure, Silvana, I'll crawl under your desk and eat crumbs from your hand. She closed the door behind me and walked over to the medicine cabinet to pick up her stethoscope. God her legs are gorgeous, I thought. Poor woman has to be on her feet all day. If she were my wife, I'd keep her at home and let the maid do the ironing. My eyes traced the curvature of her shins. I noticed a faint beauty mark just below her hemline.

"So Mr. Lipschitz, what can I do for you?" She opened my chart and read through my medical history. Her broad back blocked my view of it so I stared at her patrician profile. She must have been intrigued by the variety of bizarre symptoms in the last few dates of entry. The nurses had made notations for warts, rashes, hangnails, hypochondriasis and more complaints of insomnia and depression. A long embarrassing pause separated us until she recognized her own handwriting, three pages back, in which she had noted complaints of lower back pain and rectal discomfort.

Swinging her left leg over her right, she rotated her swivel chair to face me and asked, "How is your back, Jeremy? Are you still in pain?"

"Thank you, Dr. Foster, my back is much better." I was dying to ask her how her own back felt, but decided to minimize the juvenile remarks and so said, "The pain in my lumbro-sacral region has diminished in intensity. I predict that any lingering discomfort will clear up within a few weeks."

"Yes, that seems to be the case with most minor back pain. If you give your muscles time, they'll loosen up."

"I'm so glad that you have a conservative approach to medicine and refrained from ordering X-rays. I've had my annual quota of exposure. I don't want to become sterile."

"And how is the problem in your private region?" she asked with a teasing smile that nearly precipitated a round of infectious laughter.

"Ah, I was just getting to that. My testicles haven't given me any trouble lately," I cried jubilantly, my eyes beaming.

"You've been taking Dalmane for the past three weeks," she interrupted curtly. "Has this medication helped you sleep?"

"After the first few nights I developed a tolerance. These days Dalmane is no more effective for me than a placebo. I need something stronger, much stronger."

"Did you take two capsules when you had unusual difficulty falling asleep?" Her probing eyes honed in on my conjunctival irritation. I knew my face looked sallow.

"Of course, but what I really need is something more potent, like Methaqualone."

"Jeremy," she whispered in an attempt to placate me while gently denying my request. "I was just thinking about you last week while attending a lecture on insomnia at Downstate Medical School. I saved a reprint of Dr. Friedman's lecture on sleep especially for you. Here, let me give it to you. She opened the lower desk drawer and thumbed through her files until she found the article and placed it on the side of her desk. "This outlines techniques of muscle relaxation through autogenic hypnosis. I think you'll find it helpful."

I was shocked to see my name pencilled in on the top corner of the cover page and knew that it wasn't a brochure from the State Mental Health Association which she routinely gave out to students. Perhaps she really has a crush on me, I considered.

A gift, I can't believe it. I'll bet you'll even play Mommy with me. You will stoop down to my level, if that's what it takes to reach me. Let's start from the beginning.

It's good to talk, isn't it, you poor little thing, her eyes spoke to me. Your family missed out on a lot of communication. I'd like to cuddle you, but as you know, my professional reputation is at stake, so I hope you'll be satisfied with a flirtatious session and understand if we postpone the real affair until I'm sixty-five and no longer on the staff of the university. By that time I don't know whether you'll find me attractive.

No, it's O.K. I can wait that long. I love the feel of cool, flaccid skin. Besides, love transcends corporeal form. My feelings towards you will never change. I love you so much. Is it wrong for a patient to love his physician? As long as you can still talk I will want to be with you. And even when your voice is too faint to whisper and your ears too weak to listen, I would be fulfilled by the sight of your vacant eyes, knowing the wisdom that rests within your soul. Just give me your breast to suck on and let me rub my nose along your loins. I will lick the grey swirl as a dutiful son.

"Wow, thanks a lot, Dr. Foster," I said disjointedly after a long pause, curling the reprint in my hands. "It's very kind of you to think of me. Most physicians forget about their patients when they're off duty but you're really special. Did anyone ever tell you that you have a therapeutic smile? I'll read this article as soon as I get home. Perhaps we can discuss it on a future date."

"Yes, I would like that, at some future date," she said icily, to cover up a hint of bashfulness in her eyes. "Anyway, Jeremy, you're welcome to drop by my office whenever you like. My door is always open. I only hope that the author's suggestions are helpful. Dr. Friedman received his Ph.D. from

Stanford and did a post-doc at Dr. Dement's Sleep and Dream Research Lab."

"This is all beneficial," I whispered pathetically, hiding my face in embarrassment, "but couldn't you give me the prescription anyway?" She turned her head to the side and frowned. "You can trust me to carry out your directions faithfully. I'll only take my qualludes after I've already gone through the entire battery of muscle relaxation exercises."

She didn't respond, choosing to eye me cautiously. Her penetrating eyes dug into my soft parts.

"Dr. Foster," I said timidly, "you remind me of my grandfather. Not in a physical sense of course, but in your conservative approach towards healing. My grandfather was also a general practitioner, among the last of a dying breed of physicians who were more concerned about their patients' long-term health than in providing symptomatic relief. He believed in the wisdom of the body and rarely resorted to heavy doses of tranquilizers of anti-inflammatory agents. Of course, my grandfather never went overboard in abstaining from the use of medications. He believed in the judicious use of drugs and surgery, but only after natural methods failed."

Her eyelids narrowed as she tried to digest everything I told her. I assumed that she was tickled pink that I appreciated her style of practice. Perhaps she would place it alongside the gift of my letter. I stared at her blankly with blurred vision, afraid that I would be paralyzed by her magnetic force if she gazed at me directly. She had the power to coerce me into worshipping her forever in a state of irreversible catatonia.

"Before emigrating to this country, my grandfather was a country doctor in a small Bavarian town. He was licensed to practice medicine at the age of twenty-three."

"Oh, really," she interjected, leaning her forearm on the desk for support and exposing the faint blue veins of her inner arm. She listened attentively, hoping, I thought, to gain a greater clue to my family history and see if there was some source of friction at home which might have contributed to my complaints of nervous tension and insomnia. "So your father's from Germany?"

"Yes, both Mom and Dad lived in Germany before they were deported to concentration camps. In 1938 my parents escaped from Dachau and fled to Holland where they were hidden by Christian families. They worked in the Underground until Holland was liberated by the Canadians in 1945. At the end of the war my parents each weighed less than ninety pounds, but Mom was strong enough to give birth to my sister, Zipporah. In 1949 my parents moved from Rotterdam to Israel where my other sister, Miriam, was born. Within a year, my father contracted lockjaw and emigrated to the United States to avoid more physical hardship. When my mother was forty, I was conceived accidentally, a high-risk infant, who nevertheless emerged with few physical imperfections. I inherited my father's slenderness and my mother's bowed legs. And so here I am, the only member of my family who was born in the U.S., the only one who can be legally elected to the office of the President of the United States."

She gazed at me suspiciously and appeared to be surprised by my patriotic fervor, before realizing that I was putting her on. Her eyes softened. It's really wonderful to see Jeremy open up to me and speak freely about his family, I thought, reading her mind. Perhaps I should tell him a story from my personal life. No, it would be terribly embarrassing if anything escaped from Hastings.

"My grandfather was a medical officer in the Kaiser's army during the First World War," I continued, my voice resonating with greater confidence. "After treating the wounded German soldiers he would cross the lines to the Russian front at night and care for the wounded soldiers on the other side. The penniless Russians were so grateful for his aid that they repaid him in their own special way by giving him hand-carved wooden dolls. These figurines were dressed in scraps of cotton and wool. The dolls were among a few treasured pieces smuggled out of Germany by my family. Whenever I visit my grandparents' house, I always study those beautiful dolls where they rest on the mantlepiece by the dining room window."

Pausing to collect my thoughts, I wondered whether I was being overly loquacious and possibly wasting Dr. Foster's precious time. However, her silent winking and nodding seemed to justify my rambling speech. She was intently absorbed in hearing my family history. It might make her job easier. She nodded for me to continue.

"My grandfather, whom we have always called Opa, was a dedicated follower of the Hippocratic Oath. He was one of the last of a vanishing breed of selfless physicians who were on call twenty-four hours a day and didn't just hang up the phone in the middle of the night when people needed him. Nor was he the type of G.P. who referred his patients to specialists before conducting a thorough physical examination of his own. Opa delivered babies in cowsheds by candlelight. He removed glass splinters from the scalps of drunken Germans whose skulls were cracked with beer mugs during tavern brawls.

"In those days there were no safe anesthetics available. My dad tells me that he could hear some patients scream out in pain from three blocks away. That's how medicine was in those days. Although he was tough enough to do what he had to, Opa was also very kind and gentle. His first priority was to relieve a patient's suffering and to avoid all unnecessary pain. Even the Nazis appreciated his healing hand and allowed my father to finish high school before deporting him to Buchenwald in 1937."

"That's fascinating, Jeremy," she whispered, pressing closer. I could tell by her watchful, adoring stare that she really empathized with me and maybe was even ready to get intimate. "Isn't it interesting to listen to your grandparents' stories?"

"Yes, especially since they're true and the characters are my own flesh and blood. I only mentioned the story of my grandfather because he reminds me of you from a humanistic perspective. I'm sure that if you were in his position at the time, you would also have helped the enemy soldiers, whether they were Albanians, Vietnamese, Croations, Egyptians, Fijians or of any other nationality. I know that you are ready to help any person in need." My stomach grumbled, a warning that my comments were effusive and could lead her to suspect that I was a guileful sycophant.

"That's very nice of you, Jeremy," she said faintly with an emphatic nod. A blush suffused her cheeks when she reached out and held my hand tightly. She squeezed my index finger tenderly, as if it were my penis inside her. Oh, her hand was so warm! "Is your grandfather still practicing or is he retired?" she asked respectfully.

"No, he doesn't practice anymore. He passed away last March, a day after my birthday. He was enfeebled for eight years with Parkinson's disease and cerebral arteriosclerosis. Eventually he contracted a nosocomial infection from an indwelling catheter that hadn't been changed for two weeks and died in the hospital shortly afterwards. Ironically, he almost died of a severe bladder infection when he was imprisoned in Buchenwald. His name is recorded in the official documents of the concentration camp. The Nazis were very meticulous about preserving medical records.

"Of all Jews, they were especially contemptuous of physicians and confiscated all of his medical equipment," I continued. "At that time he was the only physician in Buchenwald. Without any medication or instruments at his disposal, he still managed to be a healer by holding people in his arms. He comforted them and gave them hope that a better world lay ahead.

"One day the Nazi guards wouldn't let him go to the outhouse and posted a sign, Dr. Lipschitz: *Eingang Verboten!* It was a great humiliation. He had to hold it in, all for the entertainment of the chuckling Nazi guards. He was only allowed to wear a thin sweater. 'And how are you feeling today, Herr Doctor?' one of the guards asked. The rest stood beside him with their rifle butts tucked securely against their hips. Opa stared at the ground and pretended not to hear them. He was in such pain.

"Late in the afternoon, when the sun was setting, they made him undress in the cold and then commanded him to urinate under the muzzles of their rifles. '*Spritz* now or you will never *spritz* again, *Juden scheisse.*' His bladder froze up, but his survival instinct told him he had better urinate now if he ever wanted to see his family again. The soldiers laughed at the sound of urine hitting the dirt. The pressure was so great that his bladder almost burst. As the sound grew louder, the Nazis laughed harder. They loved to see the anguish in his face. They allowed him to survive, as if that dignified their sport. How many Hitler Youth did he treat between 1933 and 1938 without charging a fee? How many babies did he deliver into the Fatherland before they got rid of this excrement of the earth, this *Juden scheisse*?

"The following day Opa developed a urinary tract infection. He was lucky. The doctor in the infirmary remembered him from medical school. Since Opa had served as an officer during the First World War and his only brother had died in the fighting, he was released from Buchenwald after a six week stay. He was fortunate to survive at a time when the Nazis were already contemplating the Final Solution.

"There's really no justice in this world. Opa helped so many people, both in Germany and later on in the United States, where he practiced for more than thirty years. And his reward was to spend his golden years with a mind crippled with arteriosclerosis. I'll always remember him from the time when he was alert. Opa was a true Renaissance man. He was a bibliophile who held many interests aside from medicine. His bookshelves were filled with works of literary criticism, art, physics, astronomy, music and poetry. He taught me to develop an unquenchable thirst for knowledge. It was such a pity that he could never enjoy his books in his retirement."

"I wish I would have had a chance to meet your Opa when he was still healthy." She gazed at me solemnly, apparently holding the highest respect for physicians who cultivated interests in the arts in addition to medicine. "It's wonderful to appreciate your grandparents. But Jeremy," she whispered, her voice modulating to a high pitch. "You're so young, so brilliant; your mind is filled with creative ideas. Why can't you try to enjoy the positive side of life? Perhaps if you went out more at night, closed your textbooks for a few hours and had some fun with your peers, then you would have less difficulty falling asleep. You should learn to . . . how do you kids say it? Party—you should learn to go out and party more often!"

Boy, she sure is hip, I thought, thrilled that she would prescribe entertainment as a remedy for insomnia.

"Are you eating?" she asked, opening her mouth wide as if she wanted to peek inside my oral groove and examine my tonsils. "You look terribly thin."

"I only take in about 1500 calories a day. I just did some reading on anorexia nervosa in the male; it's very rare. I get a thrill out of being the exception to the rule. It's not that I don't enjoy eating, nor do I like being called 'Twiggy' by members of the crew team."

"What do you like to eat?"

"Sesame balls, non-kosher foods like oysters and pork lo mein. Eating a ham and cheese sandwich gives me a sacreligious thrill, but otherwise I have no appetite for anything."

"When was the last time you checked your weight?" She rolled her chair closer and stared at me intently, winking at me with one eye and nodding her head rhythmically.

"Last time I weighed in at Hastings at 118 pounds. That's more than thirty pounds underweight for my height and frame. I also have food allergies, especially to corn, soy, and strawberries. If I eat any of those, I break out in hives."

"Then what are your major sources of protein?"

"I really have none. I'm living off the protein matrix of my lean muscle tissue. I'm working my way through college as a hunger artist." I tried to laugh at my forced Kafkaesque joke, but she didn't laugh along, so I too looked grim.

"What did you have for breakfast?"

"Orange juice and toast with a slice of bacon." Her keen attention to my diet made me feel as if I were regressing to an infantile stage. I relished the thought of her becoming my dietician, even if it were a step down professionally.

"What did you have last night for dinner?"

"Ham steak and cabbage."

"What did you drink with it?"

"Ice water," I barked defiantly.

"Water doesn't have any calories. What did you have for lunch?"

"I didn't have anything. I skipped lunch yesterday because I was feeling depressed. I've always had problems with food. As a young boy, I wouldn't eat the sandwiches my mother put in my lunchbox. Instead, I would bring them home after school and urinate on them behind the oil tank, where they created an incredible stench."

"Go on."

"I don't know what leads me to self-starvation. Perhaps it's a form of transference in which I'm trying to relive my parents' experience during the war. I can't let myself have the food that my grandparents never had.

My mother's father died in a concentration camp in the French Pyrennes. That was my other Opa. He was a kind, sensitive man, a highly respected attorney in Germany. When my parents were my age, they were hiding from the Nazis in Holland. During the last days of the war, there was nothing to eat but turnips, tulip bulbs occasionally, a potato, if you had the strength to dig and find one buried in the ground. My father often told me that Hitler took away the best years of his life. He had won a full scholarship to Julliard and could have been a concert pianist, but preferred to stay with my mother in Europe. It was a real love story. When the war was over, he was so grateful to God for having survived the Nazi occupation that he vowed to devote the rest of his life to Judaism. Each time I fork a piece of meat and bring it to my lips I feel terribly guilty. I can't assimilate their pain since I was born in an entirely different era. I try to be a refugee in affluent, suburban America, but it's only a self-imposed exile.

"I'd love to snap out of it and become a healthy person. But there is also something romantic about being in hiding. At times, I wish that I was in my father's place, forty years ago, lying in the eaves between the floor of the attic and the living room ceiling with barely enough room to roll over. My mother was very courageous and saved my father's life several times.

"One day the occupation forces announced that they were conscripting all able-bodied men to work in the gun factories in Mannheim. The Nazis conducted a house-to-house search, for all men between the ages of fourteen and fifty. Any man who had not previously come forward for conscription was shot. When they came to the house where my parents were hiding, my mother opened the door. Her hair was dyed red, and the top button of her blouse was opened, which caught the eye of the commandant. She spoke to him in Dutch, trying to hide any traces of her German accent. My father was lying on his back in his hiding place, listening to every word of their conversation. She opened the doors to the closet, cellar and attic to show him that there was no one hiding anywhere. Fortunately, they came without dogs. The soldier seemed satisfied. Just as he was getting ready to leave, he extended his hand, but Mom wouldn't shake it. Her parents had been murdered by the Nazis. My father was so scared that he defecated in his pants. But Mother's courageous instincts prevailed. She apologized to him for being so shy and reserved with men and blamed it on her sheltered upbringing. The commandant was satisfied with her explanation and left without searching the house further. Four months later Holland was liberated.

"I'm so proud of my parents for having survived. They gave me the gift of life. But out here, in America, there's no challenge, no blatant anti-Semitism which would deprive me of my youth, as Hitler stole the youth of my parents from them. There's no underground or political movement to join without feeling like a used fool. That's what leads me to rebel against myself. That's why I don't eat. I can't eat the food my parents never had when they were my age."

"Come now, Jeremy, let's not get carried away. I don't think you feel this way all the time. There must be some foods which you enjoy, like ice cream. There's no reason to feel guilty. I'm sure your parents have told you many times how grateful they are that you don't have to live through those hard times. Deep down, you know that your parents are very proud of their son. They have reason to be proud. You're a very valuable person. And it's time you started to take care of your body. Don't you think it's worth caring for, to feed it and treat it right?"

"This is something I'll have to learn for myself."

"That's right. Well, I have one more word of advice: Never rebel against yourself. You'll only make yourself more depressed."

"Thank you Dr. Foster. That's a good, cheap lesson in mental hygiene. But it's more than insomnia and anorexia nervosa that bothers me. There may be a physical factor too. Some nights I get terribly feverish simply from studying so hard. You might say that my brain gets overheated." I allowed myself to giggle as soon as she smiled. Dr. Foster was a shrewd physician who considered laughter a therapeutic reflex as long as it wasn't at the expense of a patient or herself.

"Sometimes," I continued, "I get an attack of wakefulness and my brain won't shut off for hours. After three consecutive nights of sleeplessness my nerves begin to fray. If you would scan my peduncles on an angiogram, there would be nothing but moo goo gai pan. You're looking at a fellow who hasn't slept for five straight nights. I'm already in the post-exhaustive stage. Whenever I get these nocturnal attacks, I perspire profusely and feel forced to hop in the shower. Ten minutes later, I'm all sweaty again. You've got to help me, Doctor!"

Her solicitous stare grew more severe when she heard my last two remarks. Excessive perspiration was a symptom she would have to consider seriously as a possible indication of hyperthyroidism.

"Hold out your hands straight in front of you," she commanded dryly. Failing to react immediately to her instructions, I fidgeted in my chair. She grew impatient with my unresponsiveness and pulled my arms outwards to observe my nervous tone. My fingertips fluttered with the intensity of hummingbird wings. She grabbed my perspiring hands and massaged the lifelines of my palms. Her hands were warm and slippery. They made me feel secure, completely under her protective wing. Her tone was dry and lacked affection. She released my hands from her soothing grasp and they trembled in the cold air.

"They're sweating, aren't they?"

She looked at me querulously, as if I deserved an unsatisfactory grade in basic diagnosis for failing to recognize something so remarkably self-evident. "Your hands are trembling," she said gravely, as if to announce that I had some terminal neuromuscular disease like Huntington's Chorea. "You have a tremor." She pronounced it "tree-more" which made her diagnosis sound even more forboding.

She's just trying to scare me, I thought. Everybody has a fine resting tremor at one time or another. Even the hands of a great neurosurgeon tremble on occasion. But when I looked up, her cold, unflinching gaze told me to stay put and listen closely to her instructions. My whole body started to perspire profusely. Beadlets of sweat streamed down my temples and collected on my upper lip.

"Are you hot in this room?" She opened the window and returned to her desk.

"Would you sit up on the examining table?" I propped myself up and swung my legs back and forth. "Keep your shirt on. I'm just going to examine your thryoid and lymph nodes. Now I don't want you to be shocked when I touch your neck. I won't be using a pin and I'm not going to choke you." She hesitated, aware that she too was forcing a joke.

"I'm not worried. As long as the window is open, people will hear me when I scream."

Two smooth fingertips touched the nape of my neck and triggered an ecstatic shiver down my spine. She palpated the skin until she felt the residual swelling of my lymph nodes, from an earlier bout of mono, then worked her fingers around the pleasurable pressure points at the base of my skull. Her deep strokes reached the crests and depressions of my cranium. She found the Neanderthal links to my occipital condile, ennervating erotoecstatic impulses throughout the pleasure center of my brain.

Closing my eyes, I immersed myself in the warmth of her touch. After several decades of clinical experience she had developed a physician's "feel" in her fingertips and could determine whether a glandular protuberance was within "normal limits" or was bulging and grainy, and possibly malignant. I felt completely at ease in her hands and wanted to hire her as my private masseuse. She searched for a hot nodule beneath my thyroid cartilage, but the swelling was not sufficient for her to suspect Grave's disease or hyperthyroidism.

"Now take off your shirt." My heart pounded audibly. I followed her instructions and slouched my shoulders. Placing a stethoscope in her ears, she warmed the disc in her palms and pressed it over my heart. She rotated the diaphragm of the stethoscope around the mitral, tricuspid and pulmonary quadrants, ausculating the pressure flow, the syncopated rhythms, the natural jazz of my heart. Then she palpated my chest and tapped a series of percussive thumps.

I held my breath and tried to accelerate my heart rate voluntarily. Perhaps this would compel her to keep her hand and stethoscope in position. The widening furrows in her forehead expressed grave concern that my pulse was now over 135.

"Jeremy, I would like a straight answer. Have you been taking amphetamines?" Her piercing stare demanded an explanation. Suddenly I realized that she was scrutinizing my every move. She walked away and looked out the window to give me a chance to express myself. My heart skipped a beat. I was so nervous that my head felt like it was on fire.

"No, Dr. Foster," I cried. "I don't take any medication which isn't prescribed for me. That would be violating medical ethics. Besides, it's against the law."

"Did you have any stimulants before coming here? Coffee? Tea?"

"No, I never drink coffee or tea, not even Pepsi—no stimulants whatsoever." She breathed easily but resumed her laserbeam stare. I buried my trembling hands between my thighs. She couldn't repress a smile and seemed extremely pleased by the way I had responded to her interrogation.

"Do you think you can slow your pulse by trying to relax?" Her eyes softened and comforted me.

"I can try. Just give me a few minutes." I reclined on the table and rested my head on the cushion. She palpated my chest, causing my purple nipples to swell. My shoulder twitched spasmodically, prompting her to massage my pectoral muscles until the shakes disappeared.

Once I had calmed down, she placed the diaphragm of the stethoscope over my heart and looked down at her watch. "Your pulse is still not slowing down. In fact, your heart is beating faster than it was at the start of the examination. Now would you please sit up and put on your shirt?

"I'm going to turn off the lights for a few minutes." As the room grew dark I focused on the pale light trickling through the venitian blinds. She removed a silver ophthalmoscope and a high-intensity flashlight from the cabinet and stood directly in front of me. Staring through the opening in her labcoat, I measured the curvature of her breasts pressing against her middle button. The scent of her provocative perfume drew me closer. I wanted to touch her lovely skin but was afraid my hand would wander within her blouse and she would break my arm. Still, I could hardly restrain myself from kissing her between the buns.

"Follow my finger," she commanded, positioning her index finger between my eyes. A bright yellow beam probed my right pupil. I stared at her finger rotating in the distance while she pressed her face close to my cheek and examined my retinal fundus. I felt her warm breath. Her face was transmuted into a black shadow when she intensified the light beam. I tried to follow her finger with my eyes, but the very proximity of her cheeks distracted me. She zoomed the bright beam in circular, laser-like paths to test the reflexes of my optic nerve and possibly locate a brain lesion responsible for my hyperadrenergic response. The black void before me precipitated a series of hallucinations: amorphous shaped objects, luminescent green and purple flickering lights, stars, pinwheels, discs, whirling balls, spindly lattice work, all floating across a sea of air. However, these were only hypnogogic hallucinations which could be easily evoked by applying pressure to the eyeballs and had no pathological etiology.

She aimed the bright pencil light in the center of my left pupil, which was forced to contract. I was glad that I had restrained my desire to kiss her on the cheek. She would have been extremely angry with me had I taken advantage of her position.

"I'm looking at all the blood vessels in the back of your eye. It's really a beautiful sight. I wish you could see this on a scanning microscope," she said gently, diverting my attention to keep me still through the course of the eye examination.

"Is my fundus beautiful too?" I asked sheepishly, hoping she would comprehend the double entendre as an indirect reference to her vulval chiasma. She acknowledged my pun by rubbing her clitoral hood against the edge of the examining table in rhythmic thrusts and then abruptly turned on the lights.

"Before you leave Hastings," she said slowly and deliberately, "I want you to stop off at the nurse's station for a blood test. Judging from the results of your last blood profile, there's no evidence of any organic disorder. You may be experiencing situational anxiety." She waited patiently to give me a chance to comprehend her diagnosis and then combed her fingers through my hair affectionately. "Maybe you're just a little nervous, Jeremy, hmmn?" She held my hand and looked me straight in the eye.

"Dr. Foster, aren't you going to fill my prescription?"

"I'm afraid I have serious reservations about prescribing Methaqualone for one of my favorite patients. It's one of the most frequently abused drugs in its class."

"Oh, you don't have to worry about that with me. My history of drug abuse is behind me. When I was thirteen, I started shooting up my grandfather's morphine sulfate with disposable syringes. My grandmother preserved his office as it had been when he was in practice, for purely sentimental reasons. She neglected to throw out any medications. I had easy access to his Demerol and morphine. You're talking to an old-timer. After my second suicide attempt at the age of fifteen, they ran a tube through my nose and pumped out my stomach. I learned a lesson. Nobody in his right mind would choose to go through gastric lavage a second time. It's worse than withdrawal. Honestly, these days I only take medication after every other remedy fails. Do you think I care for hypnotic drugs? Downers are absolutely the worst high. If I take too many sedatives, I suffer a hangover for three days and find myself unable to function for the rest of the week."

I wondered whether she noticed that she was rubbing her thumb over my knuckles affectionately. "What a terrible waste of time and energy. It's so depressing when I see kids who get high on downers. Some of them are so hard up for any drug that they wind up snitching Valium from their mothers' medicine cabinets. But that's all behind me now," I boasted.

"Is that what you do when you're home? Take your mother's Valium, hmmm?"

"Of course not. I'm much more interested in finding a natural solution to my problem. I'll read Professor Friedman's article and if this doesn't put me to sleep, only then, as a last resort, will I pop a Sopor. If it were my choice, Dr. Foster, I wouldn't take any drugs at all, not white wine, rhubarb, nor the Ordeal Bean of Calabar. But in my present state I must choose between the lesser of two evils, lack of sleep or pharmaceuticals, and believe me, I'd rather take the pharmaceuticals."

Her smile was erased by a scalding stare. I was afraid that she was ready to consider me a big bullshit artist, a common, run-of-the-mill drug freak, who wheedled prescriptions out of sympathetic physicians and combined sedatives with methadone to bring on his daily high. Deceiving a physician was the most abominable sin a patient could commit. But doctors, I thought, were trained to meet all sorts of kooks. These were the risks of the profession, but made practice so much more interesting.

"Have you been exercising lately?"

"Well, at least once in a while. I walked here today."

"Clear across town?" She was facetious.

"Yep, clear across town. I need my morning constitution. Please, Dr. Foster," I pleaded, "I'm in desperate straits. Don't make me go out in the street and buy medication on the Black Market. I'll be broke by the end of the month and then I'll have to move in with you. I wasn't going to tell you this but lately I've felt so unstable upstairs that I registered as an out-patient at the local Mental Health Center. After evaluating me, the attending physician placed my name at the top of the waiting list for the psychiatric ward. I convinced him that it would be more convenient for me to live there as an in-patient. He also promised that he could arrange for me to get day passes so I could attend classes and not fall behind on my schoolwork. They have a special program for ambulatory schizophrenics." She looked at me incredulously as I focused on her bosom.

Actually, I had never registered at the Mental Health Center but used the story as a ploy. I hoped she wouldn't allow herself to be upstaged by another clinic in the University, but would be compelled to give me a private room at Hastings instead. If I didn't like the dinners at Hastings, I could always ask for more soft *Goyische* bread with butter and jelly, the usual substitute for vegetarians. Even if she didn't reserve a room for me, I could bring in a sleeping bag and camp out on the third floor, which had recently been condemned because it lacked a fire escape. Dust and cobwebs lined the once immaculate yellow tiled walls. I savored the idea of having an entire hospital wing to myself, even if it was obsolete.

Yes, if she wouldn't give me a room, I would be a squatter in her infirmary. In my mind's eye, I was playing my own jazz composition, *Spasmodic Torticollis*, on the infirmary piano. A team of psychedelic candy-striped groupies surrounded me. They were lower echelon members of the White Lightning Medical Group. Iridescent, psychedelic posters pulsated under the strobe light. A lighted marquee rolled past the announcement: Jeremy Lipschitz—Live at Hastings.

Silvana Foster was standing in the stairwell, a tray of blood samples cradled in her arms, when she heard music coming from an unfamiliar source upstairs. She hadn't been on the third floor since it had been condemned three years earlier. Who could be upstairs, playing on the piano? She quickly hurried up the steps. When she opened the door, she found me leaning over the piano. She was amazed by my cross-motor manual control, especially my jive left hand and walking bass lines. What had happened to my fine, resting tremor? I put every interpretive drop of emotion into the command performance, molding my inventions so she would be completely titillated. When the composition was over, I put my hand over her mouth and gagged her. No one could hear her desperate cries. I tied her arms behind her back and forced her down on a plastic covered mattress without sheets. Then I unbuttoned her white satin lace blouse and revealed her black bra. Oh, I have to have therapy. After all, I'm in a hospital. You gave me shelter. Hoo hoo hoo hoo. Yoidle, doidle doo doo. I am sick. I am sick. Yes, hoo hoo. Permanent relapse—unconditional insanity. (That's a legal not a medical term.)

But then I am paralyzed with fear. I am no longer the raper but the rapee, and my urinary incontinence dribbles out of my phallus. Send him over to acute psychiatric cases! Do you like my skinny, hairy body, Silvana? Am I a cute, toilet-trained orangutan? You have the face of a capuchin monkey. Your eyes are so beautiful, hazel. Oh, I watched you through my binoculars, while you were sipping iced tea on the patio. But you never came out on the terrace to answer my call, grant forgiveness. Oh, I didn't mean to ruin your reputation, your professional reputation? Are you going to sue me for all I'm worth? After all, I did it because I loved you. I still do. Please hold me in your arms. Oh, Silvana!

"Jeremy," she whispered, shaking my arm so I would withdraw from my stupor. "Are you all right? Can I get you a glass of water?"

"What? I'm fine. No, I mean I'm in terrible shape. I must complete this semester successfully. If I drop out now, I'll never be accepted by any medical school, not even one in the Dominican Republic. I must get my beauty sleep for sufficient neuroreplenishment. Do you want me to climb up the walls and tear my hair out?"

"Relax, Jeremy, I'm sure you have the grades to get in," she said, finally finding an opening to *schmaltz* up my ego. "And remember what I said: speak kindly to yourself, as to someone whom you cherish. Otherwise you'll get depressed. Now tell me, which medical schools did you apply to?"

"I applied to Downstate Medical College, Tufts, Stanford, Loma Linda and Mt. Sinai. I think I have the best chance at Mr. Sinai because Dr. La Vigne, who's a member of the admissions committee, remembers me from the time I was a patient in the children's psychiatric ward. The child psych unit is associated with the parent medical school. Last month, when I appeared for my interview, I told them that it was their moral responsibility, as physicians, to give me the opportunity to rehabilitate myself completely by accepting me as a fully matriculated student in their medical school."

She broke into a wide grin, obviously pleased by my exceptional drive. It seemed as though she was even more determined now to keep me away from institutionalized care. "Isn't that amazing. It must have been at least ten years since you were a patient at Mt. Sinai. They have an excellent medical school. I did a year of post-graduate work there myself. Did Dr. La Vigne really remember you?"

"You bet he remembered me. I broke the record at the time for receiving the highest dose of Mellaril. You know how some doctors think; the more the better. Test the threshold until you knock 'em out. I retaliated by stealing the Sandoz 'smiley button' from the lapel of his white coat, hanging in the closet of the physicians' lunch room. I also directed the hospital production of the Wizard of Oz which was attended by hundreds of people wearing white coats, most of whom were M.D.s. I don't think the hospital has ever witnessed a show quite like it," I said enthusiastically. "None of the occupational therapists on the ward knew anything about dramatics, so I adapted the screenplay, appointed myself director, and doubled as a Munchkin and the Wizard. I was ten at the time."

She looked dazed, astounded that I was able to produce the show. Too bad she had missed the performance.

"But not everyone on the Admissions Committee at Mt. Sinai has positive memories of my stay at their child psych ward. Dr. Gladys Trautwein, who has been the director of the ward for the past fifteen years, remembered me as an incorrigible terror. I used to interrupt group therapy sessions by urinating in the garbage can and performing other coprophilic acts of defiance. One time I even took a leak on her high-heeled shoes. Boy, that really pissed her off. It's amazing how some physicians never forget their patients. After that, all of the kids respected me and called me Captain Jeremy. But Dr. Trautwein aborted my healthy rebellion by tripling my dosage of Mellaril. No wonder I have insomnia now. All the drugs I ingested over the years must have affected the firing rate of my neurotransmitters."

My shoulder twitched uncontrollably. She rubbed my collarbone with her warm soothing hand until my nervous quivering disappeared. "It's not good that you're experiencing so much anxiety, Jeremy. I don't intend to sound condescending, but would you like me to refer you to a psychiatrist? I know a good one; a real professional."

"No thank you," I interrupted. "I've already seen far too many of them. Most of the shrinks I know are just clock-watching businessmen who couldn't hack it in physical medicine. They lack any kind of bedside manner. Some of them don't even know how to listen without pretending to be attentive. Half the time they're daydreaming about their investments, and their practices do especially well in a bear market. What I really need is a good internist like you, Dr. Foster. You're the best. Your natural insight and understanding makes you more sensitive to your patient's feelings. You're not victimized by psychiatric training. Besides, it's terribly frustrating shopping around for a shrink in the yellow pages or the Directory of Medical Specialists. Freudian, Jungian, Adlerian, eclectic . . . what does it all mean? I guess eclectic means Shepherd's Pie. Groping blindly for a shrink is like playing Russian Roulette. One always spends the first three sessions giving them a comprehensive psychiatric history without even having a chance to evaluate them and before you know it, $300 has gone down the drain. With that kind of money I could buy myself a new lens for my dissecting microscope. But you've been very kind to me, Dr. Foster, I'm very fond of you, perhaps too fond for my own good. You're my only friend. I have no friends, only doctors."

Was it really healthy to take such a strong interest in this young man, I imagined she was thinking. Perhaps if I'm too kind to him, he may put me in the role of surrogate mother. Should I detach myself from him emotionally for his own protection? No, it would be too cruel to avoid him completely. These are the normal responses of lonely students living away from home for the first time. I bet he misses his parents.

"Jeremy," she whispered, running her smooth fingers through my wavy hair. "You're too valuable to lose. Please hold on. We're all very fond of you here at Hastings. You're a brilliant young man who will make enormous contributions to the scientific community. You owe it to your parents and yourself."

My head had been bent down, trying to hold back a diabolical smile. When my facial muscles relaxed, I rose to meet her eyes. My lower lip still held the dental impression of a stifled smile.

"I have a hunch that you will be famous some day. That's why you need to be strong and overcome your emotional problems now. Any time lost during this critical period of your life may impede your full potential."

Now I eased into a long overdue grin. Looking up into her glassy, hazel eyes, I wanted to kiss her softly on her cheek and lick her lashes, but my lips were chapped and peeling and I didn't have the guts to lean forward, so I asked, "Dr. Foster, would you please reconsider my request for Quaaludes?" She sighed disappointedly. I sensed that she could not resist my suppliant whimperings and would give in to my request. She opened her copy of the *Physician's Desk Reference*, but only to tease me. I could tell she was bluffing because the page was only turned to the drug identification chart.

"It looks like you've conned me into giving you a prescription, Mr. Lipschitz." She laughed curtly, signing her name and writing instructions to the pharmacist to dispense a placebo instead of Quaaludes in hurried, illegible strokes. "I'm giving you just ten tablets, only for an emergency. And, as I'm sure you already know, you can't combine them with alcohol. Remember, I want you to discontinue this medication as soon as possible. I get very balky when patients ask me for refills for sleeping pills."

"I'll follow your instructions faithfully," I said solemnly, touched by her ethics in prescribing a placebo. Then I folded the prescription neatly in half and tucked it away in my shirt pocket. I would preserve her signature as a love note under my pillow and never take it to a pharmacy. I only wanted to collect replicas of her name, to play doctor with her graven image.

Now that I had achieved my goals for the visit, I saved her the effort of asking me to leave and rose from my chair. We shook hands, which showed me that she was ready to be my friend and confidante. "Thanks again, Dr. Foster," I said, walking abruptly towards the door. "I'll keep you informed of my progress."

"Fine, Jeremy, I hope you feel better. And let's hear from you," she called behind me, extending the long goodbye. "My door is always open. Whenever you feel the need to talk, please don't hesitate to call."

"Bye bye!" I cried, waving to her from the doorway. I waited a few seconds to catch a final glimpse of her, but ducked out the door, afraid that too prolonged a goodbye would bring tears to my eyes.

"Bye Bye, dear."

I felt elated as I walked out of Hastings. Boy, did she know how to relieve depression. Dr. Foster was the best role model I could ever wish for. I was glad that I had exercised restraint by not pressing against her breasts. My instincts appraised her as a physician whose training would forbid romance with a patient, but then again, maybe not, if the patient were someone special, like me.

When I returned to my room, I read Dr. Friedman's paper and practiced a series of muscle relaxation exercises. Within a week all of my symptoms had cleared up dramatically. Now I was able to sleep for eight or nine hours a night and feel refreshed in the morning, without resorting to medication. Even my nervous quivers went away. I was so excited by my progress that I decided to surprise my Science Mother by writing a research paper on my own on the subject of insomnia. I would also attach a thank you letter for her loving kindness and generosity. It was her devoted concern which enabled me to fall asleep effortlessly every night. Before the week was over, I sealed the letter and article in a large manila envelope and mailed it to her home.

The Slice Is Right

Dear Dr. Foster:

Thank you for saving me from a relapse. I'm not referring to your prescription, but your encouraging words, which have enabled me to cling to my self-sustaining lifestyle, instead of collapsing into a hospital bed in a state of total dependency.

Every person needs a motivating influence in order to pursue a desired goal. If one is swept along without hearing an inspiriting voice, then he may crash against the concrete walls in entropic disarray, fall back to the beginning, where he renews an infantile struggle. But that doesn't concern me now! My psychotic episodes are ancient history for me. As of this week, my sleeping habits have improved dramatically. I have developed my unconscious powers for overcoming insomnia without the assistance of medication. Even my muscle twitches and shock reactions are under control.

You told me that I was "too valuable to lose." It meant so much to me to hear these kind, supportive words from you. Everyone naturally feels that he, himself, is too valuable to lose, but the fear of indulging in self-pity made me wonder whether I was really valuable to anyone else. You gave me 400 milligrams of confidence (taken sparingly, as needed), which worked synergistically with the prescribed hypnotic and helped produce one of the happiest weeks of my life. After a few days, I was able to discontinue the medication and bury the bottle in my dresser.

Before seeing you, I stood on the edge of a precipice without a rail, afraid that I would throw myself over into the breaking waves. But having survived a previous suicide attempt, I finally understood that I was indeed, "too valuable to lose." Someone must have wanted me to live. You told me to hang on, and I did . . .

You initiated the momentum by which I would attempt to overcome insomnia through non-medical means. I locked myself in the medical library and read the most recent articles in sleep research. Instead of tossing and turning in bed, I sat alertly at my desk in search of a permanent solution. I'm convinced that most forms of insomnia can be treated successfully through progressive muscle relaxation exercises and autogenic hypnosis.

Writing down my conceptions on paper is a therapeutic crutch which enables me to concentrate on my problems, rather than letting the insights dissipate into forgetfulness. But I really wrote this paper for you. I don't want you to think that I'm simply grabbing for the convenient bottle of sedatives. You were the one who turned me around. Those few words were more effective than intensive psychotherapy.

Should I ever become a licensed physician, I will always remember your ethical approach towards dispensing medications. Your hesitation to sign a prescription reveals your concern for your patients' long-term prognosis. The greatest resources for healing psychological problems lie in the love and concern from others. Besides, who wants to be dependent on an impersonal pharmaceutical? I think I'll take a nap right now. Looking forward to hearing from you.

Sincerely,
Jeremy Lipschitz

Each morning I sat on the front steps of my rooming house, waiting for the mail to arrive. Whenever I saw a large manila envelope in the mailman's satchel, I prayed that it would be Dr. Foster's reply, but it always turned out to be junk mail for someone else in the house. To soothe my distress, I composed my own letters of reply and signed them, "Yours, Silvana Foster, M.D."

Through one of these fictitious letters, I invited myself to a buffet luncheon for members of the American Society of Women Physicians, which was to be held at Dr. Foster's spacious house. In my eagerness to attend the affair, I came two hours early and helped the hostess prepare the hors d'oeuvres and set the buffet table. I even cleaned the bedroom rugs with her twin-engine, turbo-charged, supersuction, vacuum cleaner. We put the house in tip-top order before the first doorbell rang.

I was the lone male guest amidst a crowd of women doctors, most of whom were middle-aged. Dr. Foster introduced me to each distinguished lady, praising my maverick research in psychosomatic medicine. As guest of honor, I was asked to read my latest article, "Insomnia Therapy: A Potpourri of Natural Sleep Remedies from Chicken Soup to Abstract Scheduling," which had been published in a leading psychiatric journal.

When I finished reading my paper, I was greeted by resounding applause. I had never seen such a heavy concentration of mature women doctors and wanted them to adopt me en masse as their model patient. Before the reception was over, I wheedled three dinner dates out of a gynecologist, a pediatrician, and a colon and rectum surgeon.

Soon I grew weary of fantasizing and writing imaginary correspondence. All hopes were crushed by the assumption that she wouldn't answer my letter. I was afraid that Dr. Foster was just like the average physician: cold, clinical and indifferent, a slick professional who snubbed all personal relationships with her patients. Why were physicians trained to be so hurtful? Of course, her most predictable response would be to dump my letter in her obsolete files, if not the trash, and ignore me forever. The letter clearly embarrassed her. Why did I have to write that stupid, immature letter? Now it had ended our relationship. Even if I came to her with double pneumonia and begged her for a shot of penicillin, she would refuse to see me and have the receptionist refer me to another physician. My thoughts were in hopeless turmoil, but deep inside I was relieved that she had not answered my letter, because it gave me an excuse to feel offended and rejected. Now I could seek revenge.

One night I awoke from a nightmare with cardiac palpitations. Cold sweat drenched my skin. I was roused so violently that it was impossible for me to fall back to sleep for the rest of the night. In most of my nightmares, I only remembered the sensation of being frightened and forgot the contents of my dreams, but the highlights of this episode lingered in my memory. I remembered walking through a tunnel beneath a train platform on my way to a pizzeria. All of a sudden someone jumped on my back, covered my mouth with a gloved hand, rammed his fingers in my throat and thrust a knife in my side. I fell to the ground in a powerless heap, feeling no pain, only the warm, benumbing sensation of blood trickling down my side. Even the cold, abrasive sidewalk that absorbed the impact of my fall felt as soft as a down-feathered pillow encased in fresh linen. A passing taxi driver shined his headlights on my body and rescued me from the dream.

My spine convulsed. I was now completely awake, ecstatic with the thought that my dream could have a practical application. The stabbing incident in the train tunnel provided me with an alibi which I would report to the nurse upon visiting Hastings Health Center with a self-inflicted wound on an evening when Dr. Foster was on call. I knew she would be compassionate and indulge me in her sensuous bedside manner, which was reserved for her favorite patients. She would stroke my skin gently, to divert my attention from the pain of a bleeding gash only inches away from my spinal cord. The imagined feel of her warm finger-tips palpating my touchy skin seemed real. What a lovely answer to my letter. Suddenly my heart palpitated wildly and I was forced to lie flat on my stomach to rid myself of tactile hallucinations.

I decided then that the time had come for me to take the initiative and dramatically change our relationship. If she was going to play hard-to-get and snub me as a vociferous wise-ass who wrote pretentious suicide notes, then I would expose her to the maniac in me by presenting her with a gaping wound. It was her professional duty to make her patients feel physically and psychologically, as comfortable as possible during a traumatic episode. She would be compelled to comfort me and assuage my fear of being permanently disfigured by an ugly scar.

I spent three weeks formulating the specific details and calculating the timing of my plan. The most crucial information was finding out which night Dr. Foster was on call for emergencies, since she had such a varied schedule. One morning, when my plans were nearly finalized, I made a surreptitious call to the receptionist at Hastings.

"Hello Mrs. Farkass, this is Eric Clapton speaking, I'm a sophomore at Kirk." I spoke loudly into the mouthpiece of the pay phone, although my voice was muffled through a fresh handkerchief, scented with Eau de Myristica, Dr. Foster's favorite perfume. "I was wondering whether you would kindly give me the night schedule of physicians on call?" I had changed my name and disguised my voice because I was afraid that she would be suspicious of anyone who might anticipate an emergency. My fingers fidgeted around the dial, while I dreaded the possibility that the rotation schedule was considered privileged information.

"Why certainly Eric," she said courteously, oblivious to my pseudonym. "Would you wait a moment, please, while I check the calendar?"

"Surely, Mrs. Farkass. Please take your time." I pushed open the door of the phone booth and breathed easily for the first time. Meditating on the tiny holes in the telephone receiver, I saw how easy it would be to perpetrate my plan and suffer a minimum of pain. New ideas flowed swiftly through my cerebral aqueduct, as if there were no psychological barrier to hinder my escapade. In my mind's eye I was standing outside the emergency entrance to Hastings. A cold, biting wind seared through the hole in my coat and dried the splotches of blood on my back. My nose was pressed against the fogged-up windows. Leaning my shoulder against the emergency buzzer, I collapsed on the steps. When I woke up I was in a warm bed, surrounded by a team of vigilant nurses and Dr. Foster herself.

"Hello! Hello, Mr. Clapton, are you with me?" she asked impatiently, clicking the dial tone button.

"Yes, Mrs. Farkass. I'm here. Excuse me, I couldn't hear you on account of the traffic. Would you know which night Dr. Foster is on call?" I asked, my voice creeping into an innocent falsetto.

"Dr. Foster, Dr. Foster, hmm, let me see," she mumbled, sliding her fingers across the rows of days on her calendar. "Yes, here it is. I just found the evening rotation. She is on call Tuesday and Friday evenings. Is there anything else you would like to know Eric?" The sound of Dr. Foster's name lingered in my ears and for the first time I saw my plan nearing fruition.

"Yes, Mrs. Farkass, if it's not too much trouble. Would you also tell me when the Health Careers Club is going to meet this week?" I already knew the answer, but wanted to divert her attention from the preceding question.

"Surely, they will be meeting at five o'clock on Thursday in the mini-conference room."

"Thanks Mrs. Farkass. You have been most helpful. Have a nice day," I said warmly, but nearly choked afterwards on the dryness of my deceitful laughter.

"You too Eric. Bye, bye."

"Goodbye," I hung up the phone and skipped home without stepping on a crack between the sidewalk slabs.

When I came home to my bedroom in the attic, I sat on the edge of the mattress and smoked a compressed bud of opium-laced cannabis, which I kept preserved in a glassine envelope and abused only on special occasions. The flower was consumed in three quick puffs, but was all that I needed to get high. Within twenty seconds my head swelled with formless energy. I grew exhilarated and giddy as the psychoactive alkaloid, THC, combined with the more potent narcotic synergist and numbed my pain receptors.

Licking my lips, I savored my first rush as the opium oozed through my arteries and made me shiver with joy. Although it was only ten o'clock in the morning, I quickly changed back into my pajamas and hibernated under the covers. I turned down the volume of the radio and reviewed my plan.

The stabbing would have to take place on a Tuesday night, because another physician might cover for her should she decide to go away for a weekend. Hygiene and timing were the critical factors. I would not allow myself to take any drugs within forty-eight hours of my injury, in the event that Dr. Foster ordered extensive blood and urine analyses. The most difficult part of the operation would be wounding myself. The cut would have to cause a minimum of pain, but still be deep enough to negate any suspicion that I had stabbed myself. A fleshy patch of tissue below my shoulder blade would be the designated site of incision.

For many days prior to the night of my self-inflicted wound, I practiced surgical procedures on the epidermal layer of skin on my buttocks with a sterile scalpel. The scratches healed completely within ten days and only left a faint, temporary scar which would disappear by the night of my emergency. The scabs looked jagged and inauthentic. I lacked the skill to make a straight incision. My assailant's hand wouldn't quiver while he thrust the knife in my back. I knew that a sloppy cut would lead her to believe that I was a danger to myself, a patient she was unwilling to handle. In order for me to acquire a steady hand and understand the mechanical resistance of flesh, I practiced surgical dissections on white laboratory rats, scavenged from the garbage bin of the Experimental Psychology Lab.

When the appointed night arrived, I opened the kitchen cupboard and removed my finest piece of cutlery, a four-inch, freshly whetted Scandinavian fruit knife, which my mother had given me as a housewarming present. I boiled the stainless steel knife in a pressure cooker for ten minutes to kill all contacting strains of bacilli and wrapped the blade in a sheath of sterile gauze. Then I taped the handle, in the event that the police would look for fingerprints on the weapon. With a pair of rusty scissors I slit holes in my woolen pullover shirt and my overcoat, at the projected point of the incision. Everything was quiet with the exception of the ticking kitchen clock. The silence made me feel alone. I slipped my arms through the satin-lined sleeves of my grandfather's old cashmere overcoat, which was at least three sizes too big for me, and checked the hole to see that it was perfectly aligned. Sliding the knife into my breast pocket, I walked down the creaking steps of the rear stairway.

I skipped and jogged towards the train station in the damp December evening. It was a perfect night to get wounded. My tongue was coated with a bitter viral phlegm. I took a short cut through an alley along a row of girders supporting the train platform. Before going inside, I stopped by a candy store and bought a chocolate bar to give myself an extra surge of energy. When no one was looking, I felt the hard object secure in my breast pocket.

When I arrived at the ground floor of the station I looked up at the stained yellow face of the giant Timex clock. The time was eight fifteen. Taxi drivers were milling around the doors, scanning the floor for people with heavy suitcases. I walked up the steps of the motionless escalator leading to the train platform and the restroom. Most of the passengers were waiting outside under the awning in the cold drizzle. A piercing whistle blew in the distance to announce the express train which soon roared down the track. Tiny raindrops shimmered under the locomotive's blinding yellow headlights. Everyone cleared the lobby, except for three stragglers, bums who were sprawled out on wooden benches. Their weathered hands clung to paper bags, covering bottles of cheap wine. Walking quickly to the men's room, I found a dime in my pocket and paid the fare for the toilet stall. Without pausing to read the graffiti, I dropped my coat on the floor and went about my business.

Remember Jerry, I warned myself, pulling my shirt over my head and hanging it over the top of the stall, the cut must be at least three-sixteenths of an inch deep and you must lose over twenty cc's of blood or the nurse won't call up Dr. Foster. She won't drive all the way to Hastings just to look at a scratch. The wound must appear to be a serious injury. And don't push the blade too deep either, or they'll send you straight to the hospital emergency room. Physicians at Hastings are not required to perform major sutures.

I tried to breathe deeply to heighten my self-confidence, but the smell of fermenting urine kept my lungs from expanding. I devoured the chocolate bar in three quick bites and felt corpuscular pressure in my sebaceous cysts. Without further delay I removed the wax bite plate I had brought from its container and positioned it securely between my teeth. I was afraid that I might bite my tongue or loosen a molar, if the pain was too great to bear.

My hands trembled while I unwound the gauze sheath and exposed the shiny blade to the pale light. I placed the knife handle on the toilet seat with the blade suspended in the air to prevent contamination. A shiny green fly buzzed overhead. My hands free, I picked up my shirt, found the slit in the material and checked to see that it was perfectly in line with the projected site of the incision, marked faintly on my back with charcoal. I measured the angle of penetration to be certain that the cut would appear on target. All I needed now was a steady hand.

In my mind's eye, Dr. Foster was sitting next to her husband on an antique love seat in their spacious, split-level living room. They were warming their feet near the crackling embers of the cedar logs roasting in their colonial fireplace. They had just finished a delicious dinner of shrimp scampi with grape leaves and stuffed mushrooms. Silvana was thumbing through a medical journal, her feet tucked snuggly under her derriere. Soon they would retire to bed and engage in Tuesday night sex, according to schedule. She appeared cozy and content. Her husband was absorbed in reading a forensic medical thriller. The smoke went up the chimney just the same. Suddenly the telephone rang on her private line. Silvana ran into her study. It was the attending nurse at Hastings.

"Hello, Dr. Foster. I'm sorry to trouble you. We have a boy here from Kirk who has just been stabbed in the back. I'm afraid it's rather serious."

"What's the patient's name?" she asked impatiently.

"Jeremy Lipschitz."

"I'll be right over," she said and hung up the phone.

"What is it, Silvana?" her husband asked when she returned to the living room. "Do they want you at Hastings? Why is it that every time we have a free evening together, one of us is called out to attend to a patient? It's a miracle that two physicians can stay married for so long."

"Alex, this is a very special patient and he has a stab wound, which doesn't happen every day. It's time you remembered your Hippocratic Oath—'I will share my substance with him and I will supply his necessities, if he be in need.' So honey, don't wait up for me. I may be away all evening. There's mocha rum cake in the frig . . . "

"Oh boy!" I cried out in ecstasy, my voice echoing against the bathroom tiles, "I can't wait to interrupt their evening together."

A powerful surge of self-confidence poured through my muscles. I was ready to begin the operation. Opening my compact first-aid kit, I removed a cotton swab and soaked it in a small vial of rubbing alcohol. Then I rested a pocket mirror on top of the toilet paper roll and leaned the top edge against the stall panel. Glancing down at the floor, I noticed a lone cockroach scurrying across the tiles in search of water. The sight didn't phase me and I resumed my work. I adjusted the angle of the mirror to bring my back into view. The fingers of my left hand trembled as I reached around and pinched a patch of flesh below my right scapula. I held tenaciously to the slippery flesh while I rubbed alcohol over the skin with my other hand. The soiled cotton ball plopped into the toilet bowl and splashed a few drops of water on my sneakers.

The knife's razor-sharp tip was now poised perfectly on target. It waited only for the thrust to drive it through all the cutaneous layers, through the superficial fascia and finally into striated muscle. My hands were perspiring so profusely that I feared my grip would slip and the trained eye of a physician would detect that the line of the incision did not match the slits in my clothes. The thought of Dr. Foster's massaging fingertips enabled me to brace myself against a cold fearful shiver running up my spine. I turned my back to the mirror, determined to follow through with the horrific procedure. My sharp incisors sank into the mouthpiece when I pushed the knife at a forty-five degree angle through the meek resistance of pubescent skin.

"The operation is simple Jerry," I tried to say in a clear, confident voice, but sounded hoarse. "Just one straight cut and you'll graduate as a licensed surgeon, M.D. F.A.C.S." I cleared my throat of phlegm and spit the gob at the cotton ball, which was swimming aimlessly around the toilet bowl. Blood trickled out in a fine, steady stream, and dripped down to my waistline before I could feel any real pain. The sight of dark beet-red blood was gratifying. I was relieved that I had the balls to follow through with my mission. "There, that's good Jerry; dig in deeper. You're making progress." The first sharp sting radiated through my back, but I was determined to press on. I worked the blade through layers of skin and flesh, against the opposing force of my hesitant wrist. In my mind's eye, Dr. Foster squirmed restlessly about on her love seat, straightening the wrinkles in her beige stockings. Her sixth sense had urged her to put down the medical journal she was reading.

The second jolt of pain was more severe and made me lurch forwards. My shoulder banged against the stall. The mirror crashed to the floor, shattering into tiny pieces. I knew it meant bad luck. Looking down at the broken mosaic, I saw the reflection of my face, fragmented and incomplete. I turned my head as far as my neck muscles could stretch to get a full view of the incision. The blood on my back had begun to coagulate. The pressure on my contracted neck muscles forced an extra gush of blood through the carotid arteries. The pain intensified, throbbing in cadence with my accelerated pulse. I opened a sealed test tube of bovine blood which I had borrowed from the hematology lab at the medical school. The sample was treated with sodium oxalate and Russel's Viper venom to prevent premature coagulation. I poured the solution over my back. It would make me look like a real emergency case. The initial fibrin clot of my own blood had begun to seal the severed capillary and vascular walls. I thought of all the endogenous microscopic allies rushing to save me: the loyal aggregating platelets which restricted the blood flow and the courageous leucocytes which engulfed the germs invading my vital organs. "The body is such a beautiful machine," I cried out loudly, listening to the echoes bounce off the walls. "Thank God I'm not a fragile hemophiliac." I noticed that the primary scab was forming and wanted to rush quickly to the infirmary to prevent infection of my wound, instead of indulging in a pseudo-psychotic stupor. I dressed carefully without staining the unaffected side of my back.

The pain started to throb violently and I wondered whether I had actually wounded myself more severely than I had intended. A surge of adrenaline oozed through my arteries. I felt ecstatic and capable of performing feats demanding extraordinary strength. No one would ever kick sand in my eyes again, not even Charles Atlas. My sentimental yearning for Dr. Foster heightened my self-confidence as well as my systolic blood pressure. I convinced myself that within an hour she would be sitting at my bedside to comfort me and dress my wound.

I dropped my bite plate in the toilet and flushed it into oblivion. The pump struggled, but finally the rusted pipes swallowed the hard object. Lifting up the porcelain panel of the tank, I dropped the knife into the bubbling water. I found a drop of blood on the broken mirror, wiped it with my pinkie and licked my finger clean. The salty, but tangy taste of my own blood gave me a cannibalistic urge and my penis stiffened unexpectedly. The pain no longer burned but felt fearfully refreshing. The skin surrounding the wound was beginning to swell. I noticed the mess around me and decided to carry out my civic duty, throwing the stained gauze in the trash can. The street lamps shimmered through the translucent windows. A car horn broke my solitude. Remembering to carry through with my mission, I hung the coat loosely over my shoulders and walked out to the lobby.

When I came into the waiting room I looked at the three hobos, who had barely moved on their benches. Each man seemed to claim his own territory. I felt like an intruder. When I turned around to inspect my appearance I felt ridiculous. My coat was not stained with blood and the hole in my back was barely visible. Even the supplementary ox blood had failed to authenticate the gash as a violent stab wound. My shirt had soaked up more sweat than blood. It looked as if my assailant had been playing Patty Cake with me.

"Oh, what difference does it make?" I snarled petulantly, uninhibited by the presence of strangers. "What do you expect from a self-inflicted wound? And besides, Jerry, if the cut was too deep, you might collapse on the way to Hastings."

Walking down the steps of the still escalator, I expected it to be in motion, but only felt the stifled thud of my shoes hitting the immobile steel stairs. I knew that a week earlier an eight year old girl had gotten her ankle crushed when her sandal strap was caught in the escalator teeth. She was afraid to get off. My childhood fear of being stuck forever on an escalator was as present as ever. When the machine was running, I was afraid that I would be swallowed up in a step which went nowhere, or crushed by the gear mesh into a macerated pile of flesh. Now that the escalator was merely a staircase, I felt out of phase in my race to the ground floor.

As soon as I reached the lobby I rushed out the door, found an empty cab and jumped in the back seat. "Hastings Health Center, Fairbanks College, and make it fast," I said urgently, but firmly, in the baritone range of my voice, slipping a five dollar bill through the plastic partition. The cabbie shifted, stepped on the accelerator and raced through the amber traffic light, his rear tires screeching and leaving a trail of rubber behind us.

The back seat was soft and plush, despite the age of the Checker Cab, and I had room to stretch my legs. Staring out the fogged-up rear window, I smelled my sour breath against the glass. The silhouette of the train station, seen through the drizzle-coated window, faded into pointilistic obscurity.

"Could you step on it man, I'm sick," I said gruffly, tapping my clammy fingers on the partition.

"This is a residential street. I'm already doing forty-five."

The traffic light turned red before he had the chance to race through. The car idled for a tortuously long time and I felt blood drying on my skin. I squirmed nervously in my seat, but forced myself to be silent because I was afraid he would ask personal questions if I started a conversation. Besides, if he found out that I was stabbed he would turn around and rush me to the emergency room of the nearest hospital, which was only three blocks away.

"What's wrong with you?" He spoke in a cold, raspy voice. His cold steel-blue eyes, bloodshot and glassy from night driving, stared at me threateningly through the rear-view mirror.

"I've got the runs real bad and I think I'm going to puke," I said breathlessly.

"Why don't you open your window?" He checked to see if there were any police in the vicinity and stepped on the gas before the light turned green. I opened the window and pretended I had to vomit out it. I watched the two-family row houses pass by in a blur.

The familiar sight of the red brick infirmary made me feel close to home. I realized that since I was one of the Hastings' staunchest supporters I would be placed in the best hands and receive preferential treatment in return for my gifts of the past. My skin felt tight and crackly from the old drying blood. When I reached in my back pocket for another loose five dollar bill, I reopened the scap and felt a painful but warm gush of fresh blood drip down my side.

"Would you please help me to the door?" I asked timidly, handing him the crumpled bill. He slipped the money in his coat pocket nonchalantly as if he expected an inordinately generous tip. Before I had a chance to catch my breath, he pivoted a daring three-point turn and parked the car in front of Hastings' emergency entrance. Gloating inside, I realized that now I was Hastings' responsibility. The driver opened the passenger door, helped me to my feet, and held my arm tightly so I couldn't collapse on the pavement. I staggered momentarily and felt my legs buckle under me.

He turned his head to the side to avoid smelling my fetid breath. When we reached the emergency entrance I leaned against the buzzer for ten seconds. We waited outside for at least two minutes in the cold drizzle. Finally a nurse I had never seen before opened the door a few inches and pouted at us for interrupting her uneventful shift.

"Yes, what is it?" she asked lazily, brushing her lacquered blond bangs in place. She inspected our faces closely, and after a long pause, finally determined that I was the college student in need of treatment.

"Would you be kind enough to open the door and let us in?" I asked meekly, shivering from a mixture of cold and fear. I looked disapprovingly at her stiff platinum hair and heavily rouged cheeks.

"Yes, of course, come in." She opened the door, but blocked the passageway, giving us only enough room to stand in the vestibule. Her name, Estelle Morrison, R.N., was engraved on a white pin alongside a service award from Mountainview Hospital. Although she was in her late forties and had a healthy, buxom figure, her expression was far too sullen for me to find attractive. I was afraid that she was inexperienced in emergency care and would barely be able to take a patient's medical history.

"The kid is sick. You can take care of him here," the driver said hurriedly, annoyed that he had been made to wait outside in the rain for a lousy ten dollars.

"Surely, oh I see, you brought him here in a taxi," she muttered, craning her neck out the door to get a good look at his car. "Thank you for helping him to the door. Are you sure you wouldn't like a cup of coffee? I have a fresh pot brewing," she offered, purposely ignoring me, as if I was the whiny type, who came to the infirmary in the middle of the night with a hangnail.

"No thanks, I have to get back to the station."

"I could put it in a styrofoam container," she persisted. I stamped my foot impatiently, but could not gain her attention.

"Thanks, but I've got to run." He turned around and walked back to his cab. Only after he had driven away did Mrs. Morrison deign to face me.

"So, what can I do for you?" she asked softly, forcing a smile through her polished teeth, "Mr. . . . "

"Lipschitz." I grabbed her wrists, kicked the door shut behind me, and cried in feigned hysterical agony, "Before you take my temperature and my pulse, let me lie down. I've just been stabbed in the back. Ahhh!" My shrieks resounded through the stairwell. Sweat beaded above my eyebrows. I could hear my heart pounding furiously.

Pretending to be unphased by my excitement, she freed her wrists from my trembling hands and calmly accepted the fact that she had to care for a patient with a stab wound. She looked at the hole in my coat, wrapped her arm around the unaffected side of my back, and supported me while I struggled to the examining room. When I felt her pillowy breast pressing against my rib cage, I held on to her neck and collapsed against her. She carried me effortlessly. There was no need for a stretcher.

The lights in the clinic were out. The entire infirmary was deserted, free of the noisy bustle of the day. She flicked on the light switch with her elbow, propped me up on a cushioned chair, and opened a bed for me, all in one unbroken moment. When she started to pull off my coat, I screamed.

"Eeee, eee, ouch, careful! That's my back. You're hurting! Let go!" I scolded, *kvetching* like a crochety spinster. I lifted the heavy coat from my shoulders and dropped it on the floor.

Her hands fidgeted when she saw the maroon blood stains on my pullover. "How am I ever going to take off his shirt?" she whispered under her breath. "I guess I'll just have to pull it over his head inside-out."

"Thank you, but I can take it off myself," I snapped when she touched my shoulder. I pulled the itchy shirt off my back and over my head, jerking the collar from my neck. A few fresh drops of blood dripped down to the small of my back. The pain forced me to bite down hard. My two emerging wisdom teeth ached from the pressure.

"Mr. Lipschitz. Lie down on your stomach with your arms extended." She spoke in a cool, indifferent tone and pointed to a bed prepared for special cases. The blood drying on my skin felt tight and limited my mobility. My head dropped in the feather pillow. I tried to think only pleasant thoughts, but suddenly I found it difficult to breathe. Each shallow breath was arrested by a searing pain. Had I probed the knife too deeply and pierced a lung, I wondered? I coughed into the pillow case but didn't find any blood within the spray of sputum. Within a minute she had wiped away the blood on the skin surrounding my wound. I squirmed around uncooperatively because I wanted to save my blood for Dr. Foster to wipe up herself.

"Answer my question! I want to know whether I'll be placed on the critical list."

"Just relax," she said curtly, as if she resented having to answer me and bathe my wound at the same time. "It might have been more serious. Dr. Foster will tell you everything when she arrives. Now just relax, son, or you'll increase the bleeding."

"Don't call me son. I'm in bad enough shape as it is without you pretending you're my mother," I grunted between clenched teeth. She pretended to ignore me and continued wiping away my precious blood, ruining the bloody spectacle I had planned for sweet Silvana. I tensed my muscles so that my back was rigid and mumbled, "Train station. He stabbed me out there." My eyelids narrowed behind welling crocodile tears before I fell into a pseudocomatose stupor.

In my mind's eye, Dr. Foster was driving over the bridge from her cozy suburb to Hastings. Her feline eyes were fiercely protective, like those of a lioness returning to her den. She wove in and out of the lanes, risking her life as if every second was vital to saving her patient's life. Pressing the accelerator pedal to the floor, she maneuvered the steering wheel and raced towards Hastings with the same competitive fervor which enabled her to finish medical school at the top of her class.

I can't wait to see her coming, I thought. Boy, will she be surprised to see me under thesse circumstances. I'd better not break out laughing.

The door opened. A cold draft wafted down the hall and tickled my legs. The sight of Dr. Foster standing in the vestibule made me feel at ease for the first time all evening. She strutted quickly into the clinic, unbuttoning her Persian lamb coat on the way to my bed. She winced when she saw me. Then her eyes turned bright and warm, assuring me that everything would be all right. I relaxed and trusted her expert surgical skill.

"Mrs. Morrison, bring my instruments over here with his chart," she commanded, and removed a pair of disposable surgical gloves from the utility cabinet.

"What class is he in?" the nurse asked submissively, straightening her cap.

"I can't remember. He has advanced standing. If you look for it, you'll find his chart."

"Should I get his immunization records too, Dr. Foster?"

"Use your own judgement," she snapped and paced around the room.

"Yes Doctor, certainly Doctor. Should I prepare a tetanus booster as well?"

"Just get me his chart," Silvana hissed and turned her attention to me. She made herself at home on the side of my bed. Her legs were spread apart. I rolled my eyes around their orbits every few seconds so I wouldn't be caught giving a low stare.

"You don't have to look up Jeremy, it's O.K.," she whispered in my ear, placing a comforting hand along the unaffected part of my back. Watery drool slid out the side of my mouth and soaked a part of the pillow case. Sliding her hand to my lower back, she tickled my spine, which touched off a coccygeal shiver. She wanted me to get used to the feel of her hands, so I wouldn't jump during surgery.

Thus my massage began, in Clinic C at eight fifty-seven p.m., under the hum of the fluorescent lamp, in a sterile medium, all according to plan. She rubbed her fingers lightly over my skin. Delicious neural impulses raced along my spinal cord, relaying the orgasmic signals to the somesthetic region of my hypothalamus. She kneaded my back muscles with her powerful fingers, thus appraising my physique before the operation. I was a perfect living example of skeletal anatomy, with all 118 pounds of me wired to a five-foot eleven-inch frame. My skinniness was a genetically transmitted result of the Holocaust, but my perversions were normal adaptations to the stimuli encountered by the average American adolescent.

I could tell by the way she dug her hands so comfortingly along the uninjured side of my back that she really loved my body and wanted to climb into my ribcage. Although I wasn't a muscular specimen, I could pass myself off as a cute, toilet-trained orangutan, an exotic closet pet who would appease her capricious tastes.

"Dr. Foster, I found Mr. Lipschitz's chart. Don't worry, he has Major Medical!"

"I don't want to know about his insurance. Just hand me his chart," she scolded and grabbed my papers from the nurse's hands. Scanning my vaccination history, she found that I had received a tetanus booster only three months earlier. "Estelle, bring me another packet of gauze, and don't hand me any opened boxes. Everything at Hastings must be absolutely sterile." Mrs. Morrison shut the door behind her.

"Jeremy, I'm sorry I haven't been able to give you my complete attention. Now I'm going to give you a mild sedative before I inspect your wound more closely," she said softly and deliberately, pouring a glass of distilled water into a dixie cup.

"Dr. Foster, don't give me any tranquilizers; I'm allergic to phenothiazines."

"Jeremy, don't worry! I'm just administering a muscle relaxant, so you feel more at ease." She held the yellow pill in her open palm and gave me the cup of water. Her nurturing eyes assured me that any medicine that she gave me was the very best stuff indeed. "Here, let's see one big swallow," she said spiritedly, as if we were about to commence breast feeding.

"Thank you, Dr. Foster," I said graciously and picked up the pill. My arm brushed against her sleeve accidentally. A warm current radiated down the length of my spine. I popped the tab and washed it down my dry pharynx with distilled water. She scrubbed her hands over the sink, partaking in the preoperative ritual.

Although I couldn't see her while lying on my stomach, I heard her approach with a heavy step. Returning to my bed, she looked at my wound and made a preliminary assessment of my injury. She palpated the perimeter of the cut. Her touch delivered a pleasant sting and seemed to blanket all memories of pain, even the pain of past lives. She picked up some gauze which had been soaking in a basin of warm salt water, and started to wash away the dried blood. The fingers of her free hand crawled along the crests and depressions of my lumpy spine, past the nape of my neck and to my scalp, tickling the fine nerve endings of cerebral ganglia.

"Jeremy, now this may be a little uncomfortable, but I need to touch the lacerated area more firmly to determine the depth of penetration. Would you roll over on your side, please?" The puppy dog in me rolled over and lapped up the special attention of his maternalistic mistress. Her rhythmic strokes loosened my taut muscles. As soon as the sedative had had time to cross the blood-brain barrier, she probed the severed skin with sterile forceps. An intense sting shot across my back, but her comforting hand kept me still. She waited for the blood to coagulate until a scab formed.

"Jeremy," she whispered affectionately, her lips hovering inches from my pricked up ear, "you've been very courageous, but I want you to prepare yourself for some further discomfort. Now this is going to sting." Her warm breath excited me so much that it provoked a spontaneous erection. I tried to roll over on my tender back, just to get a glance at her compassionate eyes. She intercepted my movement by positioning me back on my stomach with a firm but gentle twist. I craned back my head, assuming dystonic contractions in my neck muscles to escape my helplessly imprisoned posture.

"You're not going to send me to a specialist, are you Dr. Foster?" I cried softly, feigning a physical agony much worse than what I was truly experiencing. "Don't send me out in the cold. He stabbed me out there!" Two welling tears crept out of my eyes and dangled on my lashes like morning dew drops. "Let me sleep," I whispered. "I'll have no trouble falling asleep now. I've cured my insomnia."

She stood up and stepped away from my bed. I was frightened by her prolonged silence and rolled my bulging eyes sideways in oculogyric spasms. When I looked up and saw her severe expression, I felt powerless and gasped for air. Had I given myself away, I wondered, mentally defibrillating the accented gallops of my heart. Did I do anything wrong? Was the surgery imprecise, or perhaps too neat for a thug? Was everything too sterile? I gave her my most *nebische* look, hoping she would reassure me in my moment of panic.

"No Jeremy," she whispered in a voice overflowing with maternal sympathy. "I wouldn't send you out in the cold, you peculiar fellow. I'm going to take care of you myself." She sat down on the side of the bed and inched her hips closer to my head. A stream of tears oozed out of my inflamed conjunctivae. "I was deeply touched by your letter and your interesting paper on insomnia," she said, running her fingers through my hair. "I hope you don't mind, but I showed your thesis to one of my colleagues, who is an associate research professor of psychiatry at the medical school. He was really impressed by your section on tryptophan. Perhaps when you feel better we can meet to discuss your fascinating theories on the subject. But right now I want you to rest." She spoke softly, ushering me to sleep with her hypnotic singsong voice. "Any excitement will increase the bleeding. You're very lucky, Jeremy, that there was no injury to the underlying structures. Now just relax. You can tell me everything that happened later on. Right now, I want you to sleep." The effects of the sedative started to work. I tried to fight it, but grew incredibly sleepy. When she saw my eyelids close, she hummed a lullaby and stroked my skin more softly than ever before. I fell asleep under her melting touch.

When I woke up I found her surgical supplies spread out neatly on the table beside me. The numbness around the wound was gone, but a throbbing pain had replaced it.

"Do I have to get stitches?" I asked groggily, fighting the hangover effect of the short-acting sedative. Although I was delirious and my tongue was coated with a film of mucus, I was certain that I had not woken up from a bad dream.

"Jeremy, while you were sleeping I closed your wound. Let's hope that it heals quickly," she said soothingly, rubbing two fingers along my spine. She handed me a mirror to see what she had done. Fourteen loops of black thread were stitched along the perimeter of my wound.

"Oh, Dr. Foster, you have the kindest bedside manner of any physician I have ever known, even my grandfather. You helped cure my insomnia. I'm so lucky you're my attending physician. Promise me that you will let me visit Hastings after I graduate from college."

"Jeremy, you're always welcome at Hastings, even for an annual checkup. Now tell me what happened to your back. I'd like to hear the full story," she said somewhat coldly, as if to compensate for a previous display of emotion. I sensed that she was embarrassed and anxious to change the conversation.

"Dr. Foster, I came to Hastings this evening instead of a hospital because I knew that the staff here respects their patients' confidentiality. You see, the person who stabbed me was an old friend of mine. I hadn't seen Larry for two years when he started shooting up heroin. It's really a shame that no one's helped him cure his addiction. He's really a very intelligent person with a strong aptitude for science and mathematics."

"Oh my goodness, I had no idea!" She shuddered, apparently astonished that I was attacked by a friend.

"Let me start from the beginning," I said cautiously, pausing to clear my throat and slide closer to the warmth of her body.

"Go right ahead Jeremy," she whispered, stroking my cheek.

"Well, after studying all day for an exam in physical chemistry, I decided to take a break for pizza. On my way to the pizzeria, I took a shortcut through the underpass of the train station. When Larry saw me in the distance, he crossed the street to greet me. I was really happy to see him, but when I reached out to shake his hand, I noticed he was wielding a knife." She narrowed her eyelids, intensifying her probing stare, which almost extracted the truth from me. "He shined the blade in my face and said, 'Sorry Jerry, but I'm strung out. Give me all the money in your wallet. Tomorrow we're taking a walk to the bank to close out your account. Don't worry Jerry, old buddy, I won't clean you out completely.' I tried to reason with him, but everything I said had a condescending ring. When I told him that he could lead a normal life once he was on the methadone program, he grabbed my shirt collar and pushed me down on the sidewalk. I was breathless and my hands were trembling."

She looked at me sympathetically and squeezed my fingers between her warm hands.

"He stood over me, shaking the knife under my chin, and said 'I want everything. Empty your pockets. Don't make me wait any longer! Give me all your money now!' I was so shaken up that I couldn't move at all, which was almost as bad as resisting. He picked me up by the collar and pushed his thumb into my throat. I thought that I would choke to death. Then the knife plunged through my coat. When he felt my flesh resist, his heart must have softened. He pulled out the blade before piercing a lung. That's why the wound is relatively superficial."

"What a terrible ordeal," she said, staring at me with disbelieving eyes. "Don't worry, Jeremy, you'll sleep safely here tonight. Tomorrow you can give the full story to the police."

"But he's my friend," I protested, "and you agreed to keep this totally confidential. I don't want to get caught in any neurofibrillary tangles."

"I have no intention of betraying your confidence, Jeremy, but this is a very serious matter, involving campus security." Her voice was very solemn. Had I pushed myself into a corner? "Oh you poor kid," she whispered, her voice modulating to its familiar sympathetic tone. She resumed her massage of the pleasurable pressure points along my spinal column. Squirming playfully under the covers, I savored the warmth of her affectionate touch.

"Dr. Foster, I've learned my lesson. I'll never walk alone again in a bad neighborhood."

"That's a good idea Jeremy, but I still think you should reconsider your decision and identify your assailant to the police. If you choose to remain silent, your fellow students may be victims of similar crimes in the future. When you begin to practice medicine Jeremy, you'll have to make many difficult decisions, often on a daily basis . . . Right now I want you to go back to sleep so you'll regain your strength and be back on your feet. You can always file a report tomorrow. Now let's go back to sleep," she said in a motherly voice, pulling an extra blanket over my legs. I had hoped that she would serve me hot milk and honey, but there was no such luck.

Her fingers walked down the nape of my neck. My penis poked its way through the paper pajamas and dangled anxiously beneath the freshly starched sheet. She was unaware of the swelling under the blanket and continued stroking me until she thought I was fast asleep.

"Dr. Foster, I can't take it anymore," I cried, kicking off the covers. "He's going to kill me as soon as I take one step outside Hastings. What am I going to do?" Rolling over on my side, I pressed my head near her warm belly in complete spontaneity.

"It's all right. You'll be safe inside." Maternal instinct compelled her to press my head against her bosom. I was too frightened to look up into her eyes. My cheekbone rubbed against a hard button in her lab coat. The discomfort forced me to withdraw. "You know, I just came back from Cornell University where my son goes to school," she said affectionately. "Tim is a biomedical engineering major. He's starting graduate school at Harvard this fall."

So she really does have a son, I thought, seething with jealousy, although I had had a hunch all along. And she probably gives him all the maternal sympathy and encouragement which motivates him to study hard enough to get into a school like Harvard. I'm sure the whole neighborhood knows about it. Who could ever disappoint a mommy like Silvana? It's not fair that he gets her for a mother. He's probably a spoiled, privileged child.

"No," I cried in agony. "I'm your only son. I emerged from your loins. Don't you realize that? Let me kiss you mother." I stared at her with such self-assurance that she couldnl't refuse the kiss which I planted on her cheek. It was a soft, semi-dry kiss, one and a half inches northwest of her upper lip, a dutiful kiss which a son gives to his mother. Then I wrapped my arm around her back and pawed her shoulder blade with arousing strokes. Her skin was palpably warm and nonresisting. I was more determined than ever to hug her closely and drink up the sweet pheromones of her elastic body.

"What are you doing?" she shrieked, pushing me away with both hands.

Stepping backwards, she covered her breasts with her hands and glared at me angrily.

"You know perfectly well what I'm doing, Silvana. Don't worry, it's all perfectly natural. Incest is relative . . . you said that you really wanted to help me and now you'll be doing just that. Come on Silvana, be a sport. It's only therapeutic."

"Now wait a minute . . . Mr. Lipschitz!"

"I've waited too long!" Lunging forward, I grabbed her by the waist and wrestled her down to the bed. "Look Silvana, no funny stuff. Don't push the nurses' buzzer and don't speak above a whisper, because if you scream, I'll make you fondle my revolver. Get the message!"

She stared at me disbelievingly until I revealed the gun under the pillow. I snaked my slender body upwards so that our waists were parallel and bumped my hips against her pelvis in rhythmic thrusts. Then I wrapped my calves around her thighs with a tight scissor kick so that her legs were immobilized and she knew that I was in control. I was so excited that I could hardly feel my wound reopening. She gazed with futile eyes at the strawberry patterns on the wallpaper. We both knew that it was highly unlikely for the nurse to barge in, unless personally summoned.

Suddenly a sour antiseptic smell coated my phlegmatic tongue and weakened my self-confidence. A few drops of urine dripped on the sheets. I cowered away, afraid that she would attack one of my painful pressure points and humiliate me.

"Jeremy Lipschitz, aren't you ashamed of yourself?" she scolded hoarsely, pushing me away to the far side of the bed. Rolling over me, she pinned her knees against my elbows. My legs kicked helplessly in the air. Her hard kneecaps shocked the funny bones of my elbows. I withdrew from her and flung myself out of bed.

"Dr. Foster, I beseech you," I cried, bending down on my knees and giving my most pitiable stare. "Please forgive me. I just got carried away. Really, you must understand my motives."

"My, you gave me such a scare. Jeremy, do you think you can control yourself now?" She sat down and tried to catch her breath.

"Yes, I think I'm under control. I promise that I won't touch you. Oh, I can't promise that, but I'll never injure you or make you do anything against your will. The gun's only a water pistol; it's not my father's revolver. You must understand why I did it, Dr. Foster. I did it because I loved you. Please, please accept my apology or I won't be able to live with myself. I'll kill myself. I love you. I really do. I couldn't restrain my . . . "

"Now, just relax," she said, resuming her responsibilities as attending physician. "Just lie down on your stomach. Everything's going to be all right. You're just a little excited right now because you were attacked."

She pressed her hand just above the wound and stroked the nape of my neck. I melted under her soft touch and obeyed the doctor's orders. My extremities tingled from the delicious impulses. She ran her fingers through my hair, hoping I would relax and be satisfied with the limited physical contact she was willing to give me. Then she tucked me in firmly with hospital sheets.

Two woolen blankets fell over my legs. I was completely mummified within her protective cocoon. When I was almost asleep, she leaned over me and kissed me lightly on the temple. Silvana had lips of paregoric which seemed to eradicate all memory of pain. I fell listlessly into a heavy sleep, feeling her warmth beside me while I lapsed into my fantasy cavern, tucked away in the soft folds of her uterus.

When Birds Fly South

Three weeks after my stitches were removed, the scar started to itch—nature's sign of healing. My depression, however, showed little sign of lifting. I could barely feed myself, let alone take care of my biological needs. Without Silvana by my side I would indulge in exercises of self-starvation. I felt that diving into an icy river would be a quick benumbing finale. It was clear to me that I needed a vacation. At the end of January, after passing my final exams with faded colors, I asked my parents if I could join them on their annual sojourn to Miami Beach and recuperate from the stressful semester. At first they were reluctant to take me along, afraid that I might pester them and spoil their vacation, but after listening to my plea they made room for another snowbird in the back seat.

After a three day drive, our Galaxy 500 rolled up the ramp of La Belle Province, a modest motel dwarfed by high-rise condominiums shadowing the length of Indian Creek Drive. We were only three blocks away from Collins Avenue and Bagel Beach. Most of the guests at our motel were French Canadians from Quebec who rarely spoke a word of English. My father preferred to mingle with the *goyim* in this secluded spot rather than be boxed-in with the *Yiddlach* at the oceanfront hotels. He was afraid that the *yentas* there would talk his ear off, once they found out he was a rabbi and a professor of Hebrew letters, no less. Questions would be asked about dietary laws and potato pancakes, the latter directed at my mother, a *rebbitsin*. At least half of the Jewish crowd in Miami Beach was from "Lonkisland," Scarsdale, Rochelle Park or New Jersey. Dad wanted to be far away from the men wearing the alligator labels on their shirts. He had seen enough of them in the Borscht Belt and was sensitive to criticism about the decadence of American Jewry. In fact, he felt more at ease amid strangers who were latent anti-Semites, as if they helped remind him of his Jewishness without beating in his head. "As long as they take out their aggressions in football stadiums," he would say, "we're safe in this country." An additional advantage at La Belle Province was that we could do our own cooking. I was perfectly satisfied with the location. Collins Avenue was a Mecca for comfortably-off older women living a life of leisure.

As soon as we arrived I put on my tropical outfit: a pair of white sailor pants, a Hawaiian shirt and Israeli sandals. The change in temperature raised my spirits. Feeling generous with myself, I splurged on a copy of the *New York Times* printed via satellite. Ten paces down Collins Avenue I paused to rest on an empty park bench and read the paper. Two peep holes flanked the center crease. Feeling comfortable with this sun umbrella, I was not ashamed to prolong my low stares as long as I liked and gazed at the assortment of mature legs strolling along the promenade. Gold and diamond jewelry glittered in the tropical sunlight, blending with red and purple varicose veins. Whenever a cloud of perfume swept by the bench I sniffed it greedily and suffused my lungs with hope for the future. The warm rays started to bake out the pneumonic phlegm encrusting my bronchial tree, my bronx.

After sitting alone for half an hour, I grew discouraged. Wasn't there at least one woman who was courageous enough to sit down beside me and share small talk about medicine, movie stars or the warm weather? The least I expected was for a seventy year old grandmother with gaseous *kishka* to sit beside me and tell me how the sun had worked wonders for her rheumatism. I would convince her that I was a third year medical student and give her a free physical. As the hours wore on and the bench remained bare I was ready to get up and prowl around. Just as I was about to leave the park bench, a young man, wearing a *yarmulke* and *tzitzis* walked by. He paused to read the headlines of the *New York Times*, looked down at the Hebraic pubic hair on my head and sat down on the far end of the bench. From the corners of my eyes, I watched him fingering the fringes of his *tzitzis*. His white, long-sleeved shirt was soaked with perspiration. Although he was too well assimilated to grow *payess* over his ears, I could tell by his nervous *shuckle* that he was a yeshiva *bocher* from New York. He seemed bewildered upon noticing the two peep holes in my newspaper. Then he stared down at my crotch, only to observe my *Zion* poking against the zipper at an oblique angle as an older woman walked by. The pace at which he was winding and unwinding the fringes of his *tzitzis* intensified. By the time I had looked up to meet his eyes directly he had already edged six inches closer to me.

"Hi, I'm Seth Teitlebaum, from Flushing. Pleased to meet you."

A layer of chicken *schmaltz* stuck to my fingers after I shook his clammy hand. I tried wiping it on the newspaper, leaving the imprint of the morning headlines on my fingers. He looked me straight in the eye as if to appraise my sexual orientation.

"Jeremy Lipschitz," I muttered, forcing a polite smile. "Where do you go to school?"

"Oh, there's a synagogue across from the Sterling Hotel. There's some good restaurants in the area too, all of them *glatt kosher*."

"*Glatt kosher*, hmm. Oh, that's very nice. Well maybe we can go there sometime for dinner. My family just arrived in Miami Beach last night. I haven't made any friends yet."

"Neither have I; it gets very lonely here sometimes. Where's your family staying?"

"Just at a small motel down on Indian Creek Drive. It's a bit cramped."

He peered down at my crotch and hid his hands in his pants pocket. I could tell by the way his pants were cut that he had wide and deep pockets with ample room to fondle his fringes. Judging by the depth of his sideburns, he was under twenty-one. The perspiration on his round, pudgy face loosened a stray whitehead. He had a pale complexion from studying the Talmud indoors when other children were playing ball outside. My parents would have considered Seth to be a perfect playmate, a good influence who would teach me Jewish values and keep me out of trouble.

"Well Jeremy, I've got to show you my place. My grandparents gave me their condo for two weeks. They're taking a vacation in Israel."

"Oh, that's very interesting. Are they taking a tour, or . . . "

"No, they're just visiting relatives. My grandfather's a millionaire. He owns a chain of haberdashery stores."

"It's wonderful that you have the whole place to yourself. My father's a rabbi. He teaches Midrash. We wouldn't have been able to make this trip were it not for the extra money he made on the High Holidays."

"Oh really, your father's a rabbi? I wouldn't have known. Why aren't you wearing a *yarmulke*?"

"Oh, I just took it off because the wind was blowing in from the beach and my bobby pin got tangled up in my hair . . . "

"I see, you need to use a bobby pin. You have long curly hair. It's very nice." His hands squirmed around in his pockets as if he were repressing an urge to stroke his fingers through my hair.

"Thanks. Both my parents have wavy hair. I guess that's why mine is so kinky."

"Yeh, it runs in the family. I wish I had hair like yours. And such luxuriant growth; it's a real natural. I once tried to have my hair styled that way, but it drooped down after the first rinsing. What kind of shampoo do you use? It smells so fresh."

I smiled agreeably, but eyed him suspiciously. God, I thought, what a creep. It's amazing the number of neurotics they're churning out of the yeshivas these days. I'm glad that I dropped out before the fourth grade. But what the hell, Jeremy, let's play along. This guy's really interesting to observe—could be good short story material. Besides, I might be able to *schnor* a few meals off him, some *matzoh* ball soup at Wolfie's and that's only for starters.

"I use a cologne-scented protein shampoo—one that has extra body. What kind do you use?"

"The same, except without the cologne. I'm allergic and very sensitive to perfume. Your scent, however, doesn't seem to irritate me." He pulled one hand out of his pocket and dabbed a handkerchief against his forehead. "So Jeremy, what are you doing this morning? Unless you have some other plans, I know a place that is better than this park bench."

"What do you mean?" I asked sternly. His hand quivered spasmodically. He leaned away from me when he realized his tone had sounded a bit forward.

"I just wanted to invite you over to my condo," he answered timidly. "Maybe play a little shuffleboard and checkers or take a swim in the heated pool before lunch. We can have corned beef sandwiches at Wolfie's or, if you like, they deliver also. They have great sour pickles; it's on me, all you can eat. I've got a projecting color T.V. with a six foot screen and remote control. Wait until you see my videotape collection; I have plenty of three-quarter inch tapes that are collector's items. I bought them for investment purposes. Come on Jeremy, what do you say? You're on vacation. Have a good time."

"Sure. Sounds great."

"Then let's go." He rose from the bench and walked in front of me with a goosestep. Ripples of gelatinous flab shook around his thighs with every step he took. Although he was only slightly on the heavy side, there was hardly an ounce of muscle on his torso. The morning sun was rising quickly, the rays reflecting on tinted glass windows of the hotels skirting the oceanfront. His hand-crocheted *yarmulke* bobbed up and down with every step. I trailed two steps behind him, observing the way his legs waddled in synch with his hunched shoulders and wondering whether he had a slight scoliosis of the spine. A salty breeze blew in from the ocean and guided me along an unknown path. All I knew was that I was miles away from home. Dear Dr. Foster was probably not too far away herself, vacationing in the Bahamas with her husband. I needed to be with someone who didn't measure the time we spent together in mere finite appointments. I needed to heal the scars of self-imposed isolation. I needed to be, just be.

I had never been inside an air-conditioned condominium, although I had seen new high-rise buildings pop up on vacant lots every year, in a boom for the retirement community. I followed Seth inside the lobby of the Seaside Beach Club. In the adjacent lounge, four groups of elderly ladies were playing mah jong. The music of Lawrence Welk was piped through the speakers and seemed to weigh down the clouds of cigarette smoke.

"This is perfect for my grandparents, Jeremy, but I need a little more action, a place more exciting. What do you think?"

"I think it's great if you like to play cards or bingo. I'm thinking of retiring by the age of twenty-seven myself. My father always told me: you can either work with your *kopf* or your *toches*."

"I agree with you completely. There's no use learning everything ass-backwards. That's why I'm studying business administration in college. Then I'll go for my M.B.A. Can't wait to inherit the business. Here's the elevator."

Both of us looked at the flashing numbers of the floor levels. We were too self-conscious to look each other in the eye. When the elevator stopped on the twelfth floor, he pushed open the door and held it until I had walked safely into the hall. He jingled his keys and unlocked the door to the apartment. I almost bumped my head on the low ceiling and wondered whether these condos had been built for dwarfs.

"Make yourself at home," he said, leading me into the adjoining master bedroom. "What can I get you from the frig? I've got a case of black cherry soda, or would you like some straight seltzer?"

"Straight seltzer is fine, on ice."

"Coming up."

Looking around the room, I saw remnants of his grandparents' possessions. An inordinate number of baby powder canisters rested on every piece of furniture in the room. I knew then that I was in for some serious business. Everything was decorated in New York-style: kitsch, plastic flowers, shiny Franz Hals prints, and dyed feathers. I sat down on the white bedspread covering the king-sized bed and turned on the T.V. for distraction. The remote control buttons were fun to play with but the only morning shows on were rerun serials.

"Here, I brought you a little lime to flavor your drink," he said, with a sly smile placing a tall frosted glass on a silver platter before me.

"Thanks Seth, you're really very hospitable," I said innocently, guzzling down the bubbling seltzer. I belched and almost choked on the seltzer; it was so strong.

"Now that's seltzer, isn't it? I put in an extra pellet of gas just for you: it's homemade."

"I'll bet it is. Hey Seth, what do you get when you drink borscht and seltzer?"

"I don't know, what?"

"You burp in technicolor."

He laughed and slapped me playfully on the shoulder. I edged closer towards him teasingly. He reclined on the bed and started doodling with a bottle of baby powder.

"So what's on T.V.? Anything interesting?"

"Nah, I may as well turn it off. Nice remote control unit you've got."

He opened his pants to let the fringes of his *tzitzis* hang out of his shirt. "You can take off your shoes and stretch out if you like."

"Thanks, I think I will. Wow, this is really a king-sized bed and judging from the firm springs, I'll bet it's posturepedic." I gulped down the last of the seltzer and swallowed my belch.

"Yeh, it even has a built-in vibrator. My grandmother uses it for her arthritis, but I find it very relaxing too. Do you want me to turn it on?"

"No, that's O.K. Let me finish my soda first."

He sprinkled a generous amount of baby powder in his hands and rubbed them together vigorously. The scent of talc reminded me of the crib and the times when I had diaper rash. Mom would sprinkle a generous amount over my rectum and dress me with a fresh pair of diapers before leaving me alone in the crib, where I played with imaginary insects.

"Boy, the air-conditioning in this place is really nice; it doesn't blast you away. You're really lucky that you have this condo all to yourself." I unbuttoned my shirt and looked down at his bulging waistline. He started to toy with his Star of David necklace which had left an imprint on his breast. His flabby belly sank down to his genitals. There was something repulsive about his lips; they were glossed and well-fed. I could tell that his mother fed him lots of chicken *schmaltz*. For some unknown reason I wanted to make nookie with him, perhaps to reconcile my bitter memories of getting molested in the hospital shower as a little boy. There was no sense in coming down on homosexuality unless I tried it once, and making it with a yeshiva *bocher* seemed to be safe enough.

He leaned towards me and stroked the hairs on my chest. Although I didn't resist his moves, I wasn't quite ready to reciprocate. I felt violated by his clammy touch, but there was also something unique to his feel.

Had he tasted a rebellion similar to my own? Wasn't it the Jews who frequently castigated the Arabs for the prevalence of homosexuality in their society? Yet here was a fellow Semite who liked to indulge in the same act. Think of all the poor single Jewish girls who couldn't find a husband. Be fruitful and multiply, the Lord said. The greatest enemies of modern Jewry were intermarriage and assimilation, I thought; they started where the Nazis left off. Each family must have three children in order to sustain the rate of procreation; otherwise the race would dwindle away. The single Jewish gay man was only keeping an eligible woman immured in her room. All she ever wished for was to bear a few children and to light the Sabbath candles with her family. She wanted the simple things of life: a family for whom she could make gefilte fish and pickled herring. The husband would slice the *challeh* and make the *motzie* and after dinner they would sing the "Song of Songs," put the children to bed and have intercourse, a double *mitzvah* on the Sabbath. All of this was healthy and natural and the Lord would reward them with more children. But who was to waste his semen in masturbation and spill the seed of Israel into the barren wastes of his own gender?

"Do you like to be stroked lightly or vigorously?" He ran his fingers around my back and down to my legs.

"Lightly is fine. I'm kind of tired right now. You don't mind if I just rest on my back."

"Sure that's fine. I told you to make yourself at home. It's amazing how men are the only ones who really know how to touch other men and make them feel good. It's because they alone understand the tender parts of the male body."

"Yes, but not too tender now. Just work on my upper torso for now."

He sprinkled baby powder in his palm and rubbed it on my chest until the sternal hairs turned grey and slippery.

"You have very soft skin, Jeremy. Does it feel nice when I rub you this way?"

"Yeh, I can't deny that it does, but don't rub me the wrong way."

"Well, would you like me to work on your calves and thighs too, or would you like to finish your soda first?"

"No, go right ahead. Let me just unbutton my pants."

"That's O.K. I'll do it for you."

He hooked his thumbs in my belt loops and unclasped the button above the zipper. While pulling off my pants, he rubbed his thumbs along my shins and smiled to himself knowlingly. I detected a hungry look in his eyes when he folded my white sailor pants neatly over the chair. He poured a generous portion of body talc in his hands and dabbed it over my legs.

"I always find that a massage is so much smoother with lots of baby powder, but your skin is naturally soft. I normally go through three canisters of baby powder every week. Do you like the way this feels?" he asked, with a twinkle in his eye, rubbing his hand closer to my groin.

In order to keep myself from feeling disgusted I pretended that he was just another masseuse. Nevertheless, there was something upsetting about the incongruity of a gay yeshiva *bocher*. Was he victimized by his training or was he only posing as a religious boy to appear more innocuous when he approached me? I liked the idea of being picked up by someone, even if it was a man. Any living force would be enough to conquer my involuted depression.

His hand crawled along my inner thigh. I allowed him to stroke my groin without resisting. He didn't seem to be the type who would grab me by the balls and force me to suck on his penis, so I let him pull down my briefs and fondle my testicles.

"Hmm, I like loose balls," he said, fingering the varicose veins in my scrotum. "Most women don't like them, because they think the guy is feeble, but what do girls know about science? Jeremy, did anyone ever suck on your balls and hum the *Star Spangled Banner*?"

"No, but I imagine one must have a difficult time relaxing by the time they get to 'The rockets' red glare, bombs bursting in air.' "

"Ha, you knew that one. You have a good sense of humor. You're cute. Did anyone ever tell you that, Jeremy? Hmmm?" With the last question he snaked his tongue over my penis and licked it up and down slowly before mouthing the tip of the aperture. "Only a man knows how to make another man feel good, because he understands the anatomy of the male body. I love teen load. Mmmn, you feel good; you taste good; you are good!" He licked my scrotum and teethed gently on the skin without biting down hard.

Although I remained on guard, I couldn't deny the pleasant sensation. As my mother once told me before I reached puberty, sex is sex. However, I think she was referring to the conventional type. The air-conditioner cooled my perspiring skin.

"You don't have to come now if you don't feel like it," he whispered with a teasing lick when he say my organ become engorged with blood. "We can take turns. I like to have my legs massaged too. Now it's my turn."

I wasn't prepared to reciprocate in the oral fashion, but I figured I would massage him a little to compensate for the trouble he had gone through. My heart beat wildly. I feared that I was violating my own instinctive drive.

What a terrible way to start off the vacation, I thought. It may take me a week to recuperate from this ordeal. I'm stuck with a consolation prize.

He peeled off his slacks and rested on his stomach with his legs apart. I kneaded my fingers into his calf muscles, remembering my father's stories about how his aunt had to work in England as a masseuse during the war, rubbing the fat bellies of rich ladies to support the family. By the end of the day her hands were inflamed.

"Oh Jeremy, that feels so good. I'm so glad you massage legs. Please continue. I've been so lonely."

Moving up to his buttocks, I sank my fingers deep into his limp flesh. A foul, gaseous cloud wafted above his rectum; it smelled worse than rotten liverwurst. I felt repelled by the grotesque act I was in the midst of performing. A burst of anger surged through my loins. I gripped his flanks tightly, digging my nails into his skin until he started to bleed.

"Ooooooh, that feels so good, but come now, let's start off more gently and work your way gradually to the painful acts. Do you whip too, or would you prefer to eat my whipped cream?"

I rolled him over on his stomach and wrestled him down with a headlock, my elbow almost crushing his temple.

"Hey," he cried, and his voice cracked like an egg, "what do you think you're doing? That hurts! Hey, I can't breathe. This isn't fun anymore."

"You're damn right this isn't fun. Who the hell do you think you are, picking up an innocent Jewish boy off the street like that, luring him into your grandparents' condo? What would they say if they saw you using their apartment for this purpose? I ought to lock you up in the closet and throw away the key."

"Uncle. Uncle. I give up!" he said, with timid insistence. "Hey, let go of me! You're hurting me."

"You should be ashamed of yourself. This is a sin. If your *rebbe* saw what you were doing, he'd kick you out of the yeshiva and hang you by the balls. Oh, you're going to suffer for this," I screamed unmollified, pressing my elbow into his temple.

"Ouch! Hey, this is no joke. You're killing me. Who do you think you are, following me up here, you self-righteous gay basher?"

"I am your father," I answered calmly, in a deep authoritarian tone. "I hate to get very familiar, but I am the Messenger of Death. There's no time to flee."

"Please Jeremy, sir, I beg of you. Have mercy on me. I'll give you everything I own, even the gold watch I got for my Bar Mitzvah, my stamp collection. Just let me live."

"You disgusting swine," I said, spitting on the pillow. I gradually released my headlock, but hovered over him so that he knew I was in command and could pin him down again, were it my whim to do so. "Have you not read the Torah? Homosexuality is a sin worse than lying, stealing, dishonoring your father and mother, bearing false witness; it's as bad as murder, although some scholars might disagree. That's why i have no reservations about your sentence. This is only Talmudic justice. Since it's a first offense, I'll be more lenient and abide by the Code of Hamurabbi: an eye for an eye, a testicle for a testicle."

"No, whatever you do, don't touch me there," he said in a strangled voice. "Please, I'll give you everything: the T.V. set, all my money, my birthright."

"Be courageous. I'm not asking you for a bowl of red lentil soup. It's only minor surgery, swift and merciful, just as the Saudis do, but without the public throng. I'll knock you out before I cut them loose. Now where are my instruments."

His face turned so white I was afraid he would pass out. I slapped his cheek and made him look me straight in the eye.

"When the two angels visited Lot in Sodom, a crowd of men surrounded his house and demanded that he share his guests with them. And Lot offered them his daughters, if they would only spare his guests. The men wouldn't be appeased. And the angels blinded all those who tried to jump on the porch and penetrate Lot's home. Didn't you read the Torah, you disgusting *chazar*. You're not worthy of anything. You should be banished to the desert or burned to a crisp of potash by the Dead Sea. Now go jerk off in the closet; it will never produce a child. I don't ever want to see your face again. If I see you wandering on the beach hand in hand with another man, why I swear, you will not live to see the sun rise again. I will turn you into a pillar of salt."

With these last words, I picked up my clothes and dressed myself in the kitchen. I heard him sobbing into a pillow and I closed the door behind me. The scent of triumph suffused my lungs. I was strong enough to beat up a weakling from a yeshiva and felt proud of it. Now I was as horny as ever. There had to be some ripe, middle-aged woman strolling along the streets, even if she was Jewish. I never insisted on a *shikse*. I needed a female companion to compensate for this dreadful experience. In the elevator I felt butterflies flutter through my stomach as I descended to the lobby. I strolled calmly along the boardwalk, and rubbed a handful of sand between my palms, as if to wash my hands of the experience.

The Collins Avenue strip was teeming with lonely women seeking an escape from their sheltered marriages. Most were snowbirds from enclaves along the eastern seaboard. I stopped in front of a beauty salon and looked through the window to watch the middle-aged women basking under hot lamps and blow dryers. They were wives of professionals, *shikses* included. Some were treating their aging complexions with mudpacks, vitamin E cream and elastin. Others were having their hair set for the third time in a week. These ladies seemed to fry their sun-bleached brains into an eggy glump of scrambled ignorance, their thoughts limited to gossip and crinkled back issues of ladies magazines. When they returned to their hotel suites, it was time to nag their husbands for money to shop for the latest fashions. Their miserable spouses consented and escaped to the brokerage houses where they read the ticker tape coming in from Wall Street over 1300 miles away.

Rose Goodman arrived in Miami Beach with her husband two weeks before I did. Morris A. Goodman, M.D., F.A.C.S., was an internationally renowned neurosurgeon and full professor of Medicine at Columbia P & S in uptown Manhattan. In his surgical practice alone, he grossed over two million dollars annually. He was envious of his ophthalmologist colleagues who performed six daily radiokeratotomies at $5,000 per eye. Dr. Goodman only performed innovative microneurosurgical procedures which could enhance his towering international reputation and justify his exorbitant fees, for fewer than twenty percent of his patients succumbed under his knife. Wealthy individuals from all corners of the globe flew to New York with their private insurance policies and paid four-figure sums simply for an initial consultation and lab analysis, not to mention his fee for scooping out a pituitary tumor. His professional income paled in comparison to his massive real estate holdings as well as gifts he received from grateful patients who felt indebted to him for the rest of their lives. The Goodmans had so much money that they didn't know how to spend a third of it, especially since they had no heirs.

In the last few years, their marriage had shown signs of strain. They were on the verge of separation. Although Dr. Goodman possessed extensive knowledge concerning neuroendocrine anomalies, he could find no solution for his state of sexual impotence. His lone functioning testicle was completely insensitive to hormone therapies and the surgical manipulations which a colleague performed in confidence behind closed curtains and recorded on his chart in invisible ink.

Rose Goodman was forty-nine years old and had a penchant for younger men. Her husband's testicular atrophy only heightened her appetite for young flesh. She feared that lack of sexual intercourse would cause her ovaries to shrivel up. Besides, most middle-aged men were bores with pot bellies and no stamina for a night full of frolicking. As Morris became totally engrossed in his medical practice, Rose withdrew completely from her flaccid mate. She hated him for having cheated her out of a normal sex life. All Morris was good for was his money. She encouraged him to purchase a broad portfolio of life insurance and purposely aggravated his arteriosclerotic heart condition by sneaking high cholesterol and high sodium foods into his diet. This way she could finish him off with a timed-release poison, cash in on his premiums and emerge as a fabulously wealthy widow.

Although Rose and Morris lived under the same roof and occasionally spent their vacations together, they managed to sleep in separate bedrooms. At a time when they were still sleeping together, Rose learned the art of medicinal massage from him. He taught her how to stimulate the pleasurable pressure points along the spine in every available style: Swedish, Esalen, Shiatsu and Trager. That was all a doctor was good for.

Rose preferred not to approach men who were younger than eighteen years old, even if they had a pineal tumor that facilitated precocious puberty. The adventurous males who were in their early and middle twenties were generally more delectable prey, having a greater output of seminal load and pelvic thrusts that would make her groan in ecstasy. She paid her young gigolos a generous sum, on a sliding scale, according to the volume of their ejaculate. Unfortunately, there was a shortage of eligible men in Greater Miami Beach, little innocent flesh into which she could sink her desirous claws.

Shortly after Morris became board-certified in neurosurgery, he purchased a three bedroom luxury condo in a building with a private dock. Whenever he had the whim to take a cruise, he simply walked through the lobby to the pier, where his sixty foot yacht, the Hippocampus, was anchored. Although the condo had originally served as a winter retreat for both Goodmans, Morris now used it as a launch pad to go boating and get away from his wife.

Rose was always nauseous at sea. She preferred to stay in the more spacious quarters of her eleven room penthouse on Sutton Place. Their East Side apartment had a private entrance and reception room where Rose could entertain her secret lovers while her husband was at the hospital. The condo in Miami, however, had only one entrance.

Rose could never forgive Morris for making her believe at the start of their marriage that she was the one who was frigid. He documented his phantom diagnosis by fabricating scientific data and playing on his wife's ignorance. Rose spent over seven years in psychoanalysis after having been led to believe that she was the one with feeble genitalia. Morris sulked whenever Rose was around, even when they locked themselves in separate bedrooms. The Goodmans brought their maid along to Miami;

her presence enabled them to avoid conversing with one another during dinner, the only time they shared together.

In spite of their attempts to live under the same roof as a separated couple, they failed. One morning Morris left a note on the kitchen table and boarded the Hippocampus for an indefinite length of time. Rose was hardly depressed by her husband's sudden departure. In fact, she was relieved that she finally had the privacy to entertain a young man should the opportunity arise.

Looking out at the rough Atlantic waves misting her picture window, she thought, it's too bad I'm in Miami Beach now. Most of the people around here are old fogies. The only youngsters on the beach are high school kids. They're much too immature for my tastes. Perhaps I should return to New York where I'm guaranteed to find a young man. Besides, I've already built up a base for my suntan and half my boobs are brown. No, that would be too much for Morris to bear. If he ever thought I ran away from him he would stipulate in his will that all his assets go to philanthropic organizations. The thought almost makes me throw up. Come on Rose, she encouraged herself, freeing her breasts from her 38D bra cups, so they sank against her chest and dipped all the way down to her navel. I'm sure you can find a few young men around here. Maybe there're some college tootsies hanging around with their parents. It's Christmas vacation. There must be one eligible guy around here who would like a little action with a rich foxy mamma.

She took the elevator down to the lobby and walked down the rear steps leading to the beach. A breeze from the ocean wetted the rouge that caked around her nasolabial folds. She took off her shoes and walked barefoot, facing the sea. A bulbous, blue, Portuguese man-of-war jellyfish beckoned to be popped, its dried-out tentacles entangled in tar-laced driftwood, yards away from the receding tide.

Rose glanced at the red polish flaking off her nagging bunions. Her toes dug into a moist crawlspace of vanishing snail holes. A white foam splashed against her ankles. The acid didn't burn, but was cool and invigorating; it made her toes tingle and nipples swell.

Shadows of seagull wings hovered around her, but she had no bread crumbs to toss into the wind. The beach was empty, except for a few elderly couples strolling along the boardwalk within close range of their nursing home. An old man sat alone on a municipal park bench with a chewed up cigar bobbing out of the side of his mouth.

Come on Rose, this is no place for you. Let's get out of here, she thought, trying to cheer up. There are no youngsters here and besides, no one will ever notice me with my hair looking like this. Let's go to the beauty parlor and splurge on the full treatment. I'm going to have my hair set, a nail manicure, and perhaps a mudpack or chicken embryo facial treatment. At least Miami Beach can revitalize my skin. I may as well look healthy.

She walked along the boardwalk to Collins Ave., but couldn't escape the sound of blaring horns from Cadillacs, Lincoln Continentals and Bentleys. The sidewalk was blocked with heavy pedestrian traffic and looked like an open-air geriatric ward. Retired widows were creaking their arthritic joints along the promenade at a pace of two blocks an hour. At 73rd Street, she stopped at the Oasis, her favorite beauty parlor.

Ah, they know me. I don't have to make an appointment in advance. I can just walk in. She pushed her way through the crowd, weaving her buxom figure between immobile people who reacted after she had already passed them.

The receptionist came up to her and asked if she had an appointment. Before Rose could answer, the owner stepped between them and asked, "Won't you have a seat, Mrs. Goodman. Roberto will be with you in just a moment." Within seconds after she had made herself comfortable, a tall, handsome man with a wide handlebar moustache escorted her to the sink. He stroked a comb through her hair, appraising its texture to determine the strength and pH of the shampoo he would use. She squeezed his hand with a ten dollar bill, hoping he would massage her scalp extensively. He didn't get the hint and even abbreviated the cream rinse.

I stood outside the Oasis Beauty Salon, my nose pressed against the window pane, surveying the women under the lamps. There was something arousing about a woman's head in a bowl. Rose was the one who had caught my attention. I was tantalized by her yellow green eyes. Ever since I had left Seth, I was determined to find an older female companion who would nullify my shame. She took hold of my desirous eyes and smiled back. I wouldn't let her be distracted by the issue of *Ladies Home Journal* saddling her thighs, and maintained my unflinching stare. A gold Cartier watch, studded with diamonds, added luster to her suntanned arms. She kept herself up extremely well for a jaded snowbird and looked healthier than most mature women. Her shoulders were held back, making her matronly breasts appear more prominent and shapely.

She strutted up to the owner, handed him a fifty dollar bill and, with a subtle twitch of her nose, refused the change. Then she lingered at the window before me. Her chin raised, she turned full circle like a fashion model and awaited my look of approval of her coiffure. Then she wiggled her hips, winked at me and walked out the door.

"I'm Jeremy Lipschitz, a lonely boy on vacation," I said feebly, extending my hand.

Fortunately for me, she didn't see my knees buckle, for timidity in the legs could be taken as a sign of sexual weakness. However, it was also preferable for me to be a little nervous. If I appeared overly confident, she might have suspected that I was an extortionist.

"Hello, Jeremy," she nodded and shook my hand. "Rose Goodman. It's a shame you should feel lonely," she whispered with a hint of maternal seduction.

When she squeezed my hand I knew by the soft scrape of her laquered nails that it was more than a courteous handshake. Her infectious smile and intermittent winks approved my lean, hard figure. We were separated by a long, silent pause.

"Rose," I said confidently, flashing my eye teeth, "there's a juice bar down the street. Would you join me in a glass of coconut milk?"

"What a marvelous idea," she said exuberantly, squeezing my hand a second time. "I haven't had a glass of coconut milk in ages." She rocked her hips from side to side and bumped my tiny ass.

Judging from the weight of her hand, I could tell that her jewelry was solid gold, not just gold-plated. She was obviously wealthier than the nouveau riche transients who cluttered the hotels on Collins Avenue during the peak season.

We walked towards the juice bar at a leisurely, but lively pace, our legs merging periodically in friendly frottage. I squeezed her hand gently, but endearingly. We were separated briefly when an old woman, blocking the flow of pedestrian traffic, hobbled down the middle of the sidewalk. When we came together, Rose stroked her nails along the length of my spine, giving me goose pimples. She pressed her face close to my ear and held my head in place so I couldn't pull away. Her complexion felt remarkably smooth and youthful, in contrast to my two-day pubescent stubble. I looked for faint scars behind her ears, but they were covered by wisps of fine grey hears. Her cosmetic surgeon had done a marvelous job.

"Are you on vacation with your parents?" she asked, leaning into me.

"Yes, my parents took me along, but I'm really here with you, Rose."

Lurching forward, I kissed her lightly on the cheek and encountered peach fuzz. Her cheek was sweet and salty, but had an aftertaste of extramarital experience. She was so stunned by my kiss that she jumped. Her forehead rammed into my lower lip and loosened a tooth. Blood trickled out of a tiny gash. I tasted the sweet, prothrombinemic gravy and sucked hard on the blood vessels to extract more juice from my injured lip. Sympathy would be a fine appetizer for what was to come.

"Oh, I'm so sorry. Forgive me, dear. I didn't mean to jump like that. I was just so startled by your kiss, darling," she said, removing a handkerchief from her pocketbook. She moistened a corner of the cloth with her saliva and dabbed it over my cut. Her amorous spit was a benumbing antiseptic. "Here now, poor fellow, did I hurt you?" she asked, pinching my cheek between two *shnipsing* fingers, a gesture commonly extended to a rabbi's son. She pressed her finger over my inner lip and inspected the tiny gash as solicitously as an attending nurse.

"Oh, I can see that it's really nothing. The cut adds color to your lips, you handsome devil. Let's keep it moist." She winked, kissed me on the mouth and we became engaged in lingual entanglement.

We were drawn by the smell of tropical fruit emanating from an open-air juice bar. I hopped up on a swivel chair and twirled around a few revolutions. Rose sat down beside me and planted her diamond studded hand on my inner thigh. Behind the bar on a shelf of shaved ice a variety of tropical fruits were displayed: papaya, mango, coconut and pineapple. A waitress, wearing a platinum blond wig was mixing a Caesar salad.

"You know something, Jeremy. I haven't been in a place like this in years. My husband's always dragging me to these stuffy restaurants. Thank God he's away at sea now."

"Is your husband a naval officer?"

"No, he's a neurosurgeon," she said, her voice slurred by a trace of ennui. "Every year we spend a couple of months in Florida to get away from the cold. Your parents probably came here for the same reason."

Wow, I thought, the wife of a neurosurgeon. Could I get his autograph?

"My family's stuck at one of the smaller motels by Indian Creek. We're only staying here for a week," I said feebly so she would suckle the poor waif.

The waitress turned around and faced us. "What would you like to order?"

"Two coconut milks please, in chilled glasses," I said boldly, proud that I could order a refreshing mocktail for a wealthy lady.

The waitress removed a bowl of coconut meat from the refrigerator, mashed the hunks through the juice press, and poured the milk into two tall glasses.

"Allow me," I begged, covering the bill with my hand. She peeked inside my change purse, which was filled mainly with pennies. As I dropped the exact change on the counter, I noticed that my hands were trembling.

"I hope I haven't cleaned you out. Remind me to reimburse you when we get back to my place."

"Don't be ridiculous, Rose. This is my treat." Slurping up the creamy head of coconut schlagg, I lifted my glass and whispered, *"L'chayim."*

We clinked glasses. A drop of juice spilled on her hands, forming a polka dot pastel with her age spots. I pressed my knee between her thighs, edging my shin deep towards her womb. She spread her legs to absorb my patellar thrust and smiled at me from the corners of her eyes. Something in her fluid smile convinced me that she was sincerely interested in me. Hoping to tease her, I turned my back and sipped my drink slowly while looking blankly into space. Rose leaned forward, rested the weight of her sagging underarm on my neck and scraped her nails along my scalp. Then she pressed her heaving breasts against the ripples of my spine. The fabric of my Hawaiian shirt was too thin to absorb the heat of her mammary glands. I shuddered. "Kiss me baby," she whispered in my ear and then teethed on the lobe voraciously with a slurping lick. The waitress stared in disbelief.

"Some people," she snickered under her breath and tied her apron strings.

"Would you kindly excuse my mother," I said, facing the waitress. "She's just a little bit excited right now. I just flew in this morning from college and we haven't seen each other since September. You know how mothers are?" I asked, nodding in synch to convey the playfulness of our situation. The waitress maintained her unflinching stare. Slipping a crisp single onto the counter, I turned to Rose and rubbed her back. My hand slid playfully under her bra strap and almost dislodged the clasp. "Come on, let's go to your place." The waitress swept up the dollar, buried it in her pocket and let her jaw drop.

We walked out the door hand in hand. Flakes of coconut meat stuck to my teeth. The bright Florida sun baked the pigments in my skin, creating the base of a suntan. I was beginning to enjoy my vacation.

"Jeremy? May I call you that, or do you prefer to be called Jerry? Oh, my little Jerry and I are going to have so much fun together real soon, under the covers. Ha, ha, ha. I just loved your story. You were simply astounding. Did you see the expression on the waitress' face?" She pulled me fiercely against her breasts. "You really crack me up. When I first saw you through the window of the beauty parlor I thought you were retarded."

I thought I had seen my parents window shopping on Collins Ave., but I was mistaken. What a surprise that would be, if we bumped into each other. I'd suggest that they join us on a double date. They'd have no reason to complain since she was Jewish. I knew that Dad was resting securely beside the swimming pool, listening to the stock report on the radio and reading Midrash at the same time. If the market went up, he was assured that he was one of the chosen people. If it went down, he would dwell on the Holocaust. I always thought he would have been better off investing in convertible bonds; that way he could hedge his bad moods.

For a moment I was afraid I had fallen into the clutches of an evil wench who had seized upon my infantile fantasies. But I was not convinced. She'll be good for you, Jerry. You need to have straight, conventional sex while you're on vacation. It's a good way to start off the *Goyische* New Year. There's nothing to fear. She's practically in your lap. Maybe she'll set up a special scholarship fund for you and have her husband use his pull to get you into medical school. She may even give you a Jaguar XKE. You never know. Do a good job now and you may be rewarded with the family jewels for being a *mensch*, just when you least expect it.

"My penthouse is over there, just three buildings down, at the beach club," she said in a wet whisper, pointing to a row of high-rise apartments along Collins Avenue. Suddenly she grabbed my chin and pulling my face towards her, commanded, "Kiss me *bubeleh!*"

I took a deep breath and kissed her firmly on the lips. My tongue darted against the roof of her mouth. Scores of elderly pedestrians stopped to stare at us. Penthouse, not bad, I thought. God must be rewarding me for something. My eyelids were forced to close by the pressure of her smothering cheeks. She squeezed me so hard that I was afraid I would suffocate.

"Jeremy, I don't think I'll be able to hold off much longer. We have to make love now, before we get to my apartment. I just can't wait any longer. I've been dying for nookie for so long. Let's go to the beach; it's closer. I know a good hide-out under the pier. I want to see your little pecker."

This is getting ridiculous, I thought. I'm sure the superintendent of her building can arrange for a toy boy. She's behaving like a real animal. If I'm not careful, we'll be arrested for indecent exposure and committing sodomy on the beach. Sodomy's a felony. They may even press the mayhem law. My father will have to bail me out of a Florida jail, use up all his vacation cash and have his bank wire emergency money.

Her hands were clasped firmly around my neck. I pulled them apart with all my strength and flung her away from me. She fell to the street, but got back on her feet within seconds. Glaring at me, she seemed ready to kill.

I wanted to compromise and muttered feebly, "Look, if you could just wait until we made it to your condomin . . . "

"Don't you talk to me," she screamed defiantly, slapping my face with the back of her hand. "If you can't make love on the beach where it's totally natural, then you're like all the other men, spoiled rotten to the core. Look, don't talk to me," she barked, waving her fist before my eyes. "I grew up during the Depression. Do you think I got this gold watch here for nothing, you fresh little bastard? Who the hell do you think you are?" She took off her shoe and started hitting me over the head. A crowd of elderly people gathered. Many cheered as the hard sole cracked down on my skull.

"We saw him try to grab your purse," a man cried. "Serves the kid right. Go ahead, keep hitting him, ma'am. We'll hold him down."

"Ouch, that really hurt." What was happening? The lady must be going totally berserk. It's amazing how she can control a crowd's emotions. How did I ever get myself caught up in this situation? Falling to the pavement, I tried to piece everything together—from the gay yeshiva *bocher* to the middle-aged nymphomaniac. I couldn't remember how I had provoked her. She pummelled me with the sole of her shoe until I was lying motionless in the gutter. Within a few seconds I passed out and only remembered waking up on a stretcher in the emergency room of the North Shore Medical Center next to two other men who were bleeding and in urgent need of medical care.

Meanwhile, Manfred Lipschitz reclined on a purple chaise lounge, basking under the sun at poolside. A straw at the side of his mouth fed him grapefruit juice and vodka. His wife, Lotte, sat on the edge of the pool kicking her legs in the water. She adjusted the straps of her one-piece bathing suit and looked around the perimeter of the pool, from the muscular young teenagers at the diving board to the senior citizens playing shuffle board by the lower end. Weak brown eyes closed behind Manfred's polarized sunglasses when he turned his face to the sun. A twelve band transistor radio tuned to Tel Aviv rested just above his navy blue swimming trunks somewhere to the south of his rotund belly. His Midrash students at the seminary said that he hadn't seen his dick in ten years. The reception was poor, so he fiddled with the AM band until he found his favorite news station. The closing stock report came on.

To his right, on a pair of chaise lounges, two women held a lively conversation. Their harsh New York voices made it hard for Manfred to hear. He'd come to Miami to get away from the assaulting sound of that voice although it was no different from his own, except for his subtle German accent. He tried to ignore them, but finally rolled over and whispered loudly, "Excuse me ladies, but could I ask you for just a few minutes of quiet."

"Con Ed . . . nineteen."

"Ladies, the stock report will be over in just a few . . . "

"Occidental Pet . . . thirty-one."

" . . . minutes." Mentally rubbing his hands with glee, he exploded, "Oh, boy, are we going to make money in the stock market this year. Someone up in the clouds must have liked my sermon on Yom Kippur."

He didn't hear the women's sharp intake of breath. They looked at him, thanked God they didn't know him, then resumed their conversation.

"We," he said out loud, meaning the family, "made at least four hundred dollars in the market today, minus commission. I'm sure it will buy a few extra days in Florida. I'm going to bring them back here next winter. I don't care how much it costs. *Dengst du nicht die Florida Sohne ist wunder bar? Es ist so gesund fur Jederman.*"

He peered quickly to his right, saw that the women weren't looking and allowed himself a quick smile. Lotte fluttered her calves in the water. Manfred's spine shivered with pleasure. He angled his face, shaped by having looked into the many narrow graves of his friends and relatives in Germany and Holland, and squinted away from any thought of it and the brightness of the sun. He groaned, pushed himself up on his elbows and called, "Lotte, come here. I have good news." His stubby fingers patted an invitation at the end of the recliner.

Lotte raised her bowed legs out of the pool and came to him, dripping water over the shiny blue tiles. She made herself comfortable on the foot of his chair, reached over and rubbed his hairy chest, located at the northern base of his belly.

"You'll never guess what happened." Manfred always twitched in pleasure when she played with the hairs on his breast. No other woman in the fifty-nine years of his life made him feel quite the way Lotte did.

"Don't tell me," she said, pinching an armpit, as if she were sixteen rather than sixty, "you made a killing in the stock market."

"What is this, E.S.P.? You must have overheard me thinking. Never mind." Manfred didn't like the way Lotte read his mind. He looked incredulously at her, patting her blue, tinted hair. "Lotte, I made four hundred dollars today, not quite a killing, but it certainly helps with the extras in our budget, like Miami. We're celebrating tonight at Wolfie's. By the way, where's Jeremy?"

"Shopping on Collins Avenue," she said lowering her hand to his groin teasingly. "When the children are away, parents are at play."

"That sissy; why doesn't he get some exercise? He looks terribly pale. I'm embarrassed to tell everyone that we took him along to Florida. He's nothing but a sluggard, a drone, a parasite." His son's penchant for staying indoors irritated him. "We'll be here for ten days and that boy still won't have a suntan. He'll look like an old widower. Aren't I getting a nice tan, Lotte? I can't wait to show the boys." Manfred turned his face up to her. Lotte pulled away from his breath, which reeked from an onion bagel.

Seeing her husband laugh at the expense of others always made Lotte sigh. She worked hard not to be disagreeable on their brief vacation, resigned to the role of attentive listener demanded of a rabbi's wife. She tried to protect Jeremy from his father's insensitivity. Jeremy was the only subject she couldn't back away from, however disagreeable it made her to her husband.

"Manfred," she said scoldingly, mentally shaking her finger, "that's not nice to say about your own son. Huh, an old widower. Next you'll be saying such things about me."

He patted her shoulder and yet the act had the quality of a farmer stroking his favorite animal. I should live so long, he wanted to tell her, but instead out of his mouth came, "Don't worry dear; you're all protected. I just took out more insurance. If anything happens to me, everyone will be in great shape financially." Suddenly Manfred's eyes begged to be cuddled.

"Manfred, Manfred, I wasn't talking about money. I only said you shouldn't call Jeremy names which are humiliating." Lotte looked out towards the bay and hoped that Manfred would change the subject. He rolled over and resumed his supine position, basking in the hot sun.

Five minutes later, he turned his bald head and its silver crescent of hair towards Lotte. "Why are you sticking up for your son, anyway? He's old enough to look after himself and develop healthier habits. When I was his age, there was nothing for me to eat. I was either in the concentration camp or in hiding. Look what he gets: a stereo, use of both cars, pocket money, free college education. Take him to Miami Beach and he doesn't even get in some sun . . . "

"Rabbi Lipschitz. Rabbi Lipschitz, you have a telephone call. Please come to the main office," the voice on the loudspeaker interrupted. Manfred sat up and wearily put on his slippers. He had seen the bellboy snicker at his torn slippers, but Manfred didn't give a damn. Saving money on clothes was one reason he had been able to work his way up from the rank of an impoverished refugee.

"I wonder who's calling now?" Manfred stuck his left arm through the sleeve of his terrycloth bathrobe.

Lotte quickened at the sight of the skin peeling on his nose, reached for the suntan lotion and remembered that she had left it in their room.

"Disturbing me on my vacation." The chaise lounge groaned as the weight of his butt released it. "Lotte, will you tie my belt?" She shifted the terrycloth belt and tied it high on his belly.

"Lotte, before I forget let me give you a few messages in the event that I'm called away. Mrs. Margolis phoned last night, you remember her, from the old congregation. Her sister passed away and she wants me to fly back to New York to conduct funeral services, but I said that I couldn't come and recommended Rabbi Lieberman to her." He farted.

Lotte pretended not to hear. A good rabbi's wife hears only what he wants her to hear. Lotte craned her neck to avoid the glare.

"If Rabbi Friedman calls when I'm gone," he said with difficult dignity, scratching his crotch and releasing his hand from the slack supporter, "tell him that he has the position and ask him to leave his number or call me person to person."

"Rabbi Lipschitz, please come to the office. You have a telephone call."

"All right, already," he cried out blindly at the public address system. "I'm coming." He turned his head towards his wife. "Lotte, I'm going now. I hope they haven't hung up."

Manfred stretched his legs, cracking the joints in his ankles and toes and dragged his slippers to the office. The bellboy pointed to the receiver lying off the hook on the table. He held the instrument inches away from his ear, in an attempt to avoid the foreign, *Goyische* odors on the mouthpiece and the germs from a potential ear infection on the opposite end.

"This is Dr. Lipschitz speaking. May I ask who's calling please?" He brought the earpiece closer so that it brushed against the edge of his earlobe and twitched away in disgust.

"This is Mrs. Huntington, from the North Shore Medical Center. Your son, Jeremy, is here. Now I don't want to alarm you, Doctor. Your son is fine. He only sustained minor cuts and bruises."

"What happened? Will you tell me what happened?" Manfred stamped his foot impatiently and pressed the telephone receiver closer to his ear to make sure that he wouldn't miss any information.

"Can you tell us, Doctor, if you have Blue Cross, Prudential or Aetna? Your son asked for a private room," the nurse said sourly. Manfred was startled to hear someone in the health profession address him as doctor. His doctorate was in Hebrew letters, not medicine, and the salaries for professionals in the two classes were not nearly equivalent. The title rabbi was far more useful, if less prestigious. For one thing, it allowed Manfred to park his car, with its clergy sticker, in a No Standing Zone and to obtain double discounts while shopping on the Lower East Side of Manhattan. If he really wanted to push his connections, he could get season box seats at Yankee Stadium. But then again, rabbis were often overcharged.

"I want to know what happened to my son. We'll talk about insurance later. Was he in an accident? Were there any serious injuries? Will you please tell me what happened?"

"Dr. Lipschitz, please don't make me repeat myself!"

"I'm not a medical doctor."

"I said your son has only sustained minor cuts and bruises. We'll give you all the details as soon as you arrive. Now I can't speak any longer. I must attend to my patients. Goodbye."

Manfred heard her hang up. He stared at the telephone disbelievingly for five long seconds and then placed it on the desk, fleeing from it as if it were an obscene thing. He walked away with an angry nervous limp.

Lotte looked up at Manfred while he came slowly back to their chairs. She sat up, sensing that this was more than a routine call and rubbed her hands up and down her thighs, eagerly awaiting the news. He loomed nervously over her and tightened his lips to hide his alarm.

"It's about Jeremy. Now don't get excited. They said he has some bruises, but it's nothing serious. Don't worry," he said nervously, grasping her shoulder. "They said he's all right."

Lotte jumped from her chair. "Who said he has bruises? Who called? Manfred, tell me, what did they say? What happened to Jeremy?" she shrieked. Her desperate call echoed against the motel walls and rebounded towards the pool. Lotte moved her head about frantically, trying to meet her husband's eyes.

"Will you just calm down," he commanded in a patriarchal tone. "The stupid nurse hung up on me. Oh, these *goyim*; they have no compassion. I believe, deep down, that they're all anti-Semites." Manfred was suddenly frightened by Lotte's fierce expression. "She just said that he's at the North Shore Medical Center and asked me if I have insurance. Jeremy's in a private room."

"Oh my God, it must be serious. Manfred, you should have said something." She stood up and glared at him defiantly. "Why couldn't you have cut in and demanded information? What kind of a man are you? Don't you know how to handle an emergency?" Lotte sighed at her husband's incompetence in dealing with family crises and tried a softer tone. "Now they said that he isn't hurt badly. Did he break any bones? What happened to him, anyway? Was he in a car accident?"

Manfred jumped before Lotte could finish her string of questions. "Lotte, I can't even get in a word edgewise with you. Are you calm now? Look, I'm just as worried about Jeremy as you are. Let's get down there already. I'll get the car ready. You change quickly into a jump suit and I'll put on a clean shirt. You brought back the last load from the cleaners, didn't you? Let's go," he said, grabbing her hand. They tried to jog on the way to the room, but ran out of breath before they reached the stairs.

At the hospital, I was sipping on a mocha ice cream soda, which one of the nurses bought for me after I had given her a lesson in clinical urology. All of a sudden, Mom and Dad walked into my room. Two hours had passed since I was admitted to the emergency room and treated for minor lacerations. Although I was a little groggy and sore, I felt quite at home in the familiar surroundings. A policeman had dropped by to tell me that I couldn't be released on my own recognizance until my parents came by. So here we were, facing each other and not knowing what to say.

Dad maintained his typical look of despair, which he had exercised countless times at the pulpit, leading Kol Nidre services on Yom Kippur. Mom eyed me cautiously from the far end of the room. She looked angry and ready to give me a paddling. The policeman approached my father as I placed the ice cream soda on the night table.

"Hello, Dr. Lipschitz, I'm Sergeant Baker. It's my duty to inform you that a woman by the name of Rose Goodman has filed a complaint against your son. She claims that he assaulted her at the corner of Seventy-second Street and Collins Avenue at one-thirty P.M. You may be hearing from her attorney in the next couple of days. What's the matter, didn't you ever teach your kid how to box? Looks like he was beaten up by a fifty year old dame." The policeman handed Dad the card of Mrs. Goldman's attorney and patted him on the shoulder sympathetically. "You're from the Northeast; aren't you?"

"That's correct officer and I'm a clergyman." Dad spoke humbly, taking a seat on the visitor's chair. "We're here on vacation for only ten days and I can see that Jeremy has spoiled it already. Can you believe that we only arrived here this morning and we already have a scene? Oh boy, officer is he going to get it on his behind. I'm going to tan his hide. Officer, do you know what it's like to have children?"

"No, I'm single," he said disarmingly and shrugged his shoulders. "Dr. Lipschitz, considering that your son is underage, we may be able to release him this afternoon, but I want you to understand the seriousness of this affair. I've already had a long talk with Jeremy. There's no excuse for his behavior. Mrs. Goodman claims that he assaulted her."

My father was so stunned when he heard the word "assault" again that he was ready to lose control. "Officer?" he asked meekly, shuffling his feet back and forth, "Can I speak with you outside in the hall?" Before they walked out, he said to my mother, "Lotte, stay here with Jeremy. If he's fresh, then smack him one across the face."

I picked up my soda and sucked on the straw with a sheepish grin while the men walked out of the room. I knew by now that neither Mom nor Dad would ever hit me. Dad left the door ajar and I was able to listen in.

"Officer, I really don't put up with any of this nonsense at home; as you can see, this reflects on the whole family and my congregation. Needless to say, my wife and I are very embarrassed. Tell me everything that happened from beginning to end. My wife can't bear to hear the truth, but I can."

"Well, I wasn't at the scene, so I can only tell you what's in the report. It says that Jeremy Lipschitz, age seventeen, willfully and maliciously assaulted Rose Goodman, a 52 year old female caucasian. The victim has filed several charges against your son, one of which is atrocious assault. If you'll pardon my French, Rabbi, your son is accused of pinching her ass and trying to pull off her panties before three eye witnesses in the middle of Collins Avenue. Mrs. Goodman retaliated by hitting him over the head with her shoe until he fell. That's when I was called to the scene and we arranged to have your son taken to the hospital for cuts and bruises."

When I heard that I was accused of taking off her panties, I jumped out of bed and ran out to the hall.

"It's a lie! I didn't try to undress her. Can't you see I'm being framed? Why don't you listen to my side of the story? She tried to undress me! God, isn't this ridiculous? Don't let them take me away Dad! I promise that from now on I'll only date girls my own age—nice, young, Orthodox Jewish girls. This charge against me is so embarrassing and it's not even true! They *would* have to pick on me. This is going to ruin my record. Don't you want me to go to medical school?"

"That's enough, young man," the policeman interrupted. "Now go back inside and shut the door behind you. Your father and I are having a private talk."

I obeyed his instructions, but stood behind the door, smiling impishly.

"Officer, please tell me, what is the actual extent of the charges against my son? Is he facing a misdemeanor? A felony? I'm a refugee and don't know much about the law." I could imagine my dad shuffling his feet nervously, figuring that his son would be castrated in any other time period of history.

"No, Dr. Lipschitz. You didn't listen to what I said earlier. Fortunately for your son and . . . " He paused to clear his throat. "Lucky for you, Mrs. Goodman decided afterwards to drop the assault charge. Off the record, Rabbi, we've had trouble with this Goodman lady before. She lures young men into her clutches and seduces them. Adolescents are especially vulnerable. She seems able to spot her victims from a distance and approaches men in juice bars. Now back to your son. Under the very worst circumstances he will be charged with a "disorderly person," which will be expunged from his record after five years, provided that he's not convicted of another offense within that time. May I remind you that reciprocity laws apply between your home state and Florida. As far as the Dade County Police are concerned, you'll be able to avoid a day in court, if you pay the fifty dollar fine and take him into your custody. I would also suggest that you write a personal apology to Mrs. Goodman, if only to appease her. I wouldn't worry about it Rabbi," he added, "many people say that they're going to consult their attorney and never follow through. Why don't you have a talk with your son in the meantime, while I draw up the forms for his release."

Dad smiled with a sigh of appreciation which carried the same intensity that he felt towards the Christian families who had saved his life in Holland during the war. "Thank you officer," he said obsequiously, shaking his hand firmly. Before he opened the door, I hopped into bed and resumed my initial pose under the covers. Mom sat beside me, but had refused to speak to me since she heard that I had tried to disrobe an older woman.

"Jeremy," my father cried, shaking his angry finger in front of my face. "You don't know how lucky you are. The policeman is so kind. He's letting you off the hook. And let me tell you, he's a very decent man. He's preparing the necessary papers and after I pay the fifty dollars we can go back to the hotel. It could be two hundred dollars and it wouldn't make any difference. Money is not the point. Jeremy, you've ruined my vacation. And I can tell you buster, you're going to pay that fine out of your own pocket money. Seventeen years old," he laughed under his breath, "you son of a gun. Let me give you one on your behind. You certainly know how to behave like a person underage."

He couldn't help but admire my ploy of posing as a minor so the police could only book me for a juvenile offense. It reminded him of his friends' attempts to forge papers to cross the border during the war.

"Starting Monday I'm cutting your allowance."

"What? My allowance? Dad, I won't be able to go out with any nice Jewish American Princesses my own age if you do that!"

"So you were going after an older woman again," he shouted furiously. "Didn't you learn at the yeshiva how to respect your elders? Why I'll teach you." He raised his hand again and for the first time in many years looked as if he were seriously considering hitting me. "Come on, roll over, bite your teeth and accept your punishment. One, two, three and it's all over. Come on Jeremy; be a man."

"Dad," I laughed. "Are you serious? You're not going to hit me now, here. First of all, you haven't spanked me since I was ten years old and secondly, you're in a hospital. They'll send out a team of orderlies to restrain you. Remember, I'm still a patient here, which means I'm fully protected."

Dad rested his arm on his lap and sighed wearily. Little did he know that in most of my masturbation fantasies, I pretended to be my father, screwing all the ladies of his congregation. In fact, some of Dad's colleagues at the seminary used to say that Lipschitz was great with women over sixty-five. He learned how to *shuckle* while praying, bowing up and down while he was getting laid by every executive member of the Sisterhood, and telling each consenting adult woman, married or not, "It's all right, what we're doing. It's all right."

The policeman walked in with the nurse and placed the documents on the night table, next to the hospital release forms, for my parents to sign. I picked up my street clothes and changed in the bathroom. My parents led me out the main entrance.

Walking to the car we passed a surgical supply store with a big sign in the window which read, Prosthetic Devices at Cut-Rate Prices. Some smart little Yiddle knows a good business in Miami Beach, I thought, admiring the naked mannequins and the girdles, trusses and back supports. A stunning older woman with a hairy, filiform wart projecting under her lip smiled at me and urged me to come inside the store. My father pulled me by the arm to cross the street, but I lingered in front of the door, planning my next coup.

Fresh Produce

On a hot, humid afternoon in the middle of May, I found myself sitting alone in my attic room. I was bored and lonely, without a single friend to console me. The Spring semester had ended abruptly. There would be no more opportunities to see Dr. Foster before classes started in September. While most students rejoiced when their exams were over and rushed home to begin their summer jobs, I remained in Middletown in the hope of bumping into Dr. Foster.

Static hiss crackled through the speaker of my old Zenith radio as I tuned in a jazz station. The whine of a tenor saxophone made me sleepy, yet another part of me was alert and eager to see Dr. Foster. Three months had passed since I had last visited her at Hastings, when she had removed the stitches from my self-inflicted wound. Now that the scar tissue had healed completely, I had no reason to come to the clinic unless I was afflicted with a new condition.

Entrenched in a terminal depression, I had barely enough energy to get out of my pajamas. I was cursed with a stunted libido. My appetite was so poor that all my vital organs were living off the protein matrix of lean muscle tissue. The circumference of one thigh was grossly smaller than the other. If only Silvana would hold my hand instead of massaging her husband's legs, I would eat like a normal human being again.

Lying awake on my back with legs spread apart, I listened to improvisations of an avant garde jazz pianist. His fingers raced up and down the keyboard, jarring me with dissonant chords interspersed with arpeggios. What wonderful, controlled chaos, I thought. Give me an avenue of self-expression to extricate me from this horrendous depression.

I decided then that it was time to realize my obsessive fantasy; it was Silvana's house or bust. I dressed in fresh clothes and flew down the steps to the garage. A yellow butterfly with black spots fluttered across the driveway to the neighbor's lawn. I tried to block the thought that came—a butterfly was difficult to catch—because I knew that the odds were against me in reaching for Silvana's silken thighs.

My bicycle was parked in the garage. I wiped the grease off the undersized three-speed English racer with a wet rag and oiled the bearings in both wheels. Although the fork was bent from a previous accident and I could never fully extend my legs while pedalling, I had grown attached to my bike for sentimental reasons.

A white-bellied spider scurried off the web that stretched across the rear wheel spokes. My fingers became ensnared in the gossamer strands as I checked the air pressure in the tires. The perfect hexagonal web collapsed. Dried-out insects fell to the floor.

I stuffed my lock and chain in the saddle bag, ready to take off. Pushing all 118 pounds against the pedals, I whizzed out the driveway, leaving a cloud of dirt behind me.

When I approached the traffic light by the Arlington Heights bridge, the traffic was snarled. In my mind's eye, Silvana was sitting comfortably on her living room sofa. She was browsing through an issue of *Scientific American* and snacking on Japanese rice crackers. This was the life. Her husband could well afford to take her on island-hopping vacations in the Caribbean or a Scandinavian cruise along the fjords whenever they could coordinate a drop in their patient load. How could I ever compete with Alex, her great provider? Silvana's cheeks disappeared like a pricked bubble as the traffic light turned green.

I pedalled beside a man revving the engine of his blue Corvette Sting Ray convertible behind a long line of traffic. He sneered at me as I pulled ahead of him in the right lane and tried to sideswipe me. Forced to swerve away from him, I lost my balance and fell to the pavement. Although I had a few scrapes, there were no major abrasions worthy of medical attention. I couldn't knock on Silvana's door and beg her to dress my wounds. Even a doctor needs an uninterrupted vacation.

In the heat of the afternoon, I found myself sitting on the asphalt between two parked cars, watching the chrome bumpers and radials rumble by beside me. Pedestrians walked by, pretending that nothing had happened. No one even stopped to ask me if I was hurt.

I remembered my mission, a reconnaissance ride around the Fosters' home, and forced myself back on the bicycle seat. The traffic was moving at a snail's pace. I decided to coast along the shoulder and made greater headway than the cars on the road. When I caught up to the Corvette, I stuck out my tongue and sneered at the driver. He was wearing one turquoise earring which matched the green tattoo on his forearm. His brown, greasy hair was slicked back, duck's ass style.

"What's the matter with you; are you sick or something?" I shouted defiantly, spitting a drop of saliva on the pavement to appear tough.

He yanked up on the emergency brake, got out and ran towards me, waving a steel chain over his head. I pressed all my weight against the pedals and cycled between two lanes of cars until I was safely in the distance.

"You goddamn runt," he snarled. "Next time I see you, I'll kill you."

"Get back in your car," I taunted, "you're holding up traffic."

The ball bearings whirled as I pedalled furiously across the suspension bridge. In the distance up the river, I noticed the landmarks of Fairbanks College with the turret of Hastings Infirmary peeking through the trees. Suddenly my anaclitic depression lifted. The vibrations of the bridge's steel grating were absorbed through the bicycle seat and felt almost as benumbing as Silvana's coccygeal massage.

At the end of the bridge the traffic light turned red, before I had the chance to race through. I felt Silvana's force from two miles away, as if there was electromagnetic energy emanating from here and I were a stray iron filing. I was sucked into the vicinity of breast-feeding aggregates congregating at her hive. Wouldn't she expel her husband, that useless drone, and take me into her inner chambers?

I tried to keep abreast of the traffic, but a sharp cramp in my right thigh forced me to switch to first gear and cycle along at a crawl. The concentration of carbon monoxide fumes made me dizzy.

Sweat poured down my face and dripped on my chest. The poor leverage I got on the pedals of my undersized English racer made my efforts seem wasteful. Aware of the futility of my scheme, I was afraid that I appeared as ridiculous as an obese housewife pedalling an exercise bicycle in an air-conditioned basement.

When I saw the street sign, I knew I was halfway home. Welcome to Arlington Heights: Est. 1783, Pop. 17460, Kiwanis Club, Lions Club, Rotary Club, Book and Needle Club. The regional YMCA was cordoned off by a brick wall. The landmarks of her town made me feel secure: the post office, the wine and fruit shop and Sal's Pizzeria. A revolving clock on a bank roof flashed its digital signals: 5:30, 76°.

Only the *Goyim* have dinner at 5:30, I thought, but I'm sure the Fosters are an exception. Doctors always come home late. The sky was free of clouds, but the sun was dipping. I had less than two hours of daylight left to spy on her house.

There was yet another hill ahead. Why must she reinforce her superiority over me, I wondered, wiping a shirt sleeve across my brow. Look down before you, Dr. Foster, and see all of the impoverished people living in the flats of Middletown on the other side of the river. But you are immune to their pain. Medicine has hardened you. You can snuggle up in your cozy house, high on the hill, after tending to the downtrodden every day. Titillate your noble conscience while living in comfort. Physicians are always so well-fed.

The Valhalla Drive street sign whizzed by me in a blur as I passed the bank tower. The Fosters lived only two blocks west on Cherry Lane and I was anxious to get there. Sweat trickled down my temples and carried a crust of condensed exhaust into my squinting eyes.

This was not my first trip to Arlington Heights. I had visited her estate from the outside several times before. On one occasion I spied on her house through a pair of close-range binoculars. That day Silvana and her husband were sitting comfortably on the patio. She was thumbing through an issue of *Medical Economics*, holding a tall, frothy glass of iced tea with a dash of mint from her garden. Since Alex was cuddling beside her I was forced to keep my distance. I wasted the rest of the afternoon sitting on a mound across the street and went home feeling defeated. This time, however, I was determined to get farther. If I could only be her backdoor man.

My stomach felt tight and hollow as Cherry Lane appeared in the distance. Balancing my bike on its kickstand, I sat down on the curb and rested until I caught my breath. I couldn't stay for long without attracting the attention of her vigilant neighbors. Perhaps someone had already warned the police of a skinny prowler seen in the neighborhood.

I needed to see Silvana ever so badly, to be granted but one peek at her flaccid, swinging underarms. Her body could be covered with long sleeves and dark stockings like the wives of pious Jews. I didn't care. I only wanted to hug her. Besides, I already had an accurate conception of her naked body after mapping out her dimensions with semi-logarithmic coordinate points on a CAD program at my college computer center.

The six o'clock siren bombarded my defenseless acoustic nerve. I plugged up my ears with my fingers to muffle out the most offensive decibels.

How awful, I thought. Who could ever live here? This is supposed to be a quiet neighborhood, replete with every upper middle-class comfort. I'll bet that half the residents within a two block radius suffer from tinnitus or insomnia due to that siren. Dr. Foster, whatever made you chose to live in this lily white bedroom community. It's much more cozy in my attic. I can order a queen-size bed where the two of us can snuggle up for the night.

Although the siren finally died out, lingering oscillations punished my eardrums and merged into a pseudoauditory hallucination. I heard voices, a chorus of middle-aged women, laughing at my timidity. Why didn't I have the balls to ask one of them out on a date? They were ready to tickle me until I died of hysteria, a greater torture than having goats lick the soles of my feet.

I pedalled slowly before reaching the fork in the road. The scent of Silvana's pheromones made me veer sharply towards her house. There were no cherry trees on Cherry Lane, not even wild cherry trees, only willows, white birches, bark-shedding sycamores and clumps of sod matted on half-acre plots. I wondered how anyone could name the street Cherry Lane. Either the developer lied to make the residences sound more attractive or he chopped down the cherry trees, or both. A blurred montage of colonial houses, green hedges and luminescent astroturf whizzed by me as I coasted down the wide, branched street. The willows whispered a restless song.

Her palatial home imbued me with feelings of awe and reverence. What a cozy nest it was. I parked my bike on a grassy knoll of undeveloped land about fifty yards from their property. Growing delirious, I rested my head on the sod, under the spell of her poppies, as if deluded by Dilaudid.

In my daydream, Cherry Lane was a fixture in Candy Land. Reversion to childhood was only possible for me in these auspicious surroundings. Since I was alone it would be safe to play my favorite infantile game, Spit and Fits, a cathartic exercise designed to expel excess self-destructive energy. Children tire quickly of Shoots and Ladders and prefer to giggle hysterically with contorted facial grimaces. I pulled down my eyelids with two fingers, widening my mouth with my thumbs, twitching my cheeks to simulate Belle's Palsy as if I were auditioning for the "Laughing Man" at the freak show. Drool dripped out the sides of my mouth. My chin was soaked with a glairy mucus. I felt like such a prize sight, groveling along the curb in this nouveau riche development.

There's a fine legal distinction between spitting and drooling. Spitting is a willful and illegal ejaculation. Drooling, by its involuntary nature, is not a conscious violation of law, and therefore cannot be punished as such. The days when there were spittoons on streetcorners are long gone. Well, enough drool for now.

I proceeded to immerse myself in a Candy Land fantasy, hopping along the magic colored squares: red, green, blue, yellow: one step, three steps or whatever push your socioeconomic group gave you to pursue a m ore comfortable standard of living. I thought they were liable to arrest me for disobeying Milton Bradley's age requirements. Candy Land was my first exposure to the steady course of advancement which molds a boy into a professional man. They teach you that shit when you're three, at the malleable age. Soon I lapsed into another fantasy which I remembered from childhood: red light, green light. May I? Yes, you may. Repressive commands from an authority figure may lead to a healthy rebellion. Ask your superior before you take any umbrella steps to the boys' room.

Dr. Foster, won't you take me into your gingerbread house? You're much too kind to bake me in an oven. You're a good witch. I will always bind my eyes to the movement of your golden scepter.

I found myself standing in front of her turreted castle. My neck felt free from not having to support the weight of heavy binoculars I had taken with me on previous peeping occasions. This visit would be different from other reconnaissance missions; it would give me more than a voyeuristic thrill.

Pink and white begonias rested on the window ledge outside the master bedroom on the third floor. The front yard was free of trees. Lush zoizia grass sloped down the hill around the stump where a wild crab apple tree once stood. The house was surrounded by trimmed hedges, standing six feet high. The dense bushes blocked the view of the wide living room window. An electric trip wire on the door could fry any resentful patient who would deign to intrude. I knew from watching soap operas that doctors cherish their privacy. Two rows of tulips flanked the cobblestone path leading to the front steps. The Fosters' family insignia, the guilded lion, was engraved above the electric buzzer.

Stationing myself between a gap in the hedges, I peered up the driveway until I caught sight of the chrome bumper of her yellow Buick Electra. It was the natural choice for her: safe, reliable, with a comfortable wheel base, but not overly ostentatious. I was enchanted with the power of her valuable M.D. license plates which gave her the privilege of parking anywhere she pleased. It was almost as good as my father's clergy sign which freed him from the Scofflaw's Club. The Fosters' patio could only be seen at an angle, across the neighbor's lawn. Today I had not come to peep, but to bump into her. I was ready to stalk her and follow her to the four corners of the earth.

I snuck up close to the house with mincing steps and squatted behind the hedges. The living room light was on behind translucent curtains. Her silhouette was unmistakenly familiar. Silvana was sitting sedately on her sofa beside a reading lamp. The garage doors were open. Alex Foster's Mercedes 300 SD was not in the driveway. I knew that she was at home alone, because the maid never stayed late on Friday afternoons.

Before I could get any closer, the living room lights went off. The fear that she would be out of reach surged through my fingertips. The rhythmic hiss of cicadas drowned out all other sounds. I hopped on my bicycle, pedalled down the street for a short distance and waited for her to come out of her nest.

Suddenly the rear screen door opened and slammed shut. I heard Silvana's footsteps moving briskly towards the car and I quickly moved my bicycle into position. A few stray pebbles were kicked back into the rock garden. She opened the car door and turned the ignition. Two brake lights lit the driveway.

I noticed she had a new hairdo as I watched her from the corners of my eyes, my head turned so that she wouldn't recognize me. She looked behind her through the rear-view mirror, saw that the boy on the bicycle was playing at a safe distance and slowly backed out the driveway. I followed closely behind her. She coasted to the end of the block at a speed of fifteen miles an hour. My path was in line with the blind spot in her mirror.

At the first traffic light she turned into the parking lot of the neighborhood supermarket.

Of course, I thought, she wants to pick up a few groceries. How quaint! It's my luck that she chose to shop in a store that has fourteen aisles and is fully air-conditioned. I've got lots of room to spy.

How am I going to make our encounter appear to be a coincidence?

I can spy on her from the end of the aisles and maybe sneak a few unwanted items into her shopping cart when she leaves it unguarded.

No, that would be terribly immature. Grow up already, Lipschitz.

What do you think she likes to eat?

Don't buy a bland pork roll, honey. Get some top sirloin, London Broil. We can have a juicy barbecue on your patio. I know how to make a fire.

I followed closely while she walked in the side entrance, but waited outside for a moment before entering the supermarket. Without allowing myself to lose sight of her, I chained my bicycle to a lamp post. She was wearing a yellow sleeveless dress. Her hips swayed through the electric doors. She grabbed a cart and strolled down the first aisle with the graceful ease of a mother walking her newborn in a perambulator.

Wheeling her carriage to the side of the aisle, she paused to review her list of groceries. I kept my distance, hiding my angular body behind a pair of buxom women. All of a sudden, she pivoted her shopping cart 180 degrees and walked briskly in my direction. I darted around the corner and nearly knocked over a soup mix display.

A butcher, standing behind the refrigerated meat rack, cleared his throat to attract my attention and glared at me with hostile eyes. His white coat was stained with fresh splotches of dried blood. The edge of a stainless steel meat cleaver was poised in line with my jugular vein. He looked ready to circumcise my head, wrap the parts in cellophane and mark it a dollar sixty a pound, *glatt kosher*.

"Can I help you, young man?" His coarse German accent startled me and scared me shitless. My thoughts were preoccupied with Silvana who had just turned down the aisle.

What's the best way to get rid of him, I wondered. I'll bet he takes me for a shoplifter, he probably thinks I'm street-wise. I'd better answer him politely and the put myself down. By debasing myself like a submissive Jew, I'll make him feel virile. Perhaps then he'll feel satisfied with himself and leave me alone.

"No thank you sir," I answered timidly, barely looking up to face him, "I'm just beginning my shopping errands. My mother asked me to pick up a few things. You were probably wondering about my strange posture. Well recently, I've had this stiff neck . . . "

"All right. I don't want to hear it. Go to your shopping," he snarled and walked into the freezer room. No one but Dr. Foster herself had the patience to listen to my *tzores*.

I rushed down the aisle by the dairy case to catch sight of Silvana. Her image was clouded by steam rising from the ice cream freezer, but I had a clear view of the groceries in her cart. A bag of gourmet potato chips was crushed beneath a loaf of whole wheat bread and a jar of malt-flavored Ovaltine. She was loyal to the Sandoz brand, the same company that made Mellaril. Hiding behind a stack of roasted nuts, only fourteen feet behind her, I watched her remove a can of imported butter cookies. Her taste buds were aroused. This compulsive shopper moved in my direction. Oh my God, she's heading for the Pecan Sandies. They're on special; how declassé. Why all of this sugar? Could she be planning a party for the weekend, restricted to physicians and their wives, or does she simply like to nosh?

My shoulder bumped against a protruding carton of lady finger cookies. The tall stack wobbled and crashed to the floor. All eyes turned towards me as I made a cowardly exit around the corner. Curiosity compelled me to return to the scene of the crime. To my amazement, Dr. Foster was helping a grocery clerk pick up the scattered boxes.

Why does she have to be such a den mother, I wondered? What a goody two-shoes. It's enough that she devotes so much of her free time in the clinic to help the medically indigent. How could she deign to help a stockboy clean up the aisle?

Later on, I found her strolling down the fresh produce aisle, her hips leaning hungrily into the metal bars of the shopping cart. Of course, I considered, as a physician, she feeds her family good, wholesome foods, especially fresh fruits and vegetables. She knows how to pick out the unblemished fruit from the rack and keep her family's gastrointestinal tracts free of unfriendly cocci.

In my mind's eye, I was perched in the upper cage of the shopping cart with baby shoes strapped to my feet. Silvana was my proud mother, walking her baby down the aisles. As soon as we returned home she opened her dress and nursed me. Suckie de mamma—warm, milky fluid.

Oh Dr. Foster, don't you understand? My feelings towards you transcend positive transference. Is it wrong for a patient to love his physician? I'm crazy about you. I exist for you. I love you so much. I would give you my left kidney, if you were in need and we were histocompatible.

But I don't need a kidney.

Well then, how about a gall bladder?

Eventually, I must learn to wean myself from your lactiferous ducts.

Pausing to inspect a head of cauliflower, she tore off a plastic bag from the overhead roller. Then she placed the best of the bunch, ever so gently in the bag so that the tender white crowns were protected from bruising. She must have handled her husband's balls the same way. A grocery clerk tied the bag with a metal clip, weighed it and jotted down the price with a thick marking pen. Silvana smiled, but he was oblivious to her warmth and simply dropped the bag in her carriage.

I watched her attentively from fifteen feet back, behind an array of blemished fruit reduced for quick sale. Don't I look ridiculous standing here without a shopping cart, I wondered. The whole scheme of bumping into her in a public place is leading me nowhere. All I need now is for someone from security to come over and ask me what I'm doing.

A steel hand grabbed my shoulder from behind, pushing me forward before I could brace myself. When I turned around, I saw a security guard in a grey uniform. He stared disapprovingly at my seven-day stubble and then met my eyes with a look of contempt. I returned a look of disapproval at his banlon leisure suit.

"What do you want from me?"

"The manager wants to see you in his office." He held his grip on my shoulder. Had I moved in any direction I could have broken my collar bone. I tried to curve my back and slip away from him, but he held on tenaciously. A crowd of rubber-necking women looked on. Some pushed their shopping carts aside to watch the commotion. I looked for a get-away lane through the electric doors, hoping to avoid a confrontation, but his hostile fingers poked my shoulder blades at painful pressure points and kept me immobilized. Then he gripped my forearm, digging his stubby nails into my skin.

Before I knew what was happening, I found myself standing at the entrance of the manager's office. The tiny cubicle was packed with store receipts, cancelled checks and returned goods from dissatisfied customers. A closed-circuit television screen was tucked between the file cabinets. The manager sat on a stool, puffing calmly on a long cigar and staring at me with cold-blue eyes. The nauseating smell of stale cigar smoke filled the room. Every time I tried to stand up straight, the guard tightened his grip. The manager blew a silver funnel of smoke hitting me between the eyes.

"Get your hands off me," I shouted defiantly, loud enough for everyone in the supermarket to hear. The clerks standing by the cash registers waited eagerly for a scene, to escape their boredom. The guard released his hand. "If you touch me again, why, I swear, I'll sue you," I screamed. Mature women made up a majority of the crowd and I knew I had some allies among them. "Get your hands off me," I repeated, "or you'll go to jail."

Dr. Foster pricked up her ears when she heard the fearful cry. It was the same cry she had heard from a patient in extreme agony at Hastings.

The manager's cigar dropped from his mouth. He was stunned by my outburst and afraid of a major scene. This would be bad for business.

"Let him go, Lou," he commanded. The guard loosened his grip, but held on to my shoulder for a few extra seconds to make sure I wouldn't run away.

"Off! Get it, Lou?" I shrieked.

"Look sonny. I don't know what you planned on doing here, shoplifting or disturbing our customers." The manager spoke sullenly. He puffed vigorously on his cigar, but it had already gone out. Stepping to the side, I turned my back to him.

"I'm talking to you, kid," he snarled, shaking his angry finger under my nose.

"Don't point," I chided. "I don't know what's troubling you. I just came here to buy some groceries. I'm not concealing any of your merchandise, so I'm obviously not a shoplifter. You've got the wrong guy."

"What were you doing knocking down the cookies?" he barked, pointing his fat, hairy finger under my nose, threatening to poke out my eyes if I showed the slightest sign of resistance.

"I knocked them over by accident. The stacks protrude into the aisle, hindering the flow of customer traffic. It's a very dangerous layout. You're very lucky I wasn't injured or there would be double damages." Gazing through the crowd of eager-eyed shoppers, I caught Silvana's stare and felt terribly embarrassed. She stared at me inquisitively and edged closer. I shrugged my shoulders helplessly.

"Listen, wise guy," the manager groaned, "whether you knocked down the boxes intentionally or by accident is a whole different story. We've been watching you on the videocamera for the past ten minutes now and we know that you're up to some mischief. One of the butchers saw you disturbing the customers."

Before I could make a peep, Dr. Foster rushed over to the front office. All eyes turned to the tall, attractive woman as she pushed her way through the crowd and faced the manager. The guard shuffled his feet nervously. He was flustered by the sight of a woman an inch taller than he was. The manager rose from his stool.

"What seems to be the problem," she asked respectfully, and took a step inside his office.

"Do you know this fellow? Are you his mother, or something?" he asked sheepishly. A smirk tightened his lips when she glared at him coldly.

"No, I'm not his mother," she hissed. "What's the problem?"

I couldn't suppress a smile, thrilled that she would risk her reputation in the community to rescue me. Her protective presence made me delirious with joy.

"Excuse me madam," the manager answered sarcastically, "you must understand that it's our policy to prevent shoplifting before it occurs. This young man's behavior was really questionable."

"Who are you to judge whether his behavior is questionable? Are you a psychotherapist?" she flared back at him with a firm voice, "I happen to find *your* behavior questionable myself."

The crowd of shoppers pressed closer. A few people cheered. Looking down at the floor, I let my attending physician take charge of the situation.

"Look lady, I've got a business to run. All I'm asking is whether you know the guy?"

"Yes," she said flatly, "he just so happens to be my patient." The crowd murmured uneasily. Several women abandoned their carts in front of the registers and walked out the door.

Before I knew what was happening, Dr. Foster grabbed me under my arm and escorted me out the door, leaving the onlookers in a daze. I followed her to the parking lot without looking back. She led me to her car.

"I'm so glad to see you, Dr. Foster. Thanks for saving me from a most ridiculous and embarrassing situation. You came just in the nick of time."

"Oh, there's no need to thank me." She laughed, covering her mouth with her hand. "Those men were a bunch of buffoons. I hope you're not hurt, Jeremy. I saw the way he was pressing his thumb into your shoulder. Would you like me to examine it?"

"No thanks, Dr. Foster. I don't think that will be necessary," I said, with a hint of conspiratorial glee, eager to end our relationship as patient and physician. "The guy was trying to pinch a nerve at the pressure point. But he doesn't even know basic neuroanatomy and was totally off-target. I'm sure his thumb hurts plenty from poking my bony shoulder. Boy, I'd like to belt that guy in the mouth."

"Now, now, Jeremy," she said, scoldingly, tugging gently on my wrist. "Be a little smarter than they are. With all of their sophisticated surveillance equipment, they can't tell the difference between a shoplifter and an innocent bystander. And he had the nerve to think your behavior was questionable. That man barely has the intelligence of a sixth grader and he puts on this 'excuse me madam, look lady' routine." She mocked his mannerisms and facial expressions with astonishing theatrical skill.

The spoon-shaped depressions in her temples flushed bright pink. I was thrilled that I had uncovered another side to her personality. Today she looked totally different, like her leisured self, without a hangup in the world to slow her down. She was sharp, quick and creative. Medicine was simply her profession and forced her to wear a different uniform.

"Dr. Foster, you sure are the hippest doctor I've ever known."

"That's the nicest compliment anyone has paid me in a long time." She couldn't repress an infectious smile spreading across her lips and patted her bosom reverently.

"But really, Dr. Foster, what you did for me was fantastic. Many people just talk, but you actually stood up to those creeps and put them in their places. And you took the risk of defending me when you weren't sure of what I was doing all along . . . "

"What were you doing all along?" she asked dryly, with a toying smile. As a pre-med student I was supposed to be more mature. She eyed me suspiciously.

My stomach grumbled. I tried to think of a lame excuse, but couldn't and so said, "I was hoping I would have a chance to bump into you."

She winced for a second, but smiled to herself knowingly. Her smile widened, revealing her gums. Now maybe she understood why I had made such frequent trips to the clinic to see her.

Jeremy's finally being honest with me, I imagined she was thinking. He's finally telling me the truth. I knew that he would open up to me eventually. Perhaps my old-fashioned medicine did the trick. He wanted to bump into me, how cute. I'll reward him with the warmth of my body.

"Jeremy," she whispered in an almost dreamy voice, "instead of trying to get into a situation where you might bump into me accidentally, why don't you come over to my house, where we can sit and *schmooze* and have some hot chocolate."

I couldn't believe what she had just said, either its content or ethnic nuance. She brushed her hand against my kidney to make sure I wouldn't refuse her invitation. The words "hot chocolate" rang in my ears, reminding me of my infantile cry, "Cocoa Mamma." I was too paralyzed with joy to speak. An adrenaline rush reminded me to break the uneasy silence lest she be tempted to withdraw her invitation.

"Certainly, I'd love to come over and talk with you, but where did you learn the word *schmooze*?"

"My husband's partner is Jewish. Our families spend vacations together. But that's neither here nor there. Jeremy, you look like you could put on a few pounds," she said teasingly, pinching my forearm. "Tell me, have you eaten supper already?" She tickled my rib cage and rubbed away a darting quiver with her warm palm.

Was this the same Dr. Foster I had known at Hastings, I wondered? I didn't want her to feel compelled to invite me to dinner, but heard my stomach grumble.

"No, I haven't eaten yet."

"Then you'll join me for dinner, I insist. My husband went to a medical convention this weekend and left me all alone. I would appreciate it if a young man would keep me company this evening."

I was at a loss for words. Boy is she a smart doctor, I thought. She gets right to the point. *Toches einem tische.* What do I do? Let's act naturally and see what happens. It's no longer necessary to gain her attention by playing psychopathological games like "cat and mouse," "wooden leg," or "suicidal pre-med."

"Dr. Foster, I'd be honored to keep you company this evening, but I don't want to put you to too much trouble. Can I help you prepare the meal?"

"No, I think I can manage by myself. Would you mind, though, if we stopped off at another supermarket? There are a few groceries I have to pick up." Her informal way of speaking put me at ease. She wasn't merely a physician who related to her patients as anatomical entities. Silvana was gay and easy going; she was a nice, likable person.

I wanted to tell her how much I had missed her, but was afraid she would consider sentimentality a sign of weakness. If I were not courageous she would shy away from me, for my own emotional protection.

"Sure, let's go for a joy ride," I said, hopping inside and buckling the seat belt. I fiddled with the radio until I found a classical music station, sensing its universal appeal. I was elated to hear Debussy's *Claire de Lune*. Her stare remained fixed on the road. She was driving more cautiously with a passenger in the front seat.

"Boy, I really look forward to a home-cooked meal," I said softly over the quiet hum of her eight cylinder engine. "I've been cooking for myself. You know how carelessly students plan their diets: a hamburger here, a pizza there. All that's in between are beans and spaghetti."

"Speaking of spaghetti, Jeremy, don't expect anything fancy tonight. I've got a hunch you'll like my meatballs. I make them from a special recipe. Will that be O.K.?"

"Sure, I love pasta and home-made meatballs. Sounds like a real treat."

She flipped up the sun visor and turned into the parking lot. Gazing at the crowsfeet around her eyes, I became momentarily aware of her age. A tiny red cyst, a preserved ladybug, rested on the edge of her left eyelid and popped up when she squinted.

"Well, I'm glad someone enjoys a home-cooked meal," she muttered under her breath. I sensed a trace of displeasure in her tone of voice and wondered whether she was irked by her husband's remark about her cooking. Woman doctors were said to be terrible cooks.

"I have an idea that may save us some time," I said enthusiastically, with unmistakable pride, leaning sideways to face her.

"What's that, Jeremy."

"Why don't we split up the shopping list? I don't know which brands of food you normally choose, but I can certainly pick up some milk, eggs, yoghurt, ricotta, scooter pies, you name it. That way we can complete our shopping lickety split. I've had my fill of supermarkets this evening and I'm sure you feel the same way. So let me know what you want me to pick up."

"That's a grand idea. Jeremy, you really are a resourceful fellow." She stroked my sore shoulder for a split second before resuming her two-handed grip on the steering wheel.

If she'll let me help with the groceries, I thought, then I'm accepted as a member of her family. Will she adopt me as a foster child? I wondered.

"I only need a few items. I did my major shopping earlier in the week. Let me take care of the fruits and vegetables. Why don't you start with the eggs. Get the jumbo; they're the best value. The American Heart Association has everyone fooled. The whole cholesterol scare's just a conspiracy to lower egg prices. Don't bother locking up," she snickered when I fiddled with her power locks.

I was relieved that she wasn't overly protective about her possessions. One thing I couldn't stand was a materialistic physician.

We went through the list in less than five minutes and headed for the express lane. Silvana looked at me fondly and smiled. "Jeremy, is there any special flavor of ice cream you prefer?"

"Vanilla or peach," I said hesitantly, wondering whether she was trying to spoil me.

"They're my favorite flavors as well. Why not get a carton of each and we can make sundaes. I have some butterscotch syrup and walnuts at home. Let's get the all-natural ice cream. I try to avoid all preservatives which are potential carcinogens."

"I can't let myself be conscious of all the bad things I eat. Otherwise I'd end up as an emaciated wastrel. Cancer phobias are also immunosuppressive. Oncologists have documented the effects of the psyche on the immune system."

"Well, it's best to be on your toes. After all, we only have one life to live." Hearing this advice from a physician erased any existential doubt that there was a post-mortem reprieve in the contract of life.

Before we could end the discussion she raced over to the freezer case, found the two flavors of ice cream and hurried back to the register with a half-gallon tub in each hand. Her contracted biceps were much larger than I had ever expected and rounded out her underarms. My initial impulse was to *shnuppel* her arm pits and have my head trapped by her embrace, but I restrained myself.

"I hope you didn't buy two cartons of ice cream on my account," I forced myself to say, resuming the role of a polite *yekische* guest.

"No, don't worry; it's no imposition at all. Ice cream is the one thing I like to gorge on when the weather is hot." Her avid taste for dairy products revived my obsession with the lactiferous ducts in her breasts. Perhaps she would breast feed me after dinner. Her breast milk had a higher butter fat content than ice cream and really carried the flavor. I would even skip the main course for my just desserts.

The clerk rang up the bill and bagged the groceries. Silvana opened her alligator wallet and slipped a crisp fifty in the cashier's palm. I could tell by her blase expression that she had few financial concerns. As long as there was a nest egg for her son's graduate education, she could feel free to spend her money on clothes, perfumes, jewelry and other luxuries, to satisfy her voracious tastes for high living. I assured myself that the Fosters' supplemental income through investments in A.M.A. growth funds, medical office buildings and clinical laboratories enabled them to live in splendid comfort.

When the food was bagged, I wheeled the groceries back to the car and loaded them in the trunk. Sliding in the front seat, I smelled her unique odor permeating the vinyl upholstery. If she ever wanted to sell her car, I would offer the best price, even if the body was shot and the engine leaked transmission fluid. I would buy up all her garments if she ever tried to give them away at a rummage sale.

Just as we drove out of the parking lot I thought that our evening together would pass by all too quickly and we would resume our normal relationship as casual acquaintances or, worse yet, as patient and physician.

"You know something, Jeremy," she said innocently, breaking a long, disconcerting silence. "Originally, I had planned to invite you over to my house one evening. Since I'm pre-med advisor at Fairbanks, I need to keep abreast of advances in the basic sciences. Of all the pre-med students who have come by my office, you struck me as the one with a limitless future in medicine. You also possess the human attributes, including the capacity to empathize with your patients. Empathy is so important in forging a therapeutic alliance. It's something they can't teach you in med school. You have to develop the 'feel.' I wish I could see you eight years from now when you're board-certified in the specialty of your choice."

"Oh, we will see each other again, Dr. Foster. Someday we will meet as colleagues and, who knows, perhaps collaborate in a research experiment. I'm sure we'll have plenty of interesting things to discuss this evening," I said confidently as we turned into Cherry Lane. Looking down at the distended veins in my hands, I tried to judge whether I was back in my attic room hallucinating or blessed by a fortuitous occasion.

Infant Stim

An eerie hum wavered through the air as we pulled up the driveway. Her stately home seemed deeper and wider from the side than from the front. The neighborhood was quiet. Only the scattered mating cries of crickets and the distant roar of an eighteen wheeler interrupted the silence.

She wetted her lips and smiled at me coyly, encouraging me to lean closer. I was tantalized by her eyes, which glowed in the moonlight.

Would she hold me in her arms and make nookie in the driveway under the light of a full moon? A part of me knew that she wouldn't neck with me in the front seat of her car, even if it made her feel like a teenager again.

"So Jeremy, would you like to come in now?" she asked with a smile of private pleasure, shutting the car door with her hips.

"Sure, that would be swell," I whispered in a soft, narrowed tone. I tapped my fingers on the roof of her car while she rummaged for the back door key in her purse. "Before I forget, Dr. Foster, I left my bicycle at the supermarket. Would you mind giving me a lift back to the market?"

"I would be glad to, dear, as long as you return and spend the evening with me." Her breathing grew heavy and would have steamed were it not for the warm air.

"I want to pick up a few odds and ends at my house before dinner. It shouldn't take me longer than an hour. This way I can get rid of my bicycle and we'll have time to change into something more comfortable. I have a bottle of Chateau Lafite which I've been saving for years."

"My goodness! That must cost well over $100. Jeremy, why aren't you saving it for a special occasion?"

"This *is* a special occasion and we're going to celebrate tonight. If you wouldn't have intervened I'd be at the police precinct by now, phoning relatives for bail money. Besides, how many patients do you know who are able to date their doctors?"

"Listen, if word gets out to the student body, you'll be sorry. You don't know my dark side. If someone crosses me, I go straight for the jugular."

"My lips are sealed. I would never betray you, Dr. Foster. Besides, you just saved me from the security guard."

"Come on, quit making such a fuss about what happened in the supermarket. I'm certain you would have done the same for me. Are you sure you have the energy to ride back on your bicycle?"

"No problem. I'm in total control of my two-wheeler. I've got fantastic hand-eye coordination. If you remember me appearing spastic during that neurological examination at Hastings, it was strictly intentional. Besides, I'm sure that I can hitch a ride back with one of the neighbors. Just give me a lift back to the supermarket where my bike is parked. Let's go before it gets dark!"

"O.K., I'll drive you right now. Do you like being called Jeremy?"

"I'd prefer it you called me Jerry, but you can call me Dr. Lipschitz for short. Dr. Foster, is it all right if I call you Silvana? Your name has such a lovely ring."

"No, I don't mind at all, as long as you call me Dr. Foster at Hastings," she answered curtly with a raised brow. "Let's get in the car." As soon as my seat belt snapped in place she released the emergency brake and backed out of the driveway.

We drove along the winding streets of her neighborhood. Through the windshield I saw the first three Sabbath stars rising in the evening sky. Suddenly one of the tires plunged into a deep pothole. Thud. The right side of the car wobbled for twenty feet before the car dragged to a grinding halt. She stepped outside and examined the punctured tire. The front end sagged along with her lower jaw.

"It looks like I have a flat. I just hope it won't spoil our evening together."

"Don't look so sad, Silvana. You have a spare in the trunk. Permit me to perform the operation." As a gentleman it was my responsibility to keep the lady's hands unspoiled. When I stepped outside to inspect the tire I felt as noble as Walter Raleigh. "Hmm, it looks like a major hemorrhage. Can I have the key to the trunk?"

She tossed me the weighty key chain, which included her house keys and the key to the medicine cabinet at Hastings. I scraped my fingernail along a serrated steel edge and thought of leaving her stranded on the side of the road and dashing off in a cab to Hastings.

No one would be there. I could climb through the window of Dr. Foster's examining room and unlock her medicine cabinet. The bottle of Demerol was now down to ten cc's, but I had the key. There would be no broken glass. On Monday morning she would find me sprawled out on the floor, surrounded by the janitor and a team of dumbfounded nurses. She would palpate my livid skin, searching for a sign of life, but my pulse would have vanished to a distant world.

Jeremy, another part of me considered, now you have the opportunity to behave like a real gentleman and help a lady in need. Think of all the times she took care of you like a doting mother at Hastings. Don't you think it's time you returned a favor? Besides, there will be lots of fun and frolic ahead. Make believe that you're her chauffeur.

"You know, I'm really very lucky to have a young man with me who can change a flat tire," she said with a wave of warm gratitude, rubbing my back with the palm of her hand. She shut the door with a slight shove of her powerful buttocks and leaned closer.

"Aw shucks, it's really nothing," I said bashfully. "Mastering human anatomy is a far more intricate challenge."

"Well, I'm sure that in due time you'll know the clinical sciences cold. You're a very well-rounded fellow." I opened the trunk and pretended not to hear her. She planted her right thigh against the back of my leg in order to maximize the frequency of covetous contact.

My head bobbed around the trunk as I searched for a lug wrench. A brand new radial tire with dangling rubber nipples was hidden under a picnic blanket. Bending forward, I lifted the tire to an upright position. My derriere brushed against her thighs. Silvana leaned over my shoulder, trapping my lower torso against the bumper. The only avenue of escape was through the caressing rebound of her inner thighs. The thick, curly hairs on my legs quivered from the delicious impulses.

"Can I help you lift out the tire?" she asked with timid insistence, demanding an opportunity to share the burden. When I turned around to face her I was mesmerized by the imbedded wrinkles under her throat.

"What am I asking you for?" she scolded herself. "Of course I'll help you lift out the tire. I don't want you to strain your back. You've just come out of a depression and you're undernourished. If you're not careful and forget to bend your knees, you might reopen the scar which has healed so nicely."

"Thanks Doctor. It's a good thing you reminded me," I said, assuring her that she was not the forgetful one.

She secured a grip on the heavy tire and bent her knees to avoid straining her lower back muscles. We placed our hands at the four quadrants of the wheel and hoisted it up on its side. Before I could count to three she grunted and lifted the tire completely by herself. I was so enthralled with her quasi-bionic strength that I only guided the tire with my fingers, without sharing a milligram of the burden. She eased the heavy tire to the ground and leaned it against the fender.

"Can you hand me the lug wrench and the jack, Silvana?" She walked to the trunk, picked up the tools and carried them to the operating theater, where I was surveying the damage to the old tire. "Forceps, sponge, scalpel . . . " I ordered to my assistant as we commenced the delicate operation. I set the jack in place and pushed the lever up and down until the front end of the car was raised off the ground. Then I loosened the wheel nuts and gazed at the sunset.

Silvana looked at me like a proud mother. I would change a hundred tires for her, in the bitter cold, on soft shoulders of the turnpike, with trucks roaring beside me, if she would only take me into her arms once. I hoisted the flat tire from the chassis, placed it on the ground and replaced it with the spare. Then I tightened the nuts with the lug wrench and kicked the hub cap into place. After putting the damaged tire in the trunk I sat down on the fender and took a moment to catch my breath.

"Well, that's that!" I said playfully, brushing my grimy hands together.

"That's a job well done, Jeremy. You deserve a reward for your efforts. I have something in mind, but I'd rather surprise you."

"Please don't go out of your way, Dr. Foster. I can walk to the supermarket from here. Let me make a suggestion: stop by a service station on your way home and drop off the old tire. I can't wait to spend the evening with you. See you in about an hour. Bye bye."

"Oh Jeremy, not so fast. I have a feeling this is going to be a very special evening. And don't forget to ride safely," she said wistfully as I started to walk away. "I'm concerned that you're not wearing light clothes. Many people can't see your reflector at night."

"Don't worry, I'll watch out," I reassured her, thrilled that I could rouse her maternal concern. I realized then for the first time that it would be possible to spend the night in bed with Dr. Foster and abort my voyeuristic frustrations. The last ripples of the seal-belly sunset were swallowed up in darkness.

I found my bicycle where I had left it chained to a lamp post. I pedalled steadily downhill, lagging behind the flow of traffic. A strong breeze wisped against my face, drying tears of joy. I felt giddy just coasting down the steep incline, but shifted into high gear anyway. Before long I had crossed the bridge and entered the slums of Middletown.

Passing through the inner city I slowed down to watch the people hanging out on the streets. A transvestite couple in matching platform shoes were holding hands under the street light. How lucky they were to realize their "perverted" dreams and enjoy each other's companionship without inhibition. There was even a place for them to congregate in public. I, however, belonged to a group of isolated single men whose sexual appetites were too outlandish to attract a following and were forced to settle for vicarious gratification through masturbatory fantasies. As a gerontophile, I was considered an even greater threat to society's sexual mores than a harmless homosexual, restoring Victorian houses in between rimming and fisting. I was more closely aligned with rapists of bald pussy, or extortionists who sold phony promises of love and marriage to susceptible widows.

My impending success with Dr. Foster brought to mind my countless nights of loneliness and frustration. Silvana was the only person who was receptive to my needs. That's the way the cookie crumbles: once you achieve something, you look back at yourself as a poor lost child, a victim of circumstance who rose to the occasion to cry, "I am alive." Now take me into your arms. Oh Silvana!

The movie house, adult book store, the dope pushers snapping their fingers on the street corners, all whizzed by me in a blur as I raced home. I've got to be with Silvana. I can't wait any longer. The familiar sight of my rooming house appeared behind the Demarest Student Center.

Frank, an acquaintance who lived in the basement, waved to me from the front porch. He sat on a rocking chair nursing a beer. A blood moon was rising in the sky.

"Hey man, can I borrow your car?" I pleaded.

"Sorry, Jerry, can't lend you my wheels. You can't even drive a stick-shift."

"Come on Frank, you're not going to let me down. I've got bundles to carry and I have to meet a very important date in half an hour."

"What's she like?" he asked hungrily, wondering whether he might have the chance to share my chick once I was finished with her.

"She's got a great bod and she really digs the shit out of me. Sorry Frank, I can't help you this time. She's not your type."

"Doesn't she have a roommate or a kid sister?"

"No. Would you be a sport anyway, and give me a lift to her house? Come on Frank, I promise I'll try to set you up with somebody else."

"Shit man, can't you ride your bike over there in the meantime. You're always riding that stupid bicycle. It seems to get you where you want to go." In the same breath he smiled and assuaged my fears of being stranded. "Yeah, all right, I'll take you there. Meet you out in front in a couple of minutes. Don't make me wait!"

"O.K., that's cool. Frank, you're a prince. Oh, and Frank, I have to stop at the Ag School greenhouse to pick up some flowers. You don't mind making the extra stop. I'll pay for the gas."

Running up the stairs to my attic room I felt the temperature rise at each landing. Sweat streamed down my cheekbones, catching at the lobes of my nose, before condensing under my chin.

I uncovered my bottle of Chateau Lafite, which was buried beneath a heap of socks and soiled underwear. The bottle was clearly a collector's item and could have been auctioned for 500 dollars or more. Uncle Menachem gave me the bottle for my Bar Mitzvah with the stipulation that it would be opened only on a special occasion, preferably at my wedding ceremony. I was sick and tired of waiting for the special woman in my life. A nice, Jewish girl would make me miserable. I needed a *shikse* who was at least twice my age. Perhaps my parents could recommend one of their own single friends to whom they sold the *chometz* on Passover and make a *shituch*.

The edges of the label were worn down by the sweat of anxious fingertips. There had been many times when I was tempted to pull the cork and experience the special taste. Now I was determined to quell my curiosity, but still honor Uncle Menachem's wish to save the bottle for a special occasion.

I recited the blessing over wine, the same melody I had learned in the yeshiva. All my thoughts turned to plucking Silvana out of her clinical shell and swallowing her as if she were a seedless grape. Would she let me stick my ovipositor under her delicate skin? I picked up my knapsack from the floor and packed the wine. Then I zipped up my stash of marijuana and smoking paraphernalia in the outside pocket and hurried down the steps. In a flash I was at street level, waiting for Frank to pull up the car.

The rattly Barricuda convertible was idling in front of the house when I jumped inside. I felt exhilarated by the progress of my adventure. Only a few hours earlier I had been sitting on the edge of my mattress, miserably isolated in my attic room. Now I was speeding along University Avenue towards the Fairbanks campus and the Kirk greenhouses.

In my mind's eye, Dr. Foster was busy setting the dinner table. Crystal wine glasses were positioned on a hand-embroidered tablecloth beside her Wedgewood China. She placed an amber vase at the center of the table between a set of silver candlesticks, each holding a yellow braided candle. The Scandinavian vase was filled with fresh lilacs, clipped from her garden. The scent rubbed off on her hands.

Looking out the window, I noticed that we were already deep inside the Fairbanks campus, at the point where it bordered on Kirk Agricultural College. We drove by the greenhouses. Rows of fluorescent lights shone through the whitewashed panes. The turret of Hastings Health Center loomed in the distance. Now that I would be seeing Silvana in her home, it was merely a sterile infirmary where we had first met.

"Pull over by the floricultural greenhouse, Frank. It's the second one on your left."

A janitor stood in the main foyer. He was sweeping up the debris which had spilled from a bag of potting soil. Flashing my college I.D. card, I motioned for him to unlock the door. He had seen me frequently before, when I was experimenting with colchicine-treated marijuana seedlings, and thought that I was a graduate student who was an expert in the propagation of cockleburs and yellow roses.

I walked into the second hothouse where my hybrid roses were growing under automatic mist in perfect environmental conditions. The mixed scent of pollen and chemicals trapped in the humid air made me dizzy. I removed a pair of shears from the tool rack and searched for the most voluptuous bunch of yellow roses. A honey bee guided me to a freak variety with peach and yellow petals. After three warm up cuts in the air, I snipped off several branches ten inches down the stem, ignoring the lateral growth of suckers. Peering into the corolla of the flower I admired the fragile design of the undisturbed sexual parts, the thin filament and the desirous pistil, waiting for a wind current or an insect to help produce a seed. I blew a thin stream of air through the flowers and watched the waxy pollen grains fall into suspension.

The sound of Frank's car horn jolted me and forced me to withdraw from my game of floral sexual intervention. I tore off a sheet of waxed paper from the overhead roller and wrapped the stems loosely together, careful to avoid blemishing a single petal. The janitor led me out the door without bothering to inspect my package.

"Next step is Arlington Heights. Step on it man, the roses are dying."

"Boy Jeremy, I can't believe you go in for that mushy romantic stuff—bringing a chick flowers. Flowers went out with the fifties, when you wore a carnation to your high school prom. Wouldn't you rather spend your money on getting a girl drunk? I'll bet she gives, doesn't she, Jer?"

"Frank, don't tell me you thought I paid for these flowers."

"Never mind. I don't think I'll ever figure you out. You're the queerest bird I've ever met at Demarest. Arlington Heights coming up."

"Thanks Frank. I really appreciate your help. Take the Boulevard to Valhalla Drive—make a right at Cherry Lane. You're familiar with the area."

He drove down the left lane of Highway 28, the quick way, passing trucks, cars, motorcycles, any vehicles in our way. Zipping between lanes, he escaped the snarled traffic of park-and-ride commuters, generic people returning to their cozy homes in the suburbs. As we started to drive up the steep hill, the Cuda's engine backfired with a loud pop. Frank pushed the gas pedal to the floor but the engine could barely sustain its momentum. The motor refused to die completely and after four struggling attempts finally carried us to the top of the hill. Within minutes we hit Cherry Lane and arrived in front of the Fosters' stately grey house.

"Jerry, is this where your red hot lover lives? This is a $500,000 home. Boy, her parents must be loaded."

"No Frank, I don't think that's the case. She's financially independent."

"What? Hey, I've been meaning to ask you, how old is she?"

"That's a woman's secret. Besides, I respect my physician's confidentiality. See you later Frank. Thanks for the ride," I laughed and slammed the door behind me.

"What did you say? Your physician's confidentiality? You really are crazy!"

I noticed the silhouette of a tall woman standing in the dimly-lit vestibule. Frank kept his car in neutral, forty yards down the street. He was still anxious to get to look at my date. I tried to wave him off, but he didn't leave until Silvana poked her head outside.

Pressing the rose petals against my cheeks, I looked up into her eyes and tried to gather my courage. My hair already smelled of nectar. When she saw the flowers she shuddered at the thought of my romantic offering. "Gee Jeremy, I see that you have *schlepped* more than a bottle of wine."

"Be careful, Silvana," I warned, pawing her shoulder awkwardly with one hand. "Watch out for the sharp thorns. I wouldn't want to scratch your beautiful hands."

She winked at me, approving of my forwardness. I let go of them only after she had secured a grip on the stems.

"I'm going to put these in water. Make yourself at home," she said disarmingly, scurrying off to the kitchen in search of a vase. The thick carpet surrendered under my foot as I took one courageous step into her spacious living room. My eyes scanned the expensive furniture. The Fosters' family odor made me captive to her hospitality.

"Jeremy, give me your jacket," she said with an emphatic nod. She touched me on the small of my back and ushered me into the living room. I couldn't believe she touched me.

Watching her, I was curious to find out why she had decided to take off her stockings and dress up so beautifully for dinner. My eyes traced the borders of her arms. Her beautiful eyes were highlighted by heavy lines of mascara. Two golden crescent earrings dangled three inches below her lobes.

The sight of her curvacious calves swerving around the coffee table aroused my little head. The sofa heaved as the weight of her hips sank down gracefully beside me. Her body heat radiated through the upholstery. I wanted to trap her thighs between my knees and wildly grab her in my arms, but I was too scared even to shake her hand. She inched closer to me, perhaps hoping I would look directly into her eyes and be spellbound.

"I've got something special for you, Silvana." I unwrapped the wine bottle, revealing its long, slender neck.

"Oh, Jeremy. I don't know how to thank you. Before I forget," she said exuberantly. She paused to inspect the gold etching on the label; it was a Chateau Lafite. "Let the wine breathe so it will be ready by the time we eat dinner. I hope you didn't spend too much money on the wine, but . . . "

"This bottle has never been for sale. It's been stored in a wine cellar for over two generations and has a special history of its own. In 1942 my uncle was living in occupied France, trying to escape from the Nazis . . . "

She coughed and almost started choking. I think she wanted to change the subject.

"German soldiers were stationed at all points. Only a few people were able to penetrate the neutral zone without being gunned down. In 1939, the Nazis were already deporting trainloads of Jewish people to Buchenwald, Bergen-Belsen and other unknown destinations. Hundreds of thousands of people were disappearing. My grandfather on my mother's side starved to death in a concentration camp in the French Pyrennees. There were no neighboring countries, other than Holland, who were willing to take in Jewish refugees. Even the Red Cross hindered the trickling flow of Jewish children smuggled into Switzerland. Uncle Menachem was a very clever man. He managed to elude a Nazi patrol by posing as a drunken peasant.

"One afternoon, just before sunset, Menachem dressed in his shabbiest clothes, smeared a blend of charcoal and dirt around his face, ruffled up his hair and covered it with a torn beret so the Nazis would think he was a harmless bum, a native of the region. He left all his possessions behind, even his family photo ablums, but carried in his satchel two bottles of wine which had been stored in the family wine cellar. On his way to the frontier he popped the cork of one bottle, to drink along the way, and packed the other in the satchel. He also carried with him a small slab of cheese and half a loaf of bread which would sustain him through his journey to Geneva, should he survive. By the time he had reached the border he had already finished two-thirds of the bottle and felt light-headed. Two brown-shirted guards with swastikas emblazoned on their sleeves were positioned at the checkpoint. Automatic rifles were strapped to their backs. The Nazis watched Menachem from a distance while he stumbled across the mountainous terrain. They laughed at him for his slovenly appearance and drunken gait. He roamed aimlessly, zigzagging his way to the frontier, pausing frequently for a swig of wine.

" 'Where are you going?' one of the guards barked.

" 'Ah, *j'ai faire une belle promenade.*' He belched as his eyes rolled listlessly from side to side.

" 'What do you have in your knapsack; something for us?' The soldier yanked the satchel from his arm and inspected the contents.

" '*Ah, un peu de vin, un peu de fromage,*' he answered meekly.

" '*Un peu de fromage,*' the other soldier laughed, mocking the peasant dialect with his coarse German accent. He tore a hunk of bread from the loaf. 'Go on your walk, you drunken swine, but be back within an hour.' And with that remark, a heavy storm trooper boot shoved Menachem past the gate across the Swiss border. He made it to Geneva the following day.

"You see Dr. Foster, Uncle Menachem was the only close relative on my father's side who survived the war. My mother was left with a sister and two second cousins. Nearly everyone else in her family perished under the Nazis. So this is the story behind the bottle of wine we are about to drink tonight. Such has been the story of our family. We are a rare bunch of survivors, it's in our genes. And this survival mentality has been passed on to my generation, to my sisters and myself, even though we ourselves never experienced life in the concentration camps."

"That's fascinating, Jeremy," she said with a sigh, hoping that I wouldn't dwell on the Holocaust and lose my appetite for the delicious dinner ahead. "So your uncle survived through keen use of common sense."

"Yes, I'm sorry, Silvana. I really didn't want to get started talking about the Holocaust. Let's cast those ugly memories aside for the moment. I reserved this bottle of wine for a special occasion and now I'm so happy to see you outside Hastings. Here's to us. What a relief to know that we can finally be ourselves and drop the roles of physician and patient. You know, aside from being an excellent doctor, you're really great—and sexy."

"Jeremy, stop with the compliments. You're beginning to sound like a drug salesman." She spoke bluntly, but then laughed and ran her fingers through my hair. She wasn't trying to hurt my feelings. On the contrary, she wanted me to relax. "I can't wait to taste this wine. I'll be right back." She brought her breasts close to me before walking away. The scent of Giorgio trailed behind her.

My eyes followed the lateral swing of her hips as she strutted towards the kitchen. I became self-conscious of my low stares and tried to look up. Gazing into the spotless kitchen, I admired the white Poggenpohl cabinets where her dishes were stored.

The dining room table was set as beautifully as I had imagined. Silver candlesticks flanked two sets of Wedgewood china engraved with blue windmills. A white tablecloth, hand-embroidered in Portugal, covered the mahogany table. Two luscious bunches of purple and green grapes lay in a sterling silver fruit bowl between the crystal wine glasses.

Why not take a piece of fruit Jerry, I coaxed myself. Might as well make myself at home, just like the doctor ordered. I plucked a purple grape off its stem and popped it in my mouth. My teeth gnashed the pit. Curling my tongue, I spit out the wet pit on the back of my hand where it adhered like a piece of snot. Why did I have to pick a purple grape instead of a seedless one, I wondered. Even Amy Vanderbilt would have difficulty with this point of etiquette. There's no way that anyone, even the most highly cultured lady, can gracefully spit out a pit and leave it on the side of her plate.

When the pit started to dry on my hand I wanted to wash it off and wandered around looking for a bathroom. I found myself walking into closets. In one of them there was a mean-looking Kirby vacuum cleaner, as wide as a pickle barrel, which looked as if it could suck me up with the carpet hairs. I finally found a bathroom near the basement steps. After washing my hands thoroughly I decided that this was an opportune time to use it.

Staring into the disinfected toilet bowl, I found a stray pubic hair with a reddish pigment and knew that it had emerged from one of Silvana's follicles. The sound of the dripping faucet gnawed on my nerves. Each successive drip fell more slowly in the rhythm of a broken metronome. I twisted the knob as tightly as I could, but it continued to drip and voided my ability to void. I opened my pants and breathed deeply.

Balancing my flaccid penis on the tip of my index finger, I intended to demonstrate reasonable marksmanship and shoot through the hoop. I tapped the crown of my penis three times to issue the green light to my burning urethra, but my bladder was frozen by subliminal fear; I was unable to piss. The only sound was the unnerving drip of the faucet.

I remembered the same feeling of pelvic immobility while standing along a row of urinals in the men's room at the Port Authority Bus Station in New York City. Derelicts stood on both sides, peering down at my groin from the corners of their eyes. After two long minutes I was forced to flush the clear water john and rent a stall. Well, what can you do? It's the same old Darwinian principle which cuts through every slice of life: survival of the fittest. But here in Silvana's home I had complete privacy. No one was looking down at my pecker. There was no reason for me to feel ill at ease in these pristine surroundings. Perhaps I would have to wash down a grape jelly sandwich with a tall glass of lemonade to initiate the micturition reflex.

Come on Jeremy, I coaxed myself. You can do it. Better piss now or it will hurt when you come later on. Your body is only asking you to get rid of the toxins. Everything's already filtered for you. Be nice to your bladder and relax. Soon you'll be seeing Silvana. All you have to do is piss.

My bladder relaxed at the sound of her name. The stream splattered against the rim of the bowl and ricocheted to the cuffs of my pants. Before long, I recovered my accuracy and finished urinating. I felt clean and rinsed, like a new man.

When I opened the bathroom door I saw Silvana pacing around the dining room, holding a vase full of the yellow roses. She smiled at me seductively and then looked away. I followed her to the love seat and sat down on the plush cushions.

"Jeremy," she whispered with a hearty, contagious smile, "these are the most beautiful roses I've ever seen. You couldn't have purchased these at a florist shop. Did you grow them yourself at Kirk?"

"You guessed it, and I grew them just for you, Silvana. This has been a long and trying experiment. I even had to pinch the buds and use artificial light so they would flower in time for this occasion."

She turned on the stereo and inched closer to me. We listened to some Barbra Streisand schmaltz of People Who Need People. I wished I had brought along my Bruce Springsteen tapes. Silvana rubbed her legs against mine; and melted away all resistance.

"You really have excellent posture, Dr. Foster. Have you always kept your back so straight?"

"Yes, I always remind myself to sit up when I find myself slouching."

"Could you slouch a little for me," I started to say, but my voice cracked. She laughed to herself like a little girl, covering her mouth with her hand until the emotion drained from her face. I reached for her shoulder, but was paralyzed in mid-air by intense fear.

I slipped my hand between the couch and her back, where it found comfortable lodging against the middle of her spine. Suddenly, the hard sofa buttons impacted my fingers when she leaned back. At first I wondered whether she was trying to sustain my embarrassment. I cowered away, leaving behind my trapped hand.

"Jeremy," she asked, leaning over me and staring me straight in the eye. Her tongue flicked out and wetted her lips. "Have you ever made love with an older woman doctor?"

God, she asked me. What does this portend? Better be truthful.

"Only in my fantasies. It's all I ever think about and it never happens. I know it's the ultimate experience. Only a woman doctor has the training to influence my physiological responses. But as you know, I'm frustrated and settle for percussion and palpation. My attraction to women doctors transcends sexual fantasy. The only way in which I can nurture myself as a child in an adult body is to remain a patient . . . "

"You're not answering my question: have you ever made love with an older woman doctor?"

Boy, this is really getting heavy.

"No, I haven't. In fact, I've never even made love with an older woman before. In all of my past relationships with younger women we were forced to break up after it became obvious that in the midst of sex I was only thinking about sleeping with their mothers. They shirked me as a pervert. I was always the one to blame."

"Do you think it would be any different sleeping with a woman twice your age?"

"How should I know?" I asked defensively in a high quavering voice. "I've yet to experience the pleasure I have sought all along."

"Would you like to learn what it's like tonight?" Her unflinching stare forced me to look down.

"I really don't know. Would you decide for me? I'm too depressed to make my own decisions."

"No, this is something which you will have to decide for yourself. You only have to answer yes or no."

"I want to lay down beside you if you think it will help me, but I also want to be strong, make my own decisions and eventually grow up."

"Do you think an older woman loses her femininity, her physical beauty?"

"No, on the contrary; a woman becomes more beautiful as she grows older and wiser. Older women are superior beings. They keep out of war and nourish their sons to pursue respectable careers."

"Are you willing to put that in writing?"

"I'm willing to sign it with my very own blood. I bled for you the night you dressed my wound at Hastings. And I would give you a transfusion of my innermost substance, down to the last drop."

"Well," she coughed, trying to suppress a laugh and maintain her piercing stare. "I don't want you to lose any sleep or blood over what we're going to do tonight, so let's call it a draw and roll in the hay. Besides, you're not my blood type." She turned her back on me in mock disdain. "Now make up your mind, already. I haven't got all night," she said in a forceful whisper, "unless you want to spend it with me.

"If you go on fantasizing about sleeping with older women doctors you'll never get over the hump. In this instance, the recommended treatment is fulfillment with a surrogate therapist, one with the proper credentials. It is written in the Bible, 'Enjoy life with the woman you love.' I'm sorry I can't give you more time. I have my own eclectic method for treating autoeroticism which should make waves among orthodox physicians, so promise me that you'll keep this strictly confidential. It's extremely rare for any physician to risk her medical license by functioning as a surrogate therapist, but I'm committed to helping you. It's time to break the cycle. I'd rather treat you this way than see you on antidepressants for nine months."

"I promise. I promise I won't say anything, Silvana. It's so very kind of you to invite me into your habitat tonight. You're such a dedicated physician. If I could afford it I would pay you $1000 an hour; only an M.D. deserves such a fee. I wouldn't consider anyone who wasn't board-certified in copulatory practice. This form of treatment is safe, fast-acting and has no side-effects. Besides, it's more cost-effective than hospitalization. By the way, they're coming out with a new DRG fee scale for surrogates. I've heard many things about male physicians, mainly psychiatrists, who have sex with their patients, but this is the first time I've seen the roles reversed. In a recent A.M.A. poll, only three percent of women psychiatrists admitted to sleeping with their patients and in the majority of cases, the patients were also women. You know, I've spent so many frustrating afternoons hanging out on campus of Womens Medical College. It's been impossible finding someone of the faculty with whom I can share an intimate conversation. My parents wanted me to join the singles' club at Hillel, but none of those girls turn me on. The problem with Jewish girls is that their cunts are too mushy and they're always kvetching. I need a *shikse* doctor. Someone like you who will take risks. And the most beautiful thing about this is that you're an internist, not a psychiatrist, so I don't have to feel paranoid about someone psychoanalyzing me in bed. In the heat of passion asking me 'What are you thinking?' I only date women doctors who are into physical medicine. How about putting your D.E.A. number on the line too. Do you have any pure coke for local anesthesia? After all, it may help me overcome my inhibitions."

"I'm sorry, Jeremy, but this is not a chemical dependency program," she said in a sarcastic, biting tone. "I don't sleep with drug addicts or alcoholics. The best therapy is straight, conventional sex."

"No, don't misunderstand me. I'm totally clean, with the exception of marijuana . . . "

"That's O.K. I was talking about hard drugs."

"No hard drugs. Please Dr. Foster, don't give up on me. I was only fantasizing. I really want to thank you for all your help . . . "

"Let's cut out the thank you's. Don't regress to your sycophantic airs; I won't tolerate a *toches lecher* in my house. Now how am I going to justify this visit on your chart?" she said with a pained sigh, thinking out loud. "Occasionally, at Hastings, I need to request a sperm test for married students with fertility problems. Jeremy, for the record, I'm only measuring for number and motility tonight. I have a calibrated test tube in my night table. At the appropriate time, you can discharge your seminal fluid into the test tube. If you want I'll freeze it for posterity's sake. You'll make an excellent husband some day. Follow me into the kitchen."

I stroked her shoulder with perspiring fingertips and stared boldly into her eyes. She didn't withdraw, but pressed closer to absorb the warmth of my touch.

"Silvana, would you like to dance?" She rose from the sofa, grabbed my free hand and led me across the living room with the grace of an experienced dance partner.

I held her firmly, one hand resting on the small of her back, the other clasping her forearm. We rocked our bodies together in cadence with the music and danced a fox trot towards the kitchen odors. The sweet aroma of meatballs met my nostrils. Unleashed gastric juices made my stomach grumble.

Resting her weight on one foot, Silvana balanced herself magnificently on her toes and whirled 360 degrees under my outstretched arm. As the music slowed we resumed our original dance position. She rested her fingertips on the outer rim of my scapula, tickling me in a trick hold. By this time my clutch had become less spasmodic. Mesmerized by her breezy dance style, I felt ready to sweep her off her feet. I stepped forward, leading with my left foot. She dropped back, pivoted a quarter turn and redirected my counterthrust. Her fluid motions guided my steps with certainty and precision. I was amazed to find that she did not resist my aggressive leads and enjoyed the variety of swirling moves.

A fast rumba rolled out of the speakers. Now I had the opportunity to witness her superior dancing skills. She obviously loved the South American rhythms, especially the hard thrust of driving cunga drums. Silvana and I danced up a storm. Her knees jabbed forward in syncopated time, pulling me with her all the time. I could barely stand up, let alone keep up with her. She looked marvelously athletic. I imagined that she had worked her way through college as a Rockette at Radio City Music Hall, one of her mini-careers before she had devoted herself entirely to medicine.

By the time the second stanza came around I was familiar with most of her patterns. I backed off a step and stood erect on the balls of my feet. Anticipating the first pause in the song, she pressed her knee between my thighs and leaned into me. I sensed no further obstructions to our limbic entanglement.

When the song ended, she tugged my arm gently and led me into the kitchen. There she opened the top of an earthenware casserole, scooped out a bubbling meatball and held it under my nose. My eyes watered before the meatball was buried in its hot bath of gravy. She turned around, and to my utter surprise, kissed me smack in the middle of my forehead.

Oh my God, she kissed me first. Wow! I took a deep breath, lurched forward and planted a small, moist kiss on her cheek. I cannot describe the ecstasy of this moment. In all the hundreds of times I had imagined kissing her, I had never discovered the true taste and porous texture of her cheek; it was as full-bodied as a Morelle mushroom that had soaked overnight. Her peach fuzz left me tingling all over. Then I honed in for the third kiss, the kiss she had been waiting for, the Man's kiss. I pressed my lips over her mouth as lightly as possible, carefully pulling back the weight of my head so as not to appear overly passionate. My lips vibrated with joy.

She kissed my eyelids and licked the crust from a dangling lash. When I felt her protective saliva bathe my conjunctivae I closed my eyes and immersed myself in the warmth of her mucous membranes. Her tongue wandered to my earlobes. My ear drums thumped with joy. Then I heard a cochlear crunch; it was time for me to reciprocate.

Diving haphazardly into her oral cavity I felt the contours of her healthy gums. Her teeth were hard and slippery, but smoothly rounded, having retained their original layer of enamel. Even as a child, Silvana had received the very best dental care.

Two hands secured my shoulders. She massaged my flying trapezius muscles, pulled my chest against her breasts and hugged me fiercely. The soft tug of her bra was only a temporary obstruction which would be removed during after-dinner foreplay. Then she kissed me voraciously in figure eights along my cheekbones, eyes, temples, forehead and for an intermezzo, nibbled on my earlobes with a teasing lick.

Boy Dr. Foster, do you know the central nervous system, I thought, drinking up her moist kisses. She knew how to stimulate the peripheral nervous system as well, the cranial and spinal nerves, all the receptors that made a man happy.

"I hate to interrupt this," she said abruptly, releasing me from her embrace, "but my sixth sense tells me that the meatballs are ready. Do you have an appetite?"

"I'm simply starved." She stirred the spaghetti before it started to stick. "Can I help you with anything?" I pleaded, holding out my hands.

"Why don't you take the wine out and let it breathe. There's a corkscrew in the middle cabinet."

Silvana loped out of the kitchen into the dining room, carrying a tray of appetizers over her shoulder; most were non-kosher delights: pigs-in-a-blanket, shrimp rollmops and diced calamari. Violating rabbinic law has always given my tastebuds a sacrilegious thrill.

I followed her, placing the wine on the table between the polished silver candlesticks. She waved me off when I offered to bring in more dishes.

Resigned to my guest status I sat down and tucked the heavy cloth napkin in my pants.

"Help yourself to some appetizers, Jeremy."

"Thanks, I will." On that note I devoured a pig in its blanket and memories of Bar Kochva tickled my palate. Gazing at the shiny plate, I winked at my own reflection and squeezed one hand with the other to convince myself that Silvana and I were getting it on.

She dished a generous helping of spaghetti on my plate, interrupting my self-indulgent reflection. Then she ladled out three global meatballs—free of hamburger helper—and smothered them with an herbal tomato sauce and sauteed mushrooms.

The scent of basil urged me to dig into the main course, but I exercised restraint. Wait until she serves herself, Jerry. Remember, you're a guest here. Be on your best behavior.

She sat down on the opposite side of the table and started a game of footsie. Her toes made the hairs on my legs stand on edge. I wondered how she had been able to prepare dinner and dress up in the brief time I had been away. Perhaps she had a secret helper, who made herself inconspicuous by disappearing through a secret staircase to her room on the third floor. However, I knew that we were truly alone. Her husband was miles away attending a symposium on hip dysplasias.

She spread the napkin over her lap and helped herself to a stuffed mushroom. I grabbed the serving fork and scooped out a healthy portion of jumbo shrimp and devoured them greedily like a *chazer*. The meatballs were next on my list. Gravy oozed out of them and mingled with the red sauce smothering the spaghetti. I forked a chunk of steaming beef and raised it to my lips which were still warm and vibrating from our last kiss. The meat was cool enough to bite after I blew on it three times. She watched the contractions of my throat while I swallowed her food and seemed extremely pleased that I approved of her cooking. Then she helped herself to the main course and plunged a forkful of pasta in her mouth. Our mandibles ground the semolina in synchronized motions. The hot sauce oozed down our esophagi, stimulating the secretion of pancreatic enzymes, all regulating the gastrointestinal pH for the spicy dinner ahead.

It was time for wine. I peeled off the seal, pulled the cork and let it breathe under our noses. The wine reminded me of her: full-bodied, with great depth and a hint of the luscious fruit. This classic Bordeaux has a tremendous fragrance that develops as it matures. Most things are consumed too young.

She slid a foot along my shins. Her legs were so long and her posture so steady that she could tickle me nonchalantly from across the table and sit up straight at the same time. I filled our glasses and prepared to make a toast.

"Silvana," I said somberly, lifting my glass to eye level. "Here's to your health and happiness. I hope you retain your impeccable figure for decades to come. Let's celebrate the new millennium together in the year 2000."

"That's very flattering, Jeremy. I want you to be happy too and not miss out on anything. For a long time, I've been aware of your intense loneliness. It's never easy to fool the trained eye of a physician. Do you think I was gullible enough to believe your story about being stabbed outside the train station? After twenty years in medicine I know a self-inflicted wound when I see one. I only led you to believe that I was fooled by your alibi because I wanted to measure the severity of your depression. And here's the diagnosis. Jeremy: you're the most well-developed pseudopsychotic patient who has ever stepped inside my office. There's nothing wrong with you, you peculiar fellow. And now," she said haltingly, pausing to raise her wine glass, "it's time to realize your true desires. What you really need is the love and guidance of an older woman who can appreciate you. It's time to displace the vacuum of solitary asexuality. I know that you masturbate twice a day routinely and constantly conjure up visions of my naked body in your fantasies. Now that you're under my care at home, I have another therapeutic option. But remember, confidentiality's a two-way street. I won't do anything against your will. You're committed here voluntarily and can sign a release whenever you like as long as you leave the premises in a wheelchair." She laughed and toed my crotch. "It's just for insurance purposes. So here's to us. Cheers!" We clinked our glasses and savored our first sips of the precious wine. "Now kiss me, Jeremy," she commanded.

I rose up quickly from my chair, dashed around the table and kissed her on the nape of her neck. Before she could respond, I kissed her ear, humming erotoecstatic sounds into her inner labyrinth.

"Oooh, Jeremy, that feels so good." She pushed me away teasingly. "Now sit down and eat your food before it gets cold."

Neither one of us said a word to each other during the main course of the dinner. I savored every forkful of spaghetti and ate the meatballs slowly to insure smooth digestion. As dinner ended Silvana didn't allow me to get up from my chair. I felt compelled to help her clean the table. She sneaked up behind me and forced me to sit down.

"Don't peek," she whispered coyly, covering my eyes with her fingertips. She placed something before me. "O.K., open your eyes now."

The tantalizing sight of Napolean a la mode made my tongue curl in delight. Crushed walnuts in butterscotch syrup smothered giant scoops of peach and vanilla ice cream. I devoured the pastry greedily in a dozen quick bites and the sugar gave me a quick rush. I no longer felt drowsy, just a wee bit hyperglycemic. After scraping up the last scoop of melted ice cream, I wiped my mouth and excused myself from the table.

While she disappeared into the kitchen to load the dishwasher, I had a ripe opportunity to snoop around her house. I wandered out to the patio and gazed at the yellow-green buds unfurling under the flood lights. A lone Persian lime tree obstructed the path to the swimming pool.

No wonder she stays so limber, I thought, my eyes following the ripples of blue water in her pool. She probably swims twice a day, knowing that it's the best form of exercise. I drank in the sights of her palace, relieved that my visions were no longer illusions, nor unsolicited flashbacks from a bum trip.

When I walked into her study I was impressed by the meticulous neatness of the room. Her study was soundproofed with cork paneling. The air was pleasantly ventilated with a pine scent. My attention was drawn to the photographs on her desk. In one of these photos her tall, handsome husband stood in his swimming trunks on the beach. He had broad pectoral muscles and looked ready to kick sand into the eyes of any ninety-five pound weakling who threatened his masculinity.

In another picture, her son wore a graduation cap with a tassel hanging beside his plastered smile. He was as tall and as ugly as I had imagined. The poor fellow had a terrible acne problem. His cheeks and forehead were covered with ruptured pimples. Wasn't there some effective prescription she could give her son to limit his sebaceous secretions? Certainly either she or her husband, with all of their professional connections, knew of a famous dermatologist who could prescribe an effective wonder drug. The boy's cavernous complexion showed that he had to settle for over-the-counter preparations. Boy was he ugly. His nose was even oilier than my own. White crowned zits covered the creases around his eyes. He looked like a math nurd with little imagination and no artistic flair, a real *nebish* who made it to Harvard on the strength of his parents' connections.

Turning to the walls of her study, I scanned the bookshelves, tracing the titles of medical textbooks and scientific journals dating back twenty years: *Pathology Today, Annals of Internal Medicine, Archives of Neurological Psychiatry, Experimental Cell Research,* special editions with translations from Russian and German—which were superfluous to her collection since she was fluent in both languages. One bookshelf was filled with cloth-bound texts with topics ranging from bioluminescence to the theory of general practice. She even had a complete set of the *Proceedings of the Cold Spring Harbor Symposiums on Recombinant D.N.A. Research,* as well as the thirty-nine volume set of the *Handbook of Physiology.* When I recognized Herrick's *The Brain of the Tiger*

Salamander, I was thrilled to see she had a taste for the biologically bizarre and especially for neurocellular cloning. This demi-God knew how to regenerate missing limbs. I would be the first person to volunteer as a subject for her experiments.

The books were stacked to the ceiling. I convinced myself that the Fosters were wealthy enough to subscribe to a wide variety of medical journals and avoided the crowd of miserly M.D.s who kept up with the literature in the med school library. I admired her leather bindings: Springer-Verlag, Williams & Wilkins, Saunders, Lippincott, Shameless Hussy Press, good WASP names. Last Christmas her husband gave her a lifetime membership to the M.D. Book of the Month Club.

Reaching up to the top shelf, I removed a book *Correlative Microneurosurgery* and beckoned for a lobotomy. The price of this limited edition was $165—a worthy tax write-off. Thumbing through plates of high-resolution photomicrographs, I realized that she belonged to an elite club of physicians. The authors and readers not only held an exclusive understanding of these pathological syndromes and their available modes of treatment, but of medical terminology, the vocabulary of life and death itself.

An assortment of paperweights cluttered her desk; they were souvenirs dropped off by sales reps of mammoth drug companies. A white princess telephone was tucked away in the corner beside a Scrimshaw whalebone, picked up during a summer vacation in Maine. I memorized her unlisted home number on the dial and repeated it so I'd never forget it.

"Won't you come into the living room, Jeremy?" she said with a tinge of irritation. Perhaps she was touchy about her professional privacy and didn't want anyone snooping around her office, not even her lover.

"Surely Silvana. I didn't mean to intrude." I looked back to catch a peek at her possessions.

She ran up to me and suddenly pressed my face against her breasts, burying my ears with cupped hands. I smelled the scent of milk-ejection hormones.

"Can we go straight to bed? I'm not in the mood for discussing medicine right now, although I wouldn't mind participating in a real-life anatomy lab, with you, dearest."

"Jeremy, I agree with you 100 percent. I never have an appetite for science after a heavy meal; it definitely impedes the digestion. My bedroom's upstairs to your left." She combed her fingers through my hair with an affectionate tub to my scalp. "I'll be with you in a moment. Just let me clean up the kitchen."

Her frank instructions startled me. Everything was proceeding so easily. Why beat around the bush with pretentious verbal foreplay, I wondered?

"Silvana, would you mind if I shower first? I'm still sweaty from bicycling."

"You took the words right out of my mouth. You'll look sexy after a hot shower. I'll get everything for you, dear."

"Thanks. Can you show me where the bathroom is?"

She stepped in front of me and led me up the stairs. Her taut calves bulged with every step. Her hips seemed disproportionately broad, given her bone structure. I was pleased that she wanted me to be clean before we inspected each other's private grottos under semi-asceptic conditions.

When we reached the top of the stairs she scraped her nails along the length of my spine. My fingers and toes tingled in the afterglow of her arousing touch. I was about to take a step into the bathroom when she gripped my shoulder gently and said, "Just one second dear, let me get you a set of towels from the linen closet. I'll get a few for myself so I can shower in the other bathroom. Sometime later, Jeremy, when your dinner is completely digested, you may want to try out the whirlpool. We have a Hubbard tank in the basement."

She opened the linen closet. Eight rows of shelves supported towels, sheets, facecloths, bottles of bubble bath, imported deodorant sticks, roll-ons, sprays, dusts, powders, hand-crocheted afghan spreads, down-filled pillows, satin sheets in red, yellow, blue and green with matching sets of pillow cases. Silvana handed me a bath towel, a face cloth and a short towel for my feet; blue for boys.

After choosing a red bath towel for herself she strutted into her bedroom, her hips wriggling fron side to side. I followed her inside, jumped up and down on the king size, posturepedic mattress and plopped down on the carpet. She pulled off the bedspread, exposing her satin yellow sheets. Then she folded the bedspread into a neat bundle and placed it squarely on the seat of a colonial rocking chair.

I unlaced my sneakers, peeled off my socks and threw them on the floor like an impatient little boy. The curls of the shag carpet snaked around my toes while I eagerly shuffled my feet. Dr. Foster, who was so meticulously neat in her practice, bent down to pick up my socks.

"Ouch," she cried in agony. "Oh my back! Lower lumbar! What am I doing? Jeremy, it's all your fault. Why did you have to throw your socks on the floor?" Her cry turned to a low moan. She lay flat on her back and spread her legs apart.

I was about to panic, afraid that our evening together would end abruptly and I would be forced to call for an ambulance. Worst of all, I dreaded the thought that she would be taken away by a para-medical team.

"Oh, this is going to hurt for months," she winced, rubbing her lower back.

"Can I get you some Demerol?" I asked lamely, hoping I could have a shot for myself.

"No thanks, Jeremy," she laughed, refusing to take me seriously. "I can bear the pain for a little while and then I'll take two Tylenol. Demerol's very dangerous, especially for doctors who have easy access to the drug. If the F.D.A. would only approve reagent-grade D.M.S.O. I may have to send you to the hobby shop for the 99.8 percent solution. Oh, I can feel the pain coming now. The last time I had a slipped disc it was simply murder. Jeremy, listen to me," she commanded, placing her hands on my shoulders. "Go into my linen closet—I think it's on the sixth shelf under the foot towels—and get me my hot water bottle."

"Sure Dr. Foster. I'll get anything you need. Stat." I wanted to show her that I had better reflexes than the nursing staff at Hastings. After rummaging through a shelf of towels I finally found the hot water bottle and unplugged the stopper.

As I filled the amorphous rubber bottle with warm water I remembered the times my mother made my tummy ache feel better by applying the compress to my abdomen. It was my first masturbatory device and almost as good as the breast. Now I had a warm pulsating heart to press against my chest.

"Oh never mind, Jeremy," she called out from the bedroom. "My back's much better. It was only an old pinched nerve; it's nothing serious. The pain will go away in a few minutes. I don't want to spoil our evening. Hurry up and take your shower. There's hypoallergenic soap and shampoo in the bathroom cabinet. Don't get any water on the rug if you can avoid it, honey," she said limping out of the bedroom.

"Don't worry," I shouted over the sound of gushing water. "I'll be out in five minutes and I won't use up the hot water. I heard the pressure's weak on this side of town."

After peeling off my clothes, I bent over the sink to examine the toothbrush rack and floss dispenser. The yellow toothbrush was engraved with Silvana's initials. Would she share her toothbrush with me, I wondered? Looking up at the magnified mirror, I found a fallen eyelash dangling on the side of my nose. I flicked it away, smiled at myself and decided that I was stunningly handsome.

The shower was custom-built in the style of a European *schwitzbath*. The high-pressure plumbing had been installed in an effort to improve her family's circulation. Stepping inside the tub I turned on the water, as hot as I could stand it. High-velocity bullets pierced the volcanic tips of shoulder acne. My skin glistened. I scrubbed away the pimple oil with a bar of scented soap. The cake slid down my pubescent chest, leaving a white film behind. I slipped the soap around my back and armpits, finally squeezing the amber disc against my gonads, which were deeply withdrawn to escape the spermicidal effects of hot water. Oh, this must be the holy *mikveh*, I thought, finally adding more cold water to the burning shower. My father always told me, "if it hurts, then it's good for you."

Now that I was confidently clean I sat down on the edge of the bathtub and dried off quickly under the sunlamp. I discarded the foot towel in the hamper, wrapped a bath towel around my waist and watched the steam float out the screen window.

A cold draft swept by me as I stepped into the hallway and waited patiently outside her bedroom door. I heard the sounds of a woman undressing, the slippery crinkle of silk rubbing against feminine skin. I was dying to catch a sight of her natural morphology and tapped my knuckles lightly on the door.

"Come in Jeremy." I pushed open the door slowly against the resistance of the thick shag carpet. Standing boldly before her, I stared at her naked body, revealed at last with all the contours, crests and depressions I had imagined before in my mind's eye. I expected her to cover her breasts with her arms, but she stood confidently before me, a naturally poised Mother Venus. Her breasts were fuller and wider, but less pendulous, than I had previously imagined. They weren't limp, nor wrinkly, as I had presumed they would be on a woman of forty-nine. As a physician she knew how to prevent tissue degeneration during pregnancy, lactation and weaning. Her depilated legs were as smooth as silk. The curly triangle between her thighs was streaked with a swirl of grey pubic hair. I was still shocked by the sight of her pulsating body. I had expected at least a thin, translucent nightgown to cover her sacred figure.

A fear that I would cop-out on her passed through me. It was expected that a patient would be a little nervous about having sex with his attending physician. As long as I was sleeping with an M.D. I had no reason to be embarrassed by my own sexual performance. A test tube reserved for my sperm sample lay on the night table within easy reach for the appropriate moment of coitus interruptus. I let the towel drop from my waist to the floor and took a long stride towards her.

I knelt down before her feet and hungrily kissed her big toe. She clasped her hands around my neck and pulled my face up towards her womb, trapping my head in a soft grip. I smelled her menstrual secretions, the 420th ovum of approaching menopause, the ooze from hot flashes, dribbling down her thighs. Leading with my nose, I *schnuppeled* around her labia majora before extending my tongue into her vulval cavern. She pressed my head closer and wrapped her thighs around the sides of my face. I started to tongue-kiss her clitoris rhythmically, hoping she would go crazy and do the same to my genitals for a longer duration.

I tried to avoid smelling the odors emanating from her vagina, but wanted to excite her sufficiently, so I pressed closer. My penis became engorged with blood and climbed to a 140 degree angle, a self-supporting paroxysmal priapism. Rolling my tongue from side to side, I stimulated the lining of her vagina, causing her to quiver periodically. Her hot clitoris flexed itself against my tongue.

She rubbed my shoulders with ultra-soft strokes, as only a physician could do. I shivered from the tingling impulses. She continued to rub me lightly all over my body, tickling my neck bones, initiating a cerebrospinal thrill through a pleasure relay system in my hippocampus, all ending in a coccygeal massage.

I was overwhelmed by her commanding power and wanted to retire forever inside her crevice. While licking the walls of her vagina, I suddenly tasted a remnant of a feminine douche. I yanked my head out of the grasp of her taut thighs and spit a mouthful of saliva onto the carpet.

"Jeremy, we have a sink, you know," she shrieked, more surprised by the release of my stimulating tongue than by my unhygienic discharge.

"I'm sorry, Silvana, but it really tasted gross," I said half apologetically.

"That's O.K. I should have warned you beforehand," she said, repositioning my head between her legs.

I had no way of knowing that throughout her twenty-six years of marriage, she had never been the recipient of oral sex. Worse yet, shortly after her son was born, her husband had become impotent from testicular feminization syndrome, a rare endocrine disorder.

Staring into the cherry pit before me, I returned to the unicellular feel of embryogenesis. I was her baby all right. My preformed limbs stretched the linings of her uterus, kicking her belly in a silent cry, "I am. I am. Let me out!" But she was protecting me in my amniotic sac. I was only in my seventh month of development, too frail to face the world. Mamma Marsupial sealed me within her placental pouch, until my organs were clearly differentiated and I had a real live penis and a foreskin ready for the *mohel's* knife, only this time I was circumcized for health reasons, rather than by religious law. She carried me in her belly for two more months, until her labor pains became frequent and her water broke. Then she called a colleague from a nearby hospital, an expert obstetrician, who delivered me into the cold, hostile universe without complications. Her stimulating touch oxygenated the blood flowing through my cerebrum and precipitated multi-colored images. I thought that I was undergoing an embryonic reversal, crossing the placental barrier into her hermetically sealed uterus.

She tugged on my hair and pressed my face between her buns. The roseate spreads on the undersides of her breasts became visible as a sex flush warmed her skin. I felt calm and secure, like a little pig in a brick house, sucking from Mama's nipple. But my real Mom never let me mix milk and meat. She wanted me to grow up to be a good Kosher boy.

I carefully worked my way towards the pinnacle of her fully extended nipple. She pressed my face closer to her rib cage, but my cheek felt nothing as hard as bone. I rested my head against the soft, firm pillows. Don't put me in a crib, Dr. Foster. Don't put me on the bottle or infant formulas. I need those essential fatty acids and immune co-factors found only in breast milk. You'll never wean me. We can kick your husband out of bed. I love to curl up within your thighs. You're the warmest living blanket in the universe. I sucked on her papillae mammae as hard as my cheeks could bear. She squirmed as I made her areolae tingle.

Opening my mouth wide, I guided the tip of her breast all the way back against my epiglottis and teethed on the lobular gland as if it were laced with blackstrap molasses. She smothered me with her inflamed boob. Her breast grew firmer and expanded against my windpipe. My trachea was completely sealed off. Only a thin stream of air wisped through my hyperventilating nostrils. My pulse slowed dramatically. I was losing consciousness. Not seeing my cyanotic face, she pressed my head against her chest more fiercely than before, until all oxygen was blocked off. I gave a final shrugging sigh to the world and collapsed with a spasm. My left leg kicked helplessly to the side. Her breast retracted and eased itself out of my mouth. When she saw the vacuous look in my eyes she positioned me flat on my back. Thank God she has a physician's instincts, I thought, as I began to indulge in a pseudocomatose stupor. She leaned over me, placing one hand under the back of my neck to support my head. With her other hand she pinched my nostrils shut and blew a strong burst of air through my lungs in an attempt to resuscitate me. I was already conscious and savored the taste of her warm breath.

She removed a stethoscope from her night table and listened to my heart sounds. I tried to feign cardiac arrythmias but remembered that the heart was an involuntary muscle. Nevertheless, I was able to consciously accelerate my pulse. When I opened my eyes Dr. Foster was standing over me, gravely concerned. The simian furrows beside her eyes were deepened with worry.

"Jeremy, are you all right? Say something," she commanded in a strange, frightened tone which I had never heard before. Keeping her stethoscope pressed to her ears she smiled when my heart beat returned to normal.

"Sure I'm O.K. I'm just a little groggy. What happened?"

She shook me playfully in her arms, comforting me with her therapeutic smile. "You're all right, Jeremy. Of course, you're all right. You just passed out for a minute. I'm so glad you're O.K. You gave me such a scare. I didn't know what I was going to say to the medical examiner." She tickled my pallid toes and pressed them between her thighs. They quickly returned to room temperature. "Why don't you sit up now? I don't want you to choke and pass out again."

I followed her instructions, propping my hips against the bed. My tailbone slid freely against her satin sheets. She gave me a few minutes to catch my breath and then decided to sustain the stimulus to my heart through other means. Opening her mouth wide, she lowered her head and licked my testicles. God, I thought, she goes right for the testicles. Only a physician knows the source of the orgasmic relay system. Then she worked her tongue into my anus, coiling it into a solid U: in and out, in and out, scrubbing my descending colon with her medicinal saliva as far as the tip of her tongue could reach. I had to pant. She wanted me to die of pleasure. Her pointed tongue crawled out of my rectum, slid around my waistline and rested on the crown of my penis. She peeked inside the aperture and stroked the head gently. A preliminary drop of milky white fluid surfaced from my vas deferens. Her lips squeezed my organ gently, but deferentially, as if it were a nitrite-free sausage. Soon she started to suck wildly, in an attempt to vacuum up the sinewy strands of seminal fluid to be deposited in the test tube for sperm culture. Semen was not only her favorite delicacy, it was nutritious as well, containing protein, riboflavin, potassium and zinc.

When I felt my first surge coming I wanted to be a man about the whole thing, and so turned away, whipped my organ from her mouth and crawled to a safe corner of the huge bed. Squatting on my heels, I panted breathlessly. Never before in the twenty years of my existence had a woman excited me with such force. I needed to relax; otherwise we would never manage intercourse. There was nothing more humiliating for a man, young or old, than premature ejaculation. Looking to the far side of the bed I watched her wink at me slyly out of the corner of her eye. She gave me a little time to prepare myself for the act of coitus. We were lying motionless on the mattress, staring at the white ceiling. I rolled towards her and rubbed my face in the pillow.

All of a sudden my strength gave way and I felt too faint to move. "Do you mind if I go to sleep right now? I'm so terribly knocked out. I need to sleep. Good night." I yawned and turned over on my right side. It was a good thing that she was lying to the left of me. Otherwise she might have interpreted my move as a snub and expelled me from her bed. I was afraid she was disappointed that I had chosen to go to sleep before the real orgasmic fun began, but then again I knew how much fun it was to have sex first thing in the morning. Morning sex was especially enjoyable because the unconscious fantasy flow lingered from dreaming. Besides, it presumably gave her great pleasure to see me overcome my insomnia problem within her very sight.

There now, look at him, she would think, as she stroked my neck like a proud, understanding mother. He's already falling asleep.

If only I had her genes I could be her son, her sole offspring and bathe in her amniotic fluid. I would have her gangly limbs, hazel eyes, height, intelligence, strong muscle fibers and healthy nervous tone. If only I had been born a Foster, I would have had carte blanche at the medical school of my choice and never have flirted with the thought of becoming an unemployed English major. Within minutes I was immersed in the slow, even-waved stage of rapid eye movement.

Life had started all over again for me. I was born a baby, an orphan after two weeks of nurturing by my natural mother, who was too poor to feed me. I was exposed to the elements, shivering in a doorstep cradle. Spacelings from another planet swooped down to Earth and carried me away. I woke up in a giant crib, surrounded by hordes of anxious older women, all of whom were dying to get a peek at the darling little Earthling, a gift of God. But no one was permitted to touch me. I now belonged to the almighty Queen Xenon, ruler of Saturn's subterranean sphere. Xenon charged exorbitant prices for a peep at the precious Earthling to her planetary citizens, 99.999999 percent of whom were female and all of whom were dying to see me. Some women gave their entire life's savings for a glance at the cradle. I had more admirers than the man in the manger.

The vast majority of Saturnian women had never been fertilized, because men were so extremely rare. The planet had experienced an epidemic of gynecologic involutionary syndrome which prompted widespread voluntary oophorectomies. Some of the women had experienced many reincarnations and were still denied the experience of sexual intercourse through scores of galactic lifetimes. Women were produced asexually, through exposure of Xenon's ovaries to the hot springs of Saturn's inner core. Gamete workers emerged from her rectum like little brown nuggets.

I was locked in a room together with a few select members of the aristocratic female elite, all of whom were waiting for the opportunity to have me suckle from their nipples. They begged their supervisor, who guarded my crib, to permit them to lower their breasts to my mouth for a chance to suckle. Some would even sacrifice their lives afterwards for the occasion. Asexual life was terribly boring and alienating.

Shortly after the peep show tickets sold out Xenon made it known that she was determined to have me all to herself and ended the show prematurely. She would have the endless pleasure of holding the poor orphan in her arms, cleansing my skin with her antiseptic tongue, stimulating my developing brain with a magic mucus, so I could be the supreme, all-knowing genius of the solar system, capable of creating and cataloging a system of knowledge in an afternoon, an effort which would take civilizations the time of their cumulative existence, before the Great Implosion would wipe the remains of their planet to a fine precipitate. Yes, I would aspire to be the most brilliant child of the universe and would have the opportunity to visit other civilizations. I would live forever until I decided that it was time for me to die and even then I would always have the chance to be reborn.

Xenon kept me under close surveillance in her chambers, which were sealed off by diamond walls ten feet thick, impervious to yttrium radiation, laser beams or other primitive weaponry threatening her inner domain. Her diamond walls were polished by multitudes of slaves, who were subject to her system of torture and execution. One day after waking up from a nap I was forced to witness her ugly methods. She picked up an unruly slave and squeezed out her intestines by enscissoring her abdomen between her calves. Xenon's legs were so powerful that it took only a few seconds for the slave to lose consciousness.

Queen Xenon had an endless pool of slaves. She kept the person's spirit alive to be channeled into more productive uses and fed the macerated flesh to her best workers. There was an endless renewal of life. She wanted to breed a certain percentage of insubordinates predestined to rebel, who would be eaten by her other slaves. Biocomputational advances provided her with slaves who could work twenty-four hour shifts. Her genetic program provided an endless supply of woman-hours. There were no lunch breaks.

Silvana moaned when she heard me cry out in my sleep. I looked over to her side of the bed and wanted to touch her. She lay motionless, absorbed in her own profound dreams. There would be no more nights of unfulfilled fantasies.

Unicellular Ooze

I woke up at dawn to the smell of swamp gas rising from the industrial meadowlands. The pair of flannel pajamas which I had borrowed from her husband were encrusted with the remains of a wet dream.

Silvana was lying comfortably on her back. The weight of her supple body was absorbed by the quilt-covered mattress. Her legs were spread apart. Reaching over to her side of the bed, I stroked the stubbly skin around her armpit. Sweat exuded from her axillary glands as she shuddered momentarily, before rolling over into her pillow and immediately falling back to sleep. Behaving like a real gentleman, I let her sleep longer so she would feel refreshed upon awakening. I didn't want to rouse her from her profound dream, lest she were dreaming of me.

Gradually, the morning sunlight filled the room with a lambent yellow glow. Resting on my back in a coiled embryonic posture, I tried to sleep, but couldn't and soon found myself perspiring and growing bored. I pulled myself out of bed and slipped off my pajamas. Standing naked in front of her full length mirror, I admired my slender body. I longed for the lost narcissism of childhood, the prepubital state when impotence was of no concern.

My chest is hairy enough for her to consider me a man, not just a boy, I thought. I've been sleeping with a woman, the most beautiful woman in the universe.

What are you talking about, pecker, you could barely keep it up. Throw in the towel, Lipschitz, and let Silvana find a man who can really satisfy her.

I swung my fists wildly in front of the mirror, hoping that a quick uppercut would knock out my pejorative superego, whose familiar face shadowed me wherever I went.

Silvana rolled over on her side, yawned, stretched for a second and shuddered. She looked so robust and wholesome, like meat and potatoes. The sight of her flaccid underarms aroused me and my organ stiffened and grew purple. Her ghost-white breasts leaned against her translucent nightgown. I wanted to slurp my tongue around her ear and waken her to the sound of Rice Krispies, but she was sleeping so peacefully that I couldn't possibly waken her. An abrupt awakening might make her grouchy for the rest of the morning.

Better let her sleep, Jerry, I reconsidered. Wasn't it a beautiful sight to watch her conicals swell and her nipples turn as bright as cherry licorice? At least my touch turned her on.

As I flirted with the sight of my emaciated body I wondered how it would feel to hold myself, Sweet Narcissus, in my arms. My lips were no longer chapped, but were moist and full. I knew that I was a good lover. My affectionate kisses would make her skin feel younger than any two week vacation in the Caribbean her husband could afford to give her. After awhile I grew bored with myself and walked over to her closet to inspect her private possessions.

The closet door was open. Photograph albums were stacked on the top shelf. There was not enough natural light penetrating through the closet for me to recognize any of the smaller objects on the shelves. The scent of her perfume drew me deeper inside. My nose brushed against her spring dresses and cotton blouses.

Surely your husband clears at least four hundred grand a year, after taxes, from setting broken bones, not to mention payoffs for providing false testimony to insurance companies. I'll bet he gives you all the money you need to appease your stylish tastes. And if you need a new leopard coat for next winter, he can always finance it through your medical Christmas club. Now I understand why you were never pressured to go into private practice. You could live like a queen just on his monthly dividends, without touching his massive portfolio of stocks and real estate. I'm really glad that your husband takes good care of you, Silvana. You deserve the best treatment.

At the end of the row I felt a starched labcoat and held the insignia to the light. After several squinting attempts I could discern the words on the patch: University Hospital, Senior Resident.

I groped aimlessly along the overhead shelves, feeling nothing but dusty boxes. I opened one of the boxes and peered at the black velvet hat inside. She must look gorgeous in an Easter outfit, I considered, before returning the box to the shelf. What nice, wholesome, Christian values she maintains. Oh Silvana, my Medical Easter Bunny. I accidently knocked over a bottle of perfume and peeked out of the closet to see if the noise had woken her up.

She growled, but remained asleep, apparently absorbed in a dream. I hope that you're dreaming about me, Silvana. Her long fingers were curled against her hips, within easy reach of an anxious clitoris.

Crouching down on my haunches, I noticed a shoe rack hung below the shelf of leather-bound photo albums. The outer row was filled with spring and summer shoes of the finest leather, open-toed pumps and sandals, some with dainty ankle bands. Her shoes had only the faintest smell, as if they had each been worn only a few times. I smelled her wonderful foot odors and became mesmerized by the scent. Perhaps I would study to be her personal podiatrist. No, she would never leave me in the lurch, even if I had a foot fetish. If worse came to worst, I would always be left with an old shoe normally reserved for a Salvation Army dumpster.

I was elated by the thought that there was a hidden realm to Silvana's world of possessions and groped further into her magic wardrobe. I picked up a sandal and rubbed the leather insole along my nose to capture her scent.

Mmmm, your feet smell so good, I hummed, as if savoring a delicious matzoh ball soup, anxious to taste the steaming broth, but cautiously saving my tongue and upper palate from a painful scalding. Let me lick your toes and the spaces between them. I'll bet no man has offered to do that for you. There's no reason to deny yourself this erotic pleasure. Your toes rank among the most sensitive parts of the body—they don't call them extremities for nothing. Just take a foot bath and I'm willing to do anything that will excite you. I am your dutiful son. Let me excite you, mother.

Silvana had since rolled onto her stomach. My penis throbbed at the sight of her bulbous derriere, waiting to be mounted. I wanted to glide my tongue along her Achilles tendon, leading to the small of her back and her spinal cord beyond. Only the greatest lovers could tongue-kiss the entire length of the body.

Perhaps I could tongue-kiss her ass and really show my appreciation for her hospitality. I was thinking about the expression "kissing ass" in its sycophantic denotation. Whoever coined the term had no appreciation of the pleasures of analinguous or salivary proctomassage. It's much more invigorating than a colonic irrigation. Kissing ass is nothing to be ashamed of. People kiss ass every day, only to rise to the top. Perhaps I'll bathe her descending colon with my medicinal saliva. I'll bet no man has ever offered that to her before. Besides, they say it helps shrink hemorrhoids.

Drool poured out of her opened lips and soaked her pillow case. "Ooooh," she yawned, shuddering erotoecstatically, opening her mouth as wide as Rosy, the hippopotamus I used to feed as a kid in the Central Park zoo. She revealed her pink, healthy gums, inviting me into her oral groove before she closed her mouth and fell back to sleep.

Better check out the photo albums before she wakes up for good next time, I thought, savoring a final glance at her ripe buttocks before slipping back to the closet, careful not to make a sound. I made myself feel at home in the forbidden surroundings, as if I had found a warm snug nest in one of her orifices.

I picked up a photo album and held it obliquely to the light. All the faces in the old black-and-white photos were unfamiliar.

On the first page there were four pictures, mounted on black hinges. Silvana was standing on the beach, holding her seven month old baby securely against her breasts. She was wonderfully photogenic, a real beach queen. In her late twenties, she was in the alleged "prime" of her beauty. The date of processing was printed in the margin: the same year I was born. I could have been the fertilized egg drifting down her fallopian tube.

Of course, now I understand why our relationship has been progressing so smoothly. I'm the same age as her son. What a wonderful reciprocal arrangement. She must have had the need to return him to her womb and considered me as a respectable replacement. What a life he must have had as an only child, receiving all of that maternal attention from a doctor. He probably escaped a turbulent adolescence. I'm sure she fulfilled all of his physical and emotional needs. I wouldn't be surprised if she slept with him in the raw before he could ejaculate to prepare him for the lovers' world, so there would be innocence, but no unnecessary embarrassment during his heterosexual initiation.

He must know all the moves by now, that lucky stinker. She was his sexual mentor. Incest is relative to one's needs, but he got his first sexual experience with a doctor when he was thirteen. I had to wait until I turned twenty and until I had undergone a fruitless rectal examination (dillberry-free), stabbed myself in the back and let myself be rejected by scores of middle-aged women, because I was either too kinky or too skinny, or both.

All of a sudden, the sense of jealousy passed. I felt light-headed and free, as if I had finished a clean defecation.

"Dr. Foster," I whispered softly, putting back the album on the shelf and rolling the closet door shut behind me, "you don't realize this, but you cured me of my hang-up with middle-aged women. Now that I'm no longer rejected, I have nothing left to fulfill, with the exception of getting into medical school."

Approaching her bed, I wetted my lips and tasted a film of mucus on my teeth. Since I had an abominable case of halitosis, I decided not to kiss her on the mouth. Instead, I lowered my tongue to her calf. She twisted her leg restlessly, but wouldn't let herself be roused. Resting my chin on the back of her knee, I peered north to the delicious inner thigh. I licked the salt exuding from her sweat glands as eagerly as a young doe. Using total athletic control, I slowly snaked my tongue along the back of her thigh, in a spiraling motion, shooting warm flashes up her spine. She groaned, looked back to see me licking her thighs and fell back to sleep.

"You don't mind if I rest my head on your buttocks Humpty Dumpty," I mumbled when her eyes opened briefly.

"No, not at all," she said groggily, drowning her words in a yawn. "Just let me sleep a little more. I had to treat seventy patients this week and you're number seventy-one. MMmmmmmmmn," she growled, shaking her hips from side to side and rubbing her lips along the pillow before burying her head in the covers.

My vision was focused on the crack between her two cheeks. Why not a little anal intercourse, I considered. I'm as clean as a whistle.

Oh no, perhaps it's too early in the morning for a tight squeeze. She may not be interested.

My organ turned into a broomstick. I almost had a paroxysmal priapism. "I can't help it," I said urgently, but softly. "It's just that I desire you so badly after I konked out early last night. You've got to invite me inside and then my depression will be cured for good."

"What?" she asked dreamily, wondering what had roused her from sleep.

"I said that I want to be a part of you. I want to look over your shoulder and then live under your skin. Don't start taking advantage of me now Silvana, when I have early-waking insomnia. You've got no right to sleep while I lie uncontrollably awake. Don't torture me. Relieve my suffering. Come, take me into your arms. Let it all be part of one continuous evening of ecstasy," I cried, and tasted a tear dripping down my cheek.

My throbbing penis pushed its head through the crack in her rump and made her shudder uneasily. Boy am I in shape, I thought. Does anyone want to play volleyball? Look at those fantastic biceps of mine, darkened by a fresh supply of red blood cells, en route special delivery from my spleen. Don't you prefer a strong, lean guy like me to a baby-faced fatso?

I stretched my legs apart so that my knees rested on her thighs. My arrow was ready to be launched. I'm going to push out the impurities from her descending colon, I thought, positioning the crown of my penis in the deep fold of her *popess.*

Her sphincter muscles hugged my penis tightly as it surged into her rectum. My thoughts wandered to the time when she examined my ass so thoroughly in her office at Hastings. I was thrilled that we each had the chance to inspect each other's rectums, even if her probe was more hygienic. I swung my hips from side to side and pushed. Suddenly her grip became alarmingly tight. I was concerned that the skin of my penis wouldn't be able to breathe, so I yanked it out without a moment's notice.

"Aw shucks," she said with a sigh of disappointment.

"Wait a minute, honey," I said breathlessly when I saw her rubbing her fingers over her clitoris. She was lubricating her vagina with a wad of saliva. "Let me wash it off first. I don't want to infect you with a feculant organism. What would your husband say if you developed vaginitis? Some of those fecal strains are resistant to the full spectrum of antibiotics. Dashing into the bathroom, I scrubbed my genitals with hexachlorophene soap until my pubic hairs were shining like the mane of a black stallion.

"Come inside, my baby," she groaned smugly, spreading apart her legs. She looked up at the ceiling while I pinned her elbows against the mattress with my knees as she had done to me on the night of my self-inflicted wound.

"Don't look so serious," she said soothingly, and planted her hands on the small of my back. I was terribly excited when she stroked the crevice of my emaciated derriere with quick little butterfly touches. "You have such cute gluteus maximi, Jeremy. Just like a little monkey." My eager chest closed in on hers. My penis dangled anxiously above her vagina.

"Wait a second, hon. Let me get the cream. It's on my night table. Get it for me, dear," she demanded and kissed me on the forehead. I found the small silver tube buried under a crinkled tissue. Dr. Foster could easily afford to push out the cream from the top of the tube because she received an endless supply of physicians' samples.

I handed her the tube and looked the other way while she smeared the spermicidal salve around her private grotto and wiped the remains on her satin sheets. Leaning over her, I teethed on her flaccid underarm and searched for a choice cut of tissue. I sucked on the juicy patch voraciously, as if it were her breast. My eye teeth tugged along the loose muscle, pretending to bite. I moved on to the site of her ruby nipple. Only I could reactivate the lactiferous ducts of her mammary glands and make her breasts leak. She would give me the hot, vitamin D enriched milk that I needed to insure the healthy development of my growing bones.

I loved the feel of being in her clutches. She could bruise the temporal lobe of my brain, by using her elbow as a vice, and paralyze me forever, if I ever again tried to force her to do anything against her will.

"Oh Jeremy," she panted, cradling my head in her arms. "I don't know what I'd ever do without you. You've made me feel young again. Promise me that you'll drop by more often, but call first."

"Of course I will, dear. This is my dream come true. Never again will I see you in the health center, that reminder of past frustrations. Now we have finally achieved a therapeutic alliance. You have filled the void of loneliness and isolation. For the first time in my life I am happy to be alive. As long as your husband continues to take off for weekend conventions we're in business. Let's make love now, Silvana. I can't hold off much longer."

"Oh, you sad precious thing," she whimpered, tickling my bellybutton.

I felt that as a man I had to take command, but I was unsure of my technique from the conventional mount position without assistance from below. I tried to remember a diagram from *A Westerner's Guide to the Kama Sutra* I had found while browsing through the ob-gyn shelves in the medical library. It was a shame that I lacked navigational ability.

She raised her lips and spread her legs apart, revealing her orifice in order to give me a better view for vaginal penetration. My penis groped around the familiar terrain, but couldn't find the appropriate hole. Slipping her hands under my thighs, she finally lost patience with my boyish ignorance and guided my missile between her labiae. Once I was securely inside, she inhaled deeply, whimpered, and massaged my testicles with her inner thighs.

How cozy can we be, I thought, pushing deep into her womb, until she quivered spasmodically. Her vaginal pulsations intensified. I poked three-fourths the length of my penis back and forth at different angles. My rhythmic pulses were syncopated, in 6:8 time, allegretto, with all the harmonic underpinnings.

Resting my entire weight on her body, I relaxed for ten seconds, released a preliminary drop of proteinacious fluid and geared myself for the impending implosion. She shook her hips, her way of telling me down below that she understood what was going on. As a physician she had developed a "feel" that let her predict the approximate time of discharge by sensing the spurts through the urethral canal. Her uterine detectors were more accurate than a seismograph stationed along the San Andreas fault. My armpits hosted a putrid colony of anaerobic bacteria. She was hardly turned off by my scent and kissed me up and down the ribcage and in the pockets under my arms.

Her thighs sucked me inwards and expelled me rhythmically in a cyclical chain of thrusts. Wrestling with her, I tried to exercise my virility by tying her wrists to the bed. We kissed each other passionately, like two iguanas lashing their forked tongues in the dust of the Mojave desert. I mounted her again and slipped my hands under her hips to accentuate the force of my thrusts.

In my skin's eye, I was bequeathed retirement in the realm of numbness. The heat of her body moved me transplacentally inside the lips of her labia majora, until I was buried snugly and securely within her cavernosum. She was a massive respirator, with a tidal air capacity large enough to supply enough oxygen for her baby and herself.

When I felt our bloodstreams fuse I tried to imagine her thoughts: We are experiencing the blissful reflexes of sexual arousal. I am in the waning stage of life. This young man has his whole life ahead of him. He has made me feel young again. No more hot flashes. There's nothing unethical about our affair. We've simply realized our desires and I have served my profession well. Sex with me is certainly better for me than a prescription for Qualudes.

"Jeremy, Jeremy, I love you, I love you," she cried in cadence with her pelvic contractions. "Promise me that you'll stay with me all day long," she pleaded, flipping me over on my back in a quick jerk, assuming the aggressive position for the first time. She wrapped her legs around my shins with the strength of an anaconda and pinned me on my back with a mean scissor kick. A wrestling coach might have called it a two-point reversal.

"Don't worry, I'm still with you dear," I whispered in her ear, licking the waxy surface. My salivating kisses must have made a crackling sound in her inner labyrinth, a cochlear crunch, like Rice Krispies in milk, resonating through her tympanic membrane. I bet it was the loudest kiss she had ever received, but it was soft and creamy too, like Land O' Lakes butter. With my tongue trilling like a flutist I initiated a fifteen second orgasm, lasting three times longer and feeling six times as intense as any she could ever have experienced with her husband. So I chose to believe.

Pumping the fluids through my vas deferens, I wondered, Jeremy, what's the difference if you come now? None whatsoever. She whimpered like a cocker spaniel puppy as I issued my innermost reserves of semen, over twenty milliliters of cultured yoghurt. Millions of spermatazoa, all relishing their fleeting slice of life, crashed against her diaphragm. How many flagellate cells would survive contact with her spermicidal salve and unite with her ovum? None at all. She sprayed them all with vaginal napalm until they were sterile, ennucleated genomes.

I suddenly heard an unfamiliar sound of footsteps coming up the driveway. "Christ, who is that?" I asked, releasing my ever-shrinking penis.

"I don't know. The paper boy was paid yesterday." She sat up against the brass bedboard, her index finger tapping pensively against her lower lip. "No one else comes to the door this early in the morning. Well, at least whoever it is wasn't rude enough to induce coitus interruptus. Jeremy, I'm glad you were able to come."

"My pleasure. I'm glad I came too. Besides, holding it back is bad for the prostate. I'm never one to turn down a prostatic digital massage at Hastings."

She sprang quickly out of bed when she heard the key turn in the door and gazed out the window. "Oh my goodness, I don't believe it. My husband's here!" she shrieked, pulling the curtain shut in a sudden, frightful jerk. "Jeremy, quick, get in the closet. Go way in the back and open the door a half inch, so you have some ventilation. Come on, quickly now, out of bed," she cried, waving her arms frantically. "We've got no time to lose!"

A sharp slap on my thigh prompted me to scurry off the bed and hide in her closet. "I know what I'll do," she mumbled, as an afterglow of sex flushed her skin. I'll pretend to be sleeping. Oh goodness, the cream. I almost forgot to put away my vaginal cream." She opened her night table drawer and buried the half-empty tube under a mound of thermometers, both oral and rectal.

Lowering her head to sniff her underarms, she dabbed a few drops of cologne around her shoulders, breasts and crevices to hide the scent of sweat, sex hormones and the other glandular secretions exuding from her ducts, which her husband would have recognized immediately. After thirty seconds of phrenetic activity she closed her eyes dreamily and mummified her body in the satin sheets. If Alex walked in she would pretend to be fast asleep.

The air inside the closet was stifling with the door shut. I peered at her through the keyhole. I knew that her husband would inevitably intrude upon our privacy, but the thought of his sudden arrival made me pound my fists against my chest in frustration. If only we could share our body heat for a few hours and recuperate from our orgasms and enjoy the afterglow.

Poor Silvana was forced to retreat within her cocoon while I stood watch to protect her from the sharp talons of predatory birds flying overhead. Don't be afraid, little wing. My butterfly will crack through her paper shell and flutter her chrysalic wings—to celebrate the joys of life. But her husband will think that it's only a common moth which flew in from the garden. He'll swat her dead against the wall, only to feel guilty for the rest of his life when he finds out that it was Silvana, incarnate.

"Silvana, hon . . . I'm home," he called from the back porch, slamming the screen door behind him. She dind't respond, but rubbed her nose in the down-feathered pillow, pretending to be absorbed in a profound sleep. "Honey, are you here? I've got a surprise for you." My stomach felt hollow. The floor creaked with each successive step he took. I was afraid that if he found me undressed with his wife in the bedroom he would take the law into his own hands. As a surgeon he would cut off my fingers Saudi

Arabian style, swiftly and mercifully, but without anesthesia, and kick me out of the house with a shoe to my coccyx, leaving me crippled from the waist down. Then I could retire at Hastings for the night.

He reached the landing of the staircase. My eyeball pressed eagerly against the keyhole. Suddenly the door handle turned and the other Dr. Foster stepped inside the bedroom. The scent of a competitive male odor exuded through his worsted suit.

"Oh, I'm sorry, hon," he said affectionately, leaning over her bed and stroking her cheek with his pink, hairy fingers. "I didn't know you were sleeping. I thought I heard you talking on the phone."

"No dear, it must have been your imagination. Unless I was talking in my sleep. Alex," she yawned, blinking her eyes rapidly as if she had just awakened, "what are you doing home so early?"

"But I'm sure I heard you talking . . . "

"Don't trouble yourself, dear. I must have been talking in my sleep. Mmmn, and it was such a nice dream."

"What were you dreaming about?"

"Oh, we were celebrating our Silver Anniversary. And all of our friends were there to honor us. Alex, I love you so much."

"I love you too." He leaned over and kissed her cheek. The moist tip of her tongue crept into his mouth.

Damn it, I thought, why does she have to do this to me; cock-teasing *shikse*.

"Well Alex, I may as well get up now and fix you breakfast," she whispered groggily. She sat up against the bedboard and sighed wearily. "Could you heat some water and make me a cup of coffee, dear? I'll be downstairs in five minutes." Looking at the digital alarm clock she pretended to be stunned that it was only eight o'clock in the morning. "Alex, what happened to your seminar?" she asked incredulously, pulling her legs out of bed and covering them with her nightgown.

"Oh, it's those damn labor unions. The hotel employees turned off the electricity after we used our own projectionist to run the A.V. equipment and wouldn't allow us to reconvene. Since we couldn't book another hotel and the turnout was poor anyway we cancelled and I took the first flight out of Philly. I really don't care as long as I get my CME credits."

"That's too bad," she said sympathetically, brushing her hand against her shoulder in light, teasing strokes.

"Well anyway, I'm glad I'm home. Nice to see you dear." He put his arm around her back, bent over and kissed her cheek. Silvana reciprocated with a dry, formal kiss on his mouth. She buried her face in the pillow and covered her shoulders with the electric blanket, shying away with a low-key snub.

"Get your fucking paws off my girl," I squeaked, my clenched teeth muffling the sound.

When Silvana heard the first sound she cleared her throat with a raspy cough to divert his attention. "Oh Alex," she said, facing him directly for the first time, "just let me get dressed. I'll cook you breakfast in just a minute. You can read the Sunday paper in the meantime. I saved the funnies for you, hon."

"That's awfully sweet of you dear, to cook me breakfast on your day off." I knew then that he was proud to be back in his castle.

Seething with rage, I was ready to roll open the door and attack him with a heavy coat hanger, but as I stood up I banged my head against the overhead bar.

"What was that noise, Silvana? Did you hear that?"

"It must be the mice. I told you to call the exterminator. Why do I have to do all the household chores? That's a man's job, anyway."

"Because my practice is busier than yours."

"Must you be so infantile. You don't even clean up your own mess. It's enough that I have to cook you breakfast every morning. And your poached eggs must be timed just right or you become irritable. As a doctor you should learn to be self-reliant. Your mamma must have spoiled you terribly."

"That's telling him Silvana," I squeaked.

"Hey, there's that sound again. Didn't you hear that? I think I'll check it out, and bring a broom while I'm at it," he said heroically, taking a step in the direction of the closet.

"One moment, honey," she said fondly, tugging his arm. "Let's make up and kiss." She kissed him on the side of the mouth and squeezed him tightly. He hugged her awkwardly, pawing at her breasts.

"That's better. Now give me two minutes to get dressed and I'll be right down to fix your eggs. Would you like them served on a slice of toast?"

"Yes, on whole wheat."

"Of course, I only serve you the very best. Now I'll be down in a minute."

Silvana nearly choked with a coughing fit to distract her husband. I rubbed my sore scalp and felt a crust of blood coagulate on my scalp. A dull pain throbbed across the right side of my skull. I felt claustrophobic in the cramped quarters.

Pushing myself up on my haunches, I groped through her dresses, feeling the layers of soft fabric: luxurious silks and rayon blends. In the last row, behind a valise, I unzipped a mothproof hanging bag and dug my fingers through her furs. The first fur felt like Persian lamb bleating under the shears. The next coat had the texture of Russian sable. Next in line was a mink coat with a satin inner lining. But this was only the beginning of her immense wardrobe. As I groped further down the row, I slipped my arms through the sleeves of a leopard coat. She helped keep the Tanzanian poaching industry alive. I coiled up in the fur like a cobra in a basket, ready to sink my fangs in Alexander's flesh and release my neurotoxic venom into his bloodstream.

The leopardess carried me transplacentally into Silvana's womb and let me drift into a deep sleep with dreams so sensuous and pleasant that I would never want to wake up. I was her endangered species. The sound of hurried footsteps walking towards the closet did not make me stir.

Silvana rolled open the closet door and found me lying peacefully on the dusty floor. She lifted my head and examined the large bump on my skull. Scattered drops of blood caked my hair, but she could discern that the wound, like my previous gash at the train station, was only superficial. I tried to pull myself off the floor, but was too lazy to stand up.

"Jeremy," she asked in a motherly tone, "are you all right? I can see you hit your head. Come out here, you poor fellow and let me take a look at your boo-boo under the light!" She tugged my arm gently while I rested limply on the floor and pretended to be in greater agony than the bruise on my head could reveal. Slipping both arms under my back, she lifted me completely off the floor and carried me to her bed.

I remember seeing a high-intensity flashlight shining into my eyes and waking up to the sight of her beautiful hazel eyes. Now she was Dr. Foster again, the fine woman doctor who took sickness so seriously and did everything she could to bring her patients back to health again. She lifted my head gently and inspected my wound closely. Then she soaked a cotton ball in alcohol and squeezed it above the gash. I savored the antiseptic sting and knew that I was in good hands.

When the procedure was completed I rolled over towards her night table and found several locks of my Jewfro hair lying on top of her red appointment book. When I touched the sore part of my scalp I felt a bald patch around the area of the abrasion and realized she had cut the hair from my scalp to prevent infection. Perhaps she had saved these kinky locks to remember me by, to twirl in the night when her husband wasn't looking.

"Now," she said abruptly, "as difficult as it may be for you to accept my instructions, I'm going to have to get you out of here before my husband finds out that there's an unwelcome guest in the master bedroom. Throw the pajamas in the hamper and put on your clothes. I've decided to keep you temporarily in my son's room. Now that Tim's away at college there's no reason for Alex to go into his room. As soon as the coast is clear I'll give you the signal for escape—three sharp taps on the door. Just walk quickly and quietly down the steps, walk out the front door and before you know it you'll be out on the street."

"Out on the street? I don't want to be left alone out there. Where do you think I've been all this time? Out on the street with the medically indigent. You have a professional responsibility to let me stay here with you until I'm fully recovered."

"Shh, Jeremy." She was flustered by my ill-timed rebelliousness and was rapidly losing patience. "Don't speak so loud or my husband will hear us and then we're both in the soup."

"But I have to be with you."

"I want to be with you too, my little dumpling. You have to keep your voice down. Alex already thought I was on the phone when he barged into the house."

"But my head hurts. I may have suffered a mild concussion, possibly a subdural hematoma. I can feel the clot forming. Do you want me to collapse on the sidewalk? What will the neighbors say when I fall flat on my face in front of your house? The Fosters are blockbusters. I live over three miles from here. I'll never make it without you. You're my attending physician. According to the rules of the hospital you're required to sign a release and escort me out the front door in a wheelchair. Now where are the forms? Nurse!"

"Just take it easy, Jeremy. You'll be all right. You only banged your head on a wooden bar. I know it hurts, baby, but we're in a tight squeeze. Listen Jeremy," she said deliberately, pausing to kiss me on the forehead. "Everything will be fine. Just make an appointment to see me at Hastings so we can plan our next engagement."

"But it will take at least three weeks before I can get an appointment. There's a waiting list a mile long to see you. You're the most popular physician on campus. Silvana, you still don't understand. I respect you. I admire you. I need to be with you all the time. I need to live under your skin. Is it wrong for a patient to love his physician? Every hour between now and the time I can schedule an appointment will be excruciating. Without you beside me I'll never catch a wink of sleep. I've got to see you sooner, or I'll plunge into an irreversible depression. Can you carry the burden of precipitating the suicide of one of your favorite patients?"

"Well if you can't wait for an appointment," she sighed, "then see me in the walk-in clinic on Tuesday morning."

"How can you be so callous? Look, I don't want to be a pain in the ass, but I really want to see you soon. I'm in love with you. Let's escape together. Let's be pragmatic and devise a compromise. I've got an idea.

Why don't you knock three times on your son's door, just as you had planned and I'll dash out of the house. So far, everything's the same, right? But once I reach the street corner I'll call you up on the phone and pretend to be the nurse at Hastings. Then, as the nurse on duty, I'll request that you come over immediately to attend to a medical emergency, namely Jeremy Lipschitz. Once we're free we can go for a morning drive in the country. I know just the place."

"Jeremy, this sounds awfully familiar." She winked at me knowingly, inferring that she was fully cognizant of my procedure to lure her from her nest to treat my self-inflicted wound on that cold, raw evening back in December. "That's right. Not a bad idea at all. We'll meet at Hastings. Now that I think about it, it's a wonderful idea," she said proudly, stroking my cheek. "And then," she chuckled under her breath, "I must be sure to tell Alex that it's a severe emergency so we can have the rest of the morning and early afternoon to ourselves. I just hope he doesn't call Hastings. Now tell me, Jeremy, where do we stand? Just name the time for us to meet at Hastings."

"No Silvana, not at Hastings. We've already spent far too much time there together. How about a change of scene? Let's try something more romantic. How about meeting me at Sal's Pizzeria. Everything's cool as long as you keep a straight face and make your story consistent. When you're on the phone just carry on a simulated conversation and walk out of the house with your little black bag. When you drive up to Sal's I'll come up to meet you. You know where it is." She nodded agreeably, but her vacuous stare was plagued by uncertainty. I clearly needed to reassure her. "Don't worry dear. I won't eat any pizza in your car or spill olive grease on your vinyl interior."

"What are you talking about, Jeremy? Maybe I'd like to have some pizza myself. You think I'm so square that I won't eat a slice of Sicilian?"

I was thrilled to see her fight with me like a serious girlfriend. She sighed, tapping her index finger against her temple as if thinking up a prescription. "Why don't you order a large pie, Neopolitan will do, with mushrooms, peppers and extra cheese. Go easy on the tomato sauce. I don't want your skin to break out tomorrow. Unless you want to season the pizza with a little tetracycline. Before we take a drive along the canal, we might pick up some wine. I know a place which is open on Sundays. I'll also pack a couple of joints . . . "

"A couple of joints? You didn't tell me that you get stoned, Silvana. Boy, you sure are the hippest M.D. this side of the Mississippi. Most of the fringe doctors I know shoot up Demerol and third generation anesthetics, but none would condescend to smoke a joint; it's too plebian. That's terrific. I can't wait to turn you on to some *Cannabis indica*. I've got some great shit which I propagated myself from third-generation Thai seeds."

"Quiet Jeremy," she interrupted. "We won't have any pizza, wine, or smoke and we won't be able to take a drive along Canal Road unless you go quickly into Tim's room. Wait there patiently until I give you the signal to leave the house," she scolded playfully, shaking her finger under my nose. "Remember, three taps on the door and you can skidaddle out the front door, faster than you can say Jackie Robinson."

"How about Jonas Salk?"

"What about Jonas Salk?"

"Faster than Jonas Salk?"

"O.K. Just skidaddle out of here, but be patient, dear. It may be a few minutes before the coast is clear. I'm sure Tim has some books in his room that you'll find interesting. I want to be certain that Alex is either in the bathroom or the basement before you go out the door."

"What happens if I have to go to the bathroom?"

"Well, you'll just have to hold it."

"But that's so unhygienic. I can't believe that you're willing to sacrifice my health for your marriage."

"Look Jeremy," she said sharply, having lost all patience with me. "I don't want to discuss this any longer. If you don't do what I tell you, I promise, I'll never speak to you again."

I took in her threat and nodded obediently. She stroked my back, rewarding my sensitivity and understanding. I responded as predictably as a rat in a Skinner Box probing for the current which stimulated the pleasure center in its hypothalamus. Dr. Foster knew all the tricks of behavior modification and rewarded her loyal subjects with positive reinforcement.

"Dr. Foster, you seem to be a woman who has everything she desires. Why don't you get one of those automatic flush toilets? My parents use them ritually, on the Sabbath. At least I've come upon my anal retentive behavior honestly. Modern Talmudists have determined that pulling down the toilet lever is an act of labor. The more sophisticated gadgets they sell in Brooklyn have a delayed-flush control." She looked at me as if I were completely deranged, but I continued. "That way I could relieve myself and escape from the house at the same time, without drawing attention to myself. The temperature of fresh urea is about ninety-eight degrees Fahrenheit. The flush mechanism is activated by any change in temperature or in the turbidity of the water."

"Jeremy, you surprise me. That's disgusting! My word, you really do have an anal fixation. Alex would definitely think something was fishy if he found someone's stool floating around the pot. Besides, it's terribly unhygienic."

"Get serious for a second." I spoke sternly, assuming command. "Your husband's waiting for you downstairs. If you follow my instructions, Alex won't hear me leave. I'll call you up as soon as I get to a pay phone and then we'll meet at Sal's pizzeria. I'm going to wait in Tim's room. We'll walk out of the bedroom together. As soon as I'm ready to open the door to Tim's room, I want you to press all your weight against the top step so it creaks audibly and then I'll turn the knob and push the door open. Alex is already suspicious so we can't take any more chances. Got it?"

"Got it partner! You know something, Jeremy, before we go, I just want to say one thing. You have made me feel so young again. I never went in for such mischief since I was a girl. For women, the real sex begins when we're over forty-five. Let's not concern ourselves with the future. Look at us now. Aren't we beautiful together? It makes no difference whether we're twenty-eight years apart. In fact, relationships between older women and younger men are currently in vogue. My father was seventeen years older than my mother, bless his soul. You and I have nothing to be ashamed of. We met each other's emotional needs and . . . " She put her hands around my neck and pressed my head against her bosom.

"That's a given, Silvana. Look, I don't want to listen to any testimonials. Let's just dig each other. You're a very hip lady, a real Renaissance woman."

For the first time I considered the possibility that she would need me more than I needed her.

No, forget it, I coaxed myself. That's nonsense. She's just a great lady and if she asks you to go steady with her, Jer, you'd better say "yes" because it's all part of the Karma you've drawn upon yourself.

"All right, quick, let's go," she laughed, and slapped my behind. "My husband's getting impatient. I have to go down and serve him breakfast."

She pointed to her son's room, waited at the landing until I was in position, pressed her foot down forcefully on the creaking step, and winked at me. I walked into her son's room and closed the door behind me.

A crimson pennant from Harvard was tacked to his corkboard wall. There were photographs from the summer vacation in Maine he had spent with his parents while still in high school and under their protective wing. I immediately disliked the boy, before I had even met him. A pile of books lay on his desk: the unabridged edition of *Webster's Collegiate Dictionary, An Introduction to Fortran Programming, Differential Equations,* and an outdated catalogue of skiing equipment—all weighed down with a jar of dried-out ball-point pens. There were no interesting books on his shelves, only a series of Hardy Boy mysteries, preserved from his youth.

Why does he get Silvana as his mother? It's not fair. How could he have such a blah personality, with her genes and the conditioning power of the home environment. I can't believe it. How did she ever give birth to such a creep? The old man must be something else, polluting her exquisite genetic pool to wind up with such a reject. God, I'm jealous. Why couldn't I be her son?

Feeling disgusted, I rested on her superfirm mattress; it was one notch softer than his parents' posturepedic. I stared at the ceiling and drifted off to forget my misery.

The sound of three short taps on the door roused me. Opening the door, I looked cautiously to both sides before crossing the threshold. When I reached the landing I heard the heavy pressure of water splashing in the kitchen sink. I hurried down the stairs with pitter-patter steps, supporting most of my weight on the banister, and surveyed the latch on the front door. Without looking behind me, I released it, slipped through the door and landed on the front steps.

As I ran down the street I tried to blend in with the Sunday morning joggers. One of her neighbors was out thatching his lawn and eyed me suspiciously. The tall sycamore trees lined lining the street reminded me of my home town. I sprinted down the street until I saw the bright sign in front of Sal's Pizzeria. My heart felt as light as a feather. Soon I would be sinking my teeth into melted mozzarella cheese and skinny dipping with my dear Silvana.

Coke and Pizza

al's Pizzeria was closed when I arrived. Most of the chairs were positioned upside-down on the tables. I saw a faint light behind the counter. The owner was in the back, speckled with tomato sauce. Two sacks of flour were sitting on the loading dock. Walking outside, he pretended not to notice me and dragged a heavy sack of flour behind him.

"I no open until eleven," he said with a heavy accent. Just as he started to pick up the last sack I grabbed the corners of the bag and pulled it into the kitchen by myself. He looked at me in disbelief.

"My good friend, this is a special occasion. It's my first wedding anniversary. My wife will be here in just a few minutes. She simply raves about your pizza and won't settle for anything less. You have the best pizza in the county and the best crust in the state. Please, won't you make a pie for us?"

"O.K., for you I open early," he said, smiling and showing his gold-capped teeth, "but you have to wait ten minutes before I put the pie in the oven. Come inside." He pulled his keys out of his pocket and led me through the kitchen to the dining area. My mouth watered as I walked past a shelf of olive oil tins and shakers of oregano and red pepper. "Have a seat." He pointed to the nicest table for two, in the corner by the window, unlocked the door and turned around the sign in the window to show that his restaurant was no open.

"Thanks so much. Your name is Sal, right? You're very nice. How long has this pizzeria been around?"

"Eighteen years."

"Wow, you've been in business that long. That's fantastic! Most pizzerias die out after five years." He walked back to the kitchen without responding.

When I saw a phone booth next to the juke box I immediately felt at ease. I waited patiently by the table, relaxing for a few minutes before calling up Silvana. Before I could get up he came back to the counter and signalled with attentive eyes his readiness to serve me.

"What kind of pie would you like?"

"I'd like to order a large Neapolitan pizza with mushrooms, half sausage and with extra cheese."

"For here or to go?" he asked, inspecting my scraggly hair and rumpled shirt. With all of the excitement at the Fosters' house I had forgotten to comb my hair and wash up.

"For here, and go easy on the olive oil." My stomach growled so loudly that he probably wondered whether the sounds were his own. I was afraid of getting indigestion from the spicy food. Sal removed a round yeast patty from the refrigerator and flattened the crust with a rolling pin.

It was time to call Silvana. Thumbing through the yellow pages I found the Directory of Physicians and Surgeons. The specialties were listed beside each physician's name, starting with the letter F: Marvin Farber; practice limited to dermatology, Robert Feinberg; psychiatry—child and adult. There were long columns of doctors' addresses, some of whom had multiple practices in different localities. A Foster was squeezed in between a trio of Feldsteins and a Frankenstein; but it was the other Dr. Foster, Dr. Alex. He had two ritzy offices in the suburbs: practice limited to orthopedic surgery. Where the hell was Silvana? Her number wasn't listed under Physicians and Surgeons. Of course, she works for the college. How would I reach her? Before I panicked I recalled from memory the unlisted number on her bedroom phone.

The touch tones registered immediately, due to the proximity of the call.

"Hello, this is Dr. Foster," Alex muttered, in an antiseptic tone. I was totally unprepared to speak to him. I sucked in my stomach in fear.

Why didn't she answer the phone? She was expecting my call. Had she abandoned me? There was no time to dwell on her mistakes. I only had a split second to respond or Dr. Alex would think that someone was making a crank call.

"Hello, Dr. Foster, this is Mrs. Morrison, from Hastings," I squeaked in a feminine falsetto. "Is the other Dr. Foster in?"

He grunted, annoyed that a nurse would call his wife on a Saturday morning and disrupt their weekend.

"Yes, she's here," he said impatiently, "hold on a second, Mrs. Morrison." He dropped the telephone receiver on the table with a jarring thud.

I waited anxiously until I heard the sound of footsteps in the distance. Her dilatory walk annoyed me and made me extremely nervous. Perhaps she was already disenchanted with me. Perhaps if I ever bothered her again she would threaten to expose me as a feeble rapist who wasn't even worthy of incarceration.

"Thank you Alex," she said faintly and picked up the telephone.

"Silvana, what are you trying to do to me? Why didn't you answer the phone? You almost gave me a myocardial infarction. Come and meet me. I'm at Sal's Pizzeria."

"Oh really, does she have a high fever? What, multiple contusions? I'll be over there in thirty minutes. Sterilize all equipment and don't touch her until I arrive." She hung up the phone before I could get a word in edgewise.

Twisting the neck of the phone in my hands I assumed a retarded grin and fought off a nervous shiver. Thirty minutes, I thought. I love it when the timing is right. She'll arrive just when the pizza is hot out of the oven. The sun is so bright and beautiful. Let's take a walk and get some fresh air.

"I'll be back in a few minutes, Sal," I said, stepping out to the sidewalk. Startled by the intensity of the glare I shaded my eyes with my hands.

Inside the pocket of my cotton Egyptian jacket I found two loose joints of Acapulco Gold I had saved for an opportune moment. I could smoke one stick now and share the other one with Silvana on our drive through the country.

Twisting the thin joint between my fingers, I remembered reading a medical report on the immunosuppressive effects of cannabinoid resins on T cells, but I was still determined to raise my blood levels of THC and get high. The joint bobbed up and down like a see-saw between my mumbling lips.

The matches in my pants were worn; most of the flint was scratched away. The first match blew out when I failed to cup my hands around the dying spark. Crouching down against the wall, I lit another match. The tiny flame struggled in the breeze, searching for something to burn so it could sustain itself. It found fuel in the joint and glowed.

Sucking on the paper cylinder, I drew a cloud of burning cannabis into the catacombs of my pulmonary chambers. The THC infiltrated my bloodstream, until it reached my nerve receptors and started to give me a buzz. My eyes teared involuntarily, a combination of joy and conjunctival irritation. I smoked a few puffs casually, breathing deeply between hits. I held the third hit in my lungs for forty-five seconds. There would be other opportunities to get high when Silvana and I could light up together. I extinguished the glowing ember with a wad of saliva, twisted the ends and slipped the long roach in my breast pocket. A car pulled up in front of the pizzeria. The front grill of her Buick Electra smiled at me. Silvana looked dashing in her sunglasses and red kerchief. I was surprised that she had come so soon. Her red hair had regained its natural shimmer since she had washed and combed it before leaving the house. She gave me a coquettish glance through the windshield.

Her eyes tantalized me. I wanted to embrace her in front of the passing traffic, but was afraid she wouldn't risk being seen by a witness who might generate an embarrassing scandal in her place of residence. She parked the car and walked over to the vacant restaurant. As soon as she stepped onto the sidewalk, I overcame all inhibitions and kissed her on the lips. To my surprise she didn't retreat, but held me closely against her bosom. We cuddled each other like two young lovers, oblivious to the world around us.

Sal looked up from the counter where he was grating a slab of mozzarella cheese and eyed us curiously as we walked inside. The pungent odor of melted cheese made our mouths water.

"Five minutes," he said in his heavy Italian accent.

Observing the travel agency posters of the Sicilian coast on the wall I thought of going on a honeymoon to the Mediterranean with Silvana. Couldn't she get away from her husband for a week and tell him that she was attending a convention on student health for general practitioners in Youngstown, Ohio. Perhaps the university would pick up her air fare. Oh, what am I dreaming about, I thought while pressing my hand over her clasped fingers. Just be satisfied that she agreed to go out on a date with you. We're indulging in a nice proletarian pleasure, pizza for breakfast. There's no reason to complain.

"I'm so glad you came," I said softly, looking down at the floor.

"Did you seriously doubt for a second that I would come join you here?" she asked sullenly. Her broad back was turned to Sal, so he could not see our hands touching.

"No, Silvana. I knew all along that you would fulfill your promise to meet me. You have always responded to my emergencies. I mean medical emergencies." She smiled knowingly at my playful airs and seemed convinced that now I was able to keep an emotional distance from her. Obviously, there were complications associated with an extended affair with a married professional on the verge of her ovarian climacteric.

I walked over to the juke box and checked the list of selections. On the lower left-hand column of the lineup I noticed a few jazz records and was amazed to find Bud Powell's "Night in Tunisia." Slipping a pure silver quarter in the slot, I pushed the selector buttons for Bud's tune. The tone arm lowered the worn sapphire needle into the groove. I waited, listening to the hiss of the oven and the sizzling pizza inside. Two seconds later the speaker rattled as the first burst of air blew through the woofer.

"Can I get you a cup of coffee, dear?"

"No, I would prefer a cold drink with the pizza."

"How about a large coke?" I asked eagerly, shaking the loose change in my pocket.

"No, it has too much sugar. I'll have a few sips and a glass of water. On second thought, why don't we share a large coke?" she said smugly, licking her lips in the same sexy manner which had always driven me crazy.

I couldn't wait to sip from the same coke through long plastic straws through which I would taste her breath in the caramel-colored soda.

"Sal," I said walking up to the counter, "I'd like a large coke and two straws, and perhaps a twist of lemon."

"One large coke coming up."

He turned his back to me, reached for a sticky carton under the counter and poured brown syrup into the soda machine. Morning fatigue weakened my brain, but the few hits of marijuana helped me stay alert. Sal paced in front of the oven, waiting to sense the exact moment when the pizza would be ready. I could tell by the way he hesitated before taking the pie out that he was a real professional and wanted it to be cooked just right, especially since it was his first pizza of the day and had the works—extra cheese and lots of trimmings. He clicked his heels together three times and opened the oven door. Then he slipped the wooden spatula under the crust and let the pie slide onto a round aluminum tray. I waited eagerly as he cut the circular blade through the crust and made eight equal slices.

Silvana picked up the cups of coke and water along with a pair of sanitary-wrapped straws and paper plates, while I filled my hands with napkins and pizza. The metal tray absorbed the heat of the pie and burned my fingertips as I hurried over to our table in a leaping dash.

"Mmmn," she hummed erotoecstatically, inhaling the pungent odors. "This smells absolutely delicious. My, you really know how to order, Jeremy. This pizza looks like it has extra cheese." She smiled to herself like an eager little girl. Her eyes moistened with tears of joy.

I cut out a medium-sized slice from the pie, watching the mozzarella cheese slide off the metal tray, where it cooled into a hard gummy mass, perfect for after-dinner tidbits. Behaving like a real gentleman, I placed the first slice on her plate before serving myself.

She grabbed my hands as I was about to dig in and said, "Wait Jeremy! Let it cool first. I don't want to burn the roof of your mouth; it might sting when I kiss you."

"It's good to have a doctor around. I really appreciate the way you practice preventive medicine." She lifted my hand to her mouth and kissed each of my knuckles, stroking the sensitive webs between my fingers with a flexed tongue. The music of Bud Powell lulled me into a sentimental mood and I savored our penultimate moment of privacy. When the pizza had cooled we bit into the unusual breakfast. Our gums were protected by coats of cool saliva. Juicy mushrooms squirmed around our palates and became entangled in a blanket of green peppers.

In my stomach's eye, Silvana and I were so close to one another that we shared a common alimentary tract, like a Siamese gorgon, supplementing each other's digestive juices in the event of an acid-alkaline imbalance. My younger organs would help her achieve homeostatic rebound whenever an ailment caused her pain and would also give her the regenerative power to clone new organelles, replacing cells sloughed away through the aging process. She could even bear another child, as a senior citizen. I would give her five years of my life so she could practice medicine and serve mankind for five years longer. Our endorphins blended beautifully along joint opium receptor sites. I would even give her my left kidney if she needed a transplant donor. That would be my life-saving sacrifice. Don't tell me that my thinking is primitive. Abraham was ready to sacrifice his own son after he was tipped off by a Bedouin that an angel would intercede at the last second. I was just looking after my mother.

Silvana wetted her napkin with her tongue and wiped the dried tomato sauce off my mouth. The cleansing feel of her saliva reminded me of the times my own mother tied a bib over my shirt and cleaned my mouth with a moist facecloth. It was great to have someone else take care of all my bodily needs. If I could only find a wife who would let me infantalize twenty-four hours a day and return to the warm, unicellular feel of embryogenesis. But what I really needed was a mother who would clean me with her own spittle and stimulate the meningeal linings of my cerebrum, so I could develop precociously into a normal American boy. But how could the son of German Jewish refugees assimilate into the *Goyische* world of Howard Johnsons and emerge without major neuroses?

"Shall we go now?" I offered her my hand.

"Yes, Jeremy, I think it would be wise," she said, squeezing my hand tightly. "I'm afraid that we can't spend too much time together today. The hour glass is emptying rapidly. Alex will call Hastings if I'm not back in four hours. I told him that I would be away for at least the rest of the morning and covered for myself by telling him that I had to make several calls at the girl's dormitory and the county hospital. Sometimes he can be so obstinate, demanding that I send all of my serious cases to the emergency room by ambulance. That takes the challenge out of medicine completely. My contract states that I'm not required to perform sutures of any kind, not even superficial ones, like your self-inflicted wound. That's why my malpractice premium's so low. I only came for you. And now . . . " She winked at me and rubbed her hand over my itchy scar. "I'd like to take you on a trip to the reservoir, before dropping you off at your rooming house." Her commiserating eyes communicated a silent understanding of my frustration. This was the gift of empathy. I knew that she had no intention of prolonging a romance beyond a fleeting night and a morning, because it would eventually crush me. Silvana was still my doctor and only wanted the best for me. Soon enough I would grow out of my adolescent turmoil and find a Jewish girl, a Naomi Goldberg with a rich daddy who could offer me the fruits of a permanent relationship and bear gifted children.

She followed me out the door and pressed a hand against my back. I opened the car door, hopped in the front seat and buckled the seatbelt. After starting the car she turned on the radio to a bouncy A.M. station playing a song by the Strawberry Alarm Clock.

"Jeremy, open my pocketbook and take out my cigarette case." Her request startled me. I had almost forgotten her promise to smoke with me. Smoking a joint would serve as a covenant of good will. The thought of injesting illicit drugs with my attending physician made me wonder whether her marijuana was treated with angel dust. Unclasping the latch of her black purse I groped along the satin lining until I felt the silver case.

"Is this case a family heirloom?" I asked.

"No, I picked it up at an auction," she said impatiently, tapping her foot lightly on the power brakes as the car rolled down the steep incline leading to the bridge to Middletown. "Come on Jeremy, don't you want to get high? Light the joint, already!"

Unclasping the latch, I looked disbelievingly at a row of thick, but tightly rolled joints, all of which were stamped with a federal seal: Controlled Substance—For Experimental Use Only: DEA# 563-421.

"Well what do you think of them, Jeremy? You're the expert when it comes to dope. I've known all along that you were a heavy user . . . smelled it on your breath every time you came to the clinic. And I can smell it now. Perhaps you can evaluate the potency of these joints. I picked them up at N.I.H. last summer. They were grown at the University of Mississippi in a fenced-off field patrolled by hungry dogs. Linnaeus would have classified them as *Cannabis americanus*."

"Well, what do you know, Mississippi green—the home grown equivalent of Maui Wowie and Sonoma Coma. The Feds really know how to roll a number." I picked out the thickest joint in the case, untwisted the end and sniffed the special variety of marijuana grown in the temperate zone.

Stopping at the red light, she leaned over to my side, opened the glove compartment and removed a gold lighter buried under a pile of road maps.

I wetted the joint so it would burn more evenly. She struck the flint and held the flame to the end of the joint. The first puffs were smooth-tasting, less harsh than any other dope I had ever tasted. Blue threads of smoke clouded up the front window and wafted above the dashboard. When the light changed she pinched the joint with two fingers and cupped it in her hands while keeping her eyes focused on the traffic.

She had amazing bi-hemispheric control—beyond the hand-eye coordination of the greatest basketball star. I had never seen her look so beautiful as when she brought the joint to her lips. She sipped gently on the smoke before drawing the white cloud into her lungs. Then she held in her breath like a soldier and slowly released the smoke through her lips in a tantalizingly feminine way. A layer of lipstick coated the wet end.

If only she wasn't driving, then we could give each other power hits, blowing smoke to each other from opposite ends of the joint. Only the burning ash and a lump of grass would separate our moist kisses.

She flicked a hanging grey ash out the window, passed the joint back to me and stroked my palm with her pinky finger. I only wanted a short hit so I could concentrate on enjoying the scenery.

We coasted down to the base of the hill and turned right on the freeway which led to the countryside. I grew sad and sentimental as I looked across the river at the familiar roof of a cigar box factory. The sweatshop had been built during the last century and was now an abandoned piece of real estate owned by a multinational bandage manufacturer who made billions during wartime, when blood was shed in quantity. Such were the costs of peace. Pigeons and seagulls perched on the roof before taking off in flight.

When we stopped at the traffic light a cop driving a motorcycle pulled up beside us and scrutinized the profile of the driver with M.D. license plates.

"Keep it down," she scolded, and looked at the joint bobbing between my lips. Before I could react to her order she grabbed the roach, buried it between her thighs, took a quick hit when the cop wasn't looking and extinguished it in the ashtray.

The traffic thinned out as we left the city. We escaped the sprawling megalopolis to a land where there were more trees than smokestacks. She changed lanes, floored the accelerator until she reached seventy-five miles per hour and then held it steadily in cruise-a-matic drive. If the police decided to pull her over she could exercise her medical privileges and tell them that we were en route to the hospital. Eight miles beyond we turned off on the road leading to the reservoir and took in the natural sights of springtime.

The old canal, obsolete for sixty years, was flanked by rows of tall sycamore trees and was now considered a historic landmark. Since I was not driving I could gaze down the banks and watch the people sailing in the bright morning sunlight. A crew of boy scouts dipped their oars in the water in martial time. I was dying to jump out of the car and breathe in the country air.

She turned at the entrance to a dirt road along a stretch of farmland.

"Where are we going?"

"It's a surprise, Jeremy. We'll be there in ten minutes."

"Boy Silvana," I said eagerly, "you're full of surprises today. I'm sure we'll have some fun."

Deigning no reply, she remained silent and secretive. We passed a group of horses grazing in a corral. The road became bumpy. She ignored a sign, Water Company—Authorized Vehicles Only—and drove on. We passed another sign: No Trespassing—Unauthorized Entry Subject to Prosecution. She gripped the steering wheel with both hands. The car wobbled on the rough terrain.

"Silvana, where are you taking me? I hope you're not going to murder me gangland style. Did you have any intention of tying bricks to my feet and dumping me in the lake? I promise that I'll tell no one about our affair."

"I thought you might enjoy taking a little dip, but not as my victim," she said slyly. "I'll bet you look like a tadpole in the water," she laughed, grabbing the crotch of my pants and scratching her nails vigorously up and down the seams of my jeans until I was hard, poised vertically like the arm of the Statue of Liberty.

"You're a pretty nice looking guppy yourself." My fingers groped through her cotton blouse and *schnipsed* her nipples. She was so stunned by the pleasurable sensation that she nearly lost control of the steering wheel. I could smell her feverish desire for me and unclasped her restrictive bra. She regained control of the car and drove around a bend in the bumpy road where the border of the Washington Reservoir came into view. This experience seemed more adventurous than crashing a suburban swim club for WASPs only.

A barbed-wire fence, over ten feet high, encircled the reservoir. The lake stretched for more than five miles. The shortest span across it was over a mile and a half. Three little islands dotted the center of the lake. A green pastel of embryonic buds tasting spring for the first time imbued the air with a regenerative scent.

Dry thistles rustled under the chassis as she drove deeper into the forest. We were making a supreme getaway from our social responsibilities. I rolled down the windows and listened to the silence around us. Fortunately, all of the employees from the water company were off duty on Saturday and the pumping station was closed. The reservoir and most of the surrounding land was deserted except for the trilling birds and insects. She parked on the edge of a clearing behind a row of bushes which camouflaged the yellow car.

Slamming the door behind her, she dashed up to the sloping cliff overlooking the lake and started to peel off her clothes. She hung her clothes over a tree limb, exposing her naked body to me and the warm sun. Her breasts flopped against her supple sternum as she climbed up the rocks with supreme agility.

I ran up to greet her and share her sense of ecstasy. Then I peeled off my socks and unbuttoned my shirt in a desperate flurry to get undressed. The moss-covered rocks tickled my toes. I felt the warmth of her flanks when we bumped buttocks.

Silvana and I strolled hand in hand under the shadows of pine needles, pencilled in between shade and sunlight. A flush of incipient, vegetative growth had just begun as winter resins dissolved in the soil. She pulled me gently by the arm and led me to a large hole in the fence surrounding the lake. Bending over backwards, she pulled herself under the fence, arriving on the other side without a scratch. I was too much of a coward to attempt a similar move by myself, afraid that I might scrape my back against the sharp rocks or be poked in the face by a protruding wire; so I lay flat on my stomach, bit the dust and slid like a skink without a backbone. By the time I pulled myself through to the other side, my body was covered with dirt.

She ran off to the edge of the clearing and leaped in the air joyfully, her feet landing on the moist black loam. Only someone like Silvana, who had a supple body as well as an expert knowledge of medicine, could take care of all her biological needs in the wild. She squatted down on the rocks at the edge of the water, her buttocks resting on a mat of smooth moss. The green carpet rubbed against her flaming clitoris as she swung one leg over the other and kicked backwards to precipitate multiple orgasms.

"Mmm," she growled, and shuddered. "I love the water. Alex rarely gives me the chance to go swimming anywhere outside the YMCA. Come, let's swim out to the islands. This land is absolutely unscathed."

"But Silvana, doesn't the water company patrol the reservoir."

"Jeremy, don't be paranoid. Have no fear, Dr. Foster is here. They know me by name and go along with my eccentric whims whenever I choose to indulge in a swim. It's one of my professional privileges. Besides, I'm a major shareholder of the water company."

"But I'm not as strong a swimmer as you are and I'm out of shape. I doubt if I can swim all the way out to the islands," I whined.

"Sure you can, Jeremy. I've just examined your muscle tone—when we were in bed last night. Consider the rigorous bicycling you did yesterday.

I'm sure that those bandy little legs of yours can lash out in a mean scissor kick in the water. Come on, Jeremy, dive in."

The sound of her command faded as she dove off the promontory. She sailed through the air like a swan, slicing the water in two. Her streamlined body disappeared into the depths of the dark water. I grew gravely nervous when, after thirty seconds, she still had not surfaced for air. I wondered whether she had dissolved herself into nothingness as if I was stuck in a protracted hallucinatory orbit.

Her head shot up suddenly, sending small rippling waves in every direction as she gasped for air. Then she dove under the surface again, releasing clusters of air bubbles at equidistant intervals. I couldn't believe she could stay submerged for so long. Was she real?

Maybe she's half wood-nymph and half mermaid, I thought. She bobbed to the surface, inhaled deeply and spun a reverse flip with the perfect grace of a ballerina capable of choreographing a team of synchronized swimmers. Then she floated on her back and kicked one foot high in the air.

"Catch me if you can," she cried playfully, in a voice which echoed across the reservoir.

Male pride forced me to accept her challenge and try to outswim her. I had already acclimated to the air temperature and geared myself for the initial shock of cold water.

Diving off the rocks, I spread my arms and crashed into the liquid realm. All terrestrial inhibitions gave way to my Piscean libido. I felt like a fish with streamlined fins. Swimming breaststroke underwater, I raced ahead towards my beloved buoy, who was gaining distance on me thirty yards ahead. I sniffed the unique Fosterian scent in the water and flexed my jaws like a hungry barricuda.

She swam circles around me and laughed at the way I was wasting my energy. I suddenly felt a sharp cramp pierce my right lung. The normal concentration of oxygen in my lungs had been displaced by the noxious blend of marijuana smoke and carbon monoxide, which had settled in my innermost alveoli. This, in turn, activated carcinoembryonic antigens, a prelude to a terminal bout with lung cancer or similar malignant neoplasm by the age of forty-five, if I didn't die sooner from unnatural causes. Looking out towards the islands, I nearly panicked at the thought that they were beyond my swimming range. I realized that I was too far from shore to turn around and swim back like a sissy. Yet I had no reason to fear drowning: my attending physician had worked for several summers as a water safety instructor. She would give me mouth-to-mouth resuscitation and pull me back to shore. If only she had been my swimming teacher, I could have made the Junior Olympic Team and developed the broad back muscles of a strapping Aryan youth.

In my mind's eye, I was a toddler swimming a doggy paddle in a desperate attempt to reach the security of Silvana's nurturing body. Every time I tried to grab her arms she stepped back a few inches, so I couldn't cling to her. Just when I was about to panic and sink under water, she dove between my legs and swept me above the surface. She waded across the sandy floor with her gangly legs, her baby on her shoulders, ready for a chicken fight with any sea monster who would invade her territory.

Mom and I devoted the rest of the swim to safe bubble-blowing games in knee-high water. Afterwards, she dried me off vigorously with a terrycloth towel, played with my penis and changed me into my playclothes. I sat down on the blanket and gobbled down a peanut butter and jelly sandwich greedily and then sucked on her breast for a half hour before retiring for my afternoon nap.

When I looked up I noticed that Silvana was now swimming nearly fifty yards ahead, and I was barely treading water. A flock of ravens hovered above and scanned our bodies as if we were bobbing crusts of bread. Their sharp "caws" reverberated against the cliffs as they flew off towards the islets of Langerhans.

"Let's go, Jeremy. I don't have all day. I have other patients who need me!" she cried playfully, floating motionless on her back for a few minutes to give me a chance to catch up. Soon enough I was within striking range of her fluttering calves. The bright sun warmed my back. The cramp in my lung had disappeared completely. It suddenly occurred to me that I could increase my endurance by swimming on my back. As soon as I turned over, Silvana spun a surface dive directly under me and pinched me playfully on my *toches*. She swam parallel to me and squirted a mouthful of water in my face, teasing me like a friendly sea lion.

Circling around her like an angry shark, I waited to take the counteroffensive. I dove under her, clung to her breast and threatened to take a bite of her underbelly. When she reached for my balls I kicked my legs furiously and resumed swimming with a flurry of backstrokes. Swimming out to the island was the ultimate challenge to my virility, even though swimming was not a sex-specific sport. Pumping my leg muscles as strenuously as the lead oarsman in the Yale-Princeton regatta, I swam on with incredible swiftness as she looked on proudly, obviously pleased by my progress in therapy. An unfamiliar source of energy empowered me with Herculean strength as I swam speedily against the tide.

Watching the cirrus clouds waft in the wind, I wanted to grab the white steam in my fists, but realized that they were only a stream of evanescent vapor. The islands were now close by. A flock of ravens were circling around a water snake. Rolling back onto my stomach, I swam on, watching this tiny pyramidal head and the pattern of waves criss-crossing behind him. We were less than six feet apart, when it suddenly assumed an aggressive position. I could tell by the shape of its jaws that it wasn't a water moccasin. I was determined to reach the island. The snaked zipped away and disappeared from sight.

"Did you see the snake, Silvana?" I asked in a hushed voice, afraid that I might disturb a den of sulky reptiles.

"Boy, that was a beautiful one. I wonder whether it's the nesting season. I've never been so close to a water snake before," she said with the eager curiosity of a field biologist, not flinching in the face of danger. She waded to the waterline and stepped onto the sandy shoal. "Looks like we have the island completely to ourselves."

The lake floor suddenly turned to mud. I stood waist deep in the water. Alginous vines pulled me down. My toes churned the quicksand desperately and dug me in deeper. Silvana returned to the water and pulled me safely to the beach.

I was relieved to find firm footing on land and reached for the branches of a thin silver birth tree. Slivers of peeling bark shimmered in the sunlight. Gazing across the expanse of the island, I saw a broad row of virgin birches with yellow-green buds unfurling. The island was so quiet that all we could hear were the trickling waves and our own breath.

"This place is so beautiful, Silvana, I never knew there was such a large body of unpolluted water in the state. How did you ever find this place? I would think that with all the industrialization there would be no natural preserves left. This has been a great spiritual awakening for me. I never thought that I would be able to swim all the way out to the islands, but you gave me the courage and energy to realize my potential. Now, for the first time, I realized that we only live once. We should make the most of what life has to offer, whatever it's worth. That's all that matters. But back to worldly matters: I must say that the sight of this island is absolutely magnificent."

"Did you see the flora on the island? Only the nicest places are closed to the public. That's why I took you here. I can see that my medicine is starting to work. You're coming out of your depression. There are fossils here from the Stone Age which make our existence seem like a mere speck of time in the history of life on this planet."

We rested on the soft sand, content in each other's arms. She blew into my face and brushed the curls from my forehead. I kissed her eyes and licked the lingering drops from her eyelids.

"I love you Jeremy," she whispered. "You will always hold a special place in my affections."

"And I will always love you, Silvana. Even when we part, my feelings towards you will always transcend positive transference. You are the most beautiful person in the universe. We have to meet again, perhaps in another incarnation, as high school classmates. We can marry and raise three wonderful children, who may grow up to be doctors or dentists or file clerks, whatever they choose to be, as long as they are happy. You will always inspire me with strength. You have infused my body with a magical spirit which has enabled me to realize my superhuman powers."

"Jeremy," she shrieked, pulling my face to her cheek. "Stop speaking nonsense. Feel me! Don't you feel my blood pulsating? You will always know whether what you see is real or imaginary when you feel a pulse beat; it's a basic tenet of medicine. I know that you suffer from hallucinations, but this is no coma within a coma. You swam all the way out to the island on your own. Feel it!"

My eyes measured the span across the reservoir to the shoreline. I was amazed by my amphibious powers. Fresh, oxygen-rich blood filled the long muscles of my legs. Now I was confident of tackling a tribe of Amazons singlehandedly under water. I would gnaw through their constricting limbs before being swallowed up in their benthic realm.

A great blue heron skirted along the water, ignoring the human intruders nearby. Now there were three endangered species on the island. I wanted to apply for an Existence Grant, sponsored by the National Wildlife Commission, in which the sole recipients were condors, bald eagles, whooping cranes, Jeremy Lipschitzes and other rare, winged species. Every week the feds would supply me with a crate of Franco-American spaghetti, and dried fruit, for roughage. I could live out my remaining days as a mere statistic to appease environmental lobbyists. My sole contribution to society would be to provide demographers with the knowledge that I was alive. The heron searched the surface for some movement in the water. Thrusting her beak into the water, she surfaced with a copper-plated fish writhing in the air, and flew off towards the cadmium-laced horizon above the meadowlands.

Silvana rolled over against me, squeezing me closely against her breasts. The aroused pink tip of her breast shivered. I kissed her ear with love whispers. She lowered my head to her breast as if I were her very own suckling.

"I'm afraid that all good things must come to an end," she said glumly, pushing me away gently from her nipple. "It's time we headed back to land. Do you feel rested, so we can swim back?"

"No problem, Silvana. The hard part will be leaving you, and yet I know that it's impossible for us to stay together forever and ever."

"Correct," she interrupted dryly. "After today, it will be very difficult, if not impossible for us to meet again. Sometimes a very brief affair can bring about the most wonderful memories. I think that in the past two days we learned many things about ourselves by risking so much and yielding to our instincts. It's only natural to give in to one's physical inclinations. Most medical scientists would agree. We're only human animals. Soon I will succumb to menopause. You have your whole life ahead of you. And now, Jeremy, it's time we moved on and returned to civilization."

Her words were swallowed in a running splash as she dove into the water and started to swim to shore with a fast-clipped crawl. I stayed two body-lengths behind her and ignored the shallow cramps in my lungs. I could tell by the angle of the sun that it was already well past noon. Perhaps Alex had tried to reach his wife at Hastings; what then? If Silvana were caught lying, I would be held responsible for ruining their marriage.

Silvana accelerated her pace. I was forced to swim faster and faster in order to stay close by. Now I felt that I had more than enough strength to swim back and forth to the island a second time, without stopping to rest. My mind was purified, free of the debilitating neuroses.

Wouldn't it be beautiful, I thought, if neither one of us returned to civilization and the authorities conducted a statewide womanhunt for a prominent missing person. I could just see the headlines. Woman Doctor Abducted by Ag Student. We could munch on the wild berries fruiting in springtime. It was such a bummer to have to return to the everyday world—the monotony of student life, the routine of general practice in a student health center. We needed something more challenging, like survival in the wilderness. What was the purpose of studying biology and medicine if we could never endure independently in the wild? If the temperature ever dipped too low at night we would conserve heat by pressing our bodies together. With our binding love, we could survive the harshest circumstances. We could build a raft and make a weekly trip to town to load up on supplies and buy monthly rations of ravioli.

For a moment I believed that she would be willing to indulge in such a scandalous disappearance and risk ruining her professional reputation for a new romance late in life. Even if they caught us lying together, exposed to the T.V. newsmen, it wouldn't be catastrophic. If anyone doubted her fidelity, she could always double-cross me by saying that this psychopathic student whom she had examined on several occasions, attacked her at gunpoint and abducted her to the reservoir. A doctor's word was as good as gold. Besides, she could always point to a previous incident to corroborate her testimony. But I didn't want to force her into making a lengthy explanation. I was ready to accept her decision to avoid seeing me forever. A cold pocket, bubbling up from the lake floor, broke my contemplation.

Looking back towards the islands, I was astounded to see the enormous distance I had covered in my effortless swim. We were already fewer than a hundred yards from land. The silver birches now were only little matchsticks, shimmering in the sunlight. Silvana slowed her Olympian pace and gave me a chance to catch up with her. I mimicked her graceful breaststroke and felt as if we belonged to the same school of androgenous tadpoles.

The water turned shallow and murky. We waded for a short distance along the rocky lake floor. The gentle undertow tugged against my ankles as I stepped out of the water onto the land.

Silvana ran up to the cliffs and shook off the water beaded on her skin. She picked up my clothes from a branch and dangled them beyond my reach. If she left me naked and exposed in the forest I would be at the mercy of some beer-drinking gay bashers who would creep in at nightfall.

She threw my pants high in the air to the next tree limb, where they became caught around a scraggly branch. The monkey in me was determined to climb the tree. I hoisted myself up the trunk with my arms and legs and grabbed my clothes from the tree limb. Before she could cry Jonas Salk I landed lightly on the ground.

"My, you really are very agile, Jeremy. Why don't you try out for the gymnastics team? You'd be great on the rings and the parallel bars. The university could use an athlete of your caliber."

"I hate intercollegiate sports. Besides, the reverse flip aggravates my migraines. Come on Silvana, stop clowning around. If you say that we have to get back soon then let's go now."

"Since when are you the one who is in a rush to leave? I'd rather stay here, if I had my choice, but circumstances are such that . . . "

"I know, I know, you have to go to the clinic at nine o'clock Monday morning and resume the old routine of playing doctor. So what else is new? It's amazing how time passes so quickly when you're in love. Everything else seems so unimportant. And now that we're going back to town you can pretend that nothing ever happened."

"No, no Jeremy. You mustn't say that. I'll always remember you. You will always be my most special lover. It's just that I've been married for twenty-three years and I have certain responsibilities towards my family. It has nothing to do with the differences in our age."

"I'm not bitter," I said dejectedly, staring down at my navel. "The outcome is consistent with every other event in my life—the same old thing: fantasy, frustration, loneliness and deprivation. But I'll also remember the good moments we had together. The memory of love is a gift which passes through time, transcending temporal phenomena. My feelings towards you will never change, but I think I'd better avoid seeing you at Hastings to avoid a relapse. You're not just another woman doctor. Oh, I don't want to dwell on this any longer. Come on Silvana, it's time to hurry up."

She slipped into her jump suit and tied her kerchief. "I'm ready," she said curtly, jingling her car keys.

"Buckle your seat belt," she commanded as soon as I closed the car door. "Those potholes are very deep and I don't have any room to maneuver if a car comes from the opposite direction." I pulled the constricting shoulder strap across my chest and felt imprisoned, as if I were sitting in a van for the handicapped. She drove over a clump of thistles which tickled the underbelly of the car. A bright red cardinal flew over the lake and disappeared into a pink dot.

Spring was in full bloom. Now that school had ended I would have ample opportunity to go camping in the mountains. She turned off the path and drove for twenty minutes along country roads, delaying the trip back so we would have time to acclimate to the change of scene. Sticking my head out the window, I drank in the fresh air greedily like a dog exposing his jowls to the wind. I knew that in a few minutes I would be stuck in the smog and industrial fumes pouring down cancer alley.

As soon as we reached the highway she accelerated to seventy-five miles an hour, confident of not getting a ticket. I was so physically exhausted that I fell asleep. When I opened my eyes we had arrived at the Arlington bridge, which led to Middletown. I felt the vibrations as the tires rolled over the steel grating and looked up at the landmarks of Fairbanks College. The most conspicuous building was Harding Hall, which looked like a giant flashcube suspended in the middle of rolling hills. Even the turret of Hastings Health Center was visible in the distance.

"Dr. Foster," I mumbled through lazy lips, "I live a block behind the Student Center. You know the Demarest campus."

"I know where you live," she said coldly, as if we had no previous personal relationship to speak of. I knew that she was trying to harden herself against a sentimental resurgence. "Don't forget, your address is printed on the back of your health chart." In the past two days she had succeeded in stripping away all of my auto-debilitating pseudodefense mechanisms. Today I could become a man, more so than when I had been Bar-Mitzvahed.

A tall, blond woman with a shapely figure and the walk of a fox strutted across the middle of the street and waited on the divider for the cars to pass before crossing. After stepping on her brakes, Silvana tapped her horn as if to warn her of the dangers of jaywalking. The woman snickered defiantly. Her long blond hair swung freely in the breeze. Staring directly into her sea-blue eyes I found myself immersed in her youthful sparkle. She turned her hips sideways as if modeling her body in the middle of the street. My eyes dropped to her freely swinging breasts.

For the first time that I could remember I found myself attracted to a younger woman. She was fresh and young, as sensitive as a fawn resting in a glen and unlike most older women, there was no midriff bulge or hanging tummy. Her lean body leaped across the divider and landed gracefully on the sidewalk. I noticed three attractive young women standing by the movie arcade. One of the girls curled a fresh issue of *Rolling Stone Magazine* in her hand and pressed it rhythmically between her legs. There would be no more frustrations for me as I searched in vain for a willing older woman. There were scores of young women filling the streets, all waiting for me to come over from my hung-up state of pinching geriatric ass. There were tons of understanding hookers and even nice Jewish girls who were looking for boyfriends, who enjoyed straight, conventional sex and were ready to ensnare my fiendish ears between their boiling breasts without accepting a dime for their favors. And here I was, behaving like a *schlemiel* all along, advertising for an older lover for sixteen dollars a week in the *New York Review of Books* and getting nothing but a livid, incontinent eighty-year-old who required intermittent catheterization after every act of intercourse. Now I was blessed with a new desire, a brand new outlook on women. Unlike the predator, who stalks new terrain when his tastiest game isn't in plentiful supply, I stayed put on my turf and opened my eyes to a new school of fish which had flickered their fins before my oblivious eyes every day.

Dr. Foster turned down the street past the college gate leading to the gym and the library. The dark bricks of the Demarest Student Center were ugly and familiar. Her moody silence suggested that she had chosen to forget about our brief affair and was simply giving me a ride home as a courtesy to her patient.

"Jeremy, now as difficult as this may be for you to accept, we must go our separate ways."

"Does that mean I won't be able to see you in the clinic?"

"I'm afraid that in the event you have an urgent need for medical care that I will have to refer you to either Dr. Craighill or Dr. Blackwell. I cannot accept you as my patient anymore. I hope you understand that I'm doing this entirely for professional reasons."

"But, Dr. Foster. I didn't think that you went for that one-night-stand shit. I didn't think you were the type who liked to kiss and run."

"Well, if that's the way you look at it, then screw you."

"I thought that you were a caring, compassionate physician. I guess I was mistaken."

"Why don't you just go up to your room, Jeremy, and jerk off. It's time to get back into the same routine. You'll never have the chance to touch me again. I won't allow it. None of this actually happened," she said in a tone with such conviction that I almost believed her. "It's only your hallucination." Remembering my lesson in the yeshiva, "Never Look Back," I walked away heartbroken, but heard her call after me, "Jeremy, go to medical school and I'll hire you to work at Hastings. See you in six years."

Epilogue

The following semester, Dr. Foster received a letter from the Dean of Kirk College informing her that one of their prize students, Jeremy Lipschitz, had died in a car accident. After stealing a few sheets of the Dean's stationery, I had accurately forged his signature and delivered it through campus mail. The following day I sent a messenger to Hastings to spy on Dr. Foster and witness her reaction to my death.

She was mildly shaken by the loss of a patient whom she had known well, but kept her composure, which was predictably consistent with her medical training. Other patients walked through her office every half-hour; I would soon be forgotten.

Someday I'll walk into Hastings and surprise her. I anticipate a joyous mother and child reunion. I'm sure she will kiss me in front of all the nurses, in spite of her resolution to avoid seeing me as her patient. I only have a faint sexy scar on my back; it was certainly worth the goof.

Glossary of Yiddish and Medical Terminology

Amniotic: Relating to the membrane around the fetus.

Analgesic: A compound capable of relieving pain without producing anesthesia or loss of consciousness.

Angiogram: X-ray obtained after the injection of a radiopaque material.

Anoxia: Absence of oxygen inspired gases, arterial blood, or tissues.

Areolae: Circular pigmented area surrounding the nipple.

Asthenic: Weak or having a slight build or slender body structure.

Auricular vein: Vein carrying blood from the ear.

Auscultate: To examine by listening, either directly or through a stethoscope or other instrument, to sounds within the body.

Autogenic: Self-generating.

Autonomic nervous system: The system of nerves and ganglia that innervates the blood vessels, heart, smooth muscles, viscera, and glands and controls their voluntary functions.

Bar Kochva: A famous Jewish fighter and leader who held off the Roman siege in 132 C.E.

Bocher: A young unmarried man.

Brumpskiss: A wet kiss applied to the abdomen with a forced exhalation. Makes a loud noise.

Borsht belt: A term used by entertainers. Applies to hotels in the Catskill Mountains in New York, with an almost entirely Jewish clientelle who are fond of borsht (beet and potato soup).

Bubeleh: Endearing term for someone you like, young or old.

Candida albicans: Thrush fungus; a species which is ordinarily a part of man's normal gastrointestinal flora, but which becomes pathogenic when there is a disturbance in the balance of flora.

Carcinoembryogenic: The origin or production of cancer.

Carminative: An agent that relieves flatulence.

Catatonia: A syndrome characterized by periods of physical rigidity, and stupor.

Cephalic vein: Vein carrying blood from the head.

Ceruminous: Relating to earwax.

Chai: Life; the numerological equivalent to eighteen.

Challeh: A braided loaf of white bread, glazed with egg white, very soft, delicate in flavor and eaten on the Sabbath.

Chazar: Pig. A glutton.

Choreiform: Resembling the irregular, spasmodic, involuntary movements made by those with diseases such as Huntington's chorea.

Chumesh: The five books of Moses.

Clavical: Collar bone.

Cocci: Bacterial form.

Coccygeal: Relating to the small triangular bone forming the lower extremity of the spinal column.

Cochlea: A cone-shaped cavity forming one of the divisions of the inner ear.

Cogentin: A drug used to counteract the spasmodic side effects induced by some major tranquilizers.

Chazzen: A cantor—i.e., the trained professional singer who assists the rabbi in religious services.

Colon-climber: Ass-kisser.

Conjunctiva: the mucous membranes covering the anterior surface of the eyeballs and lining the lids.

Contraindication: Any special symptom or circumstance that renders the use of a remedy or carrying out of a procedure inadvisable.

Cyanotic: Marked by a dark bluish or purplish coloration of the skin and mucous membrane due to deficient oxygenation of the blood.

Dalmane: A sleeping pill belonging to the family of benzodiazepines, or minor tranquilizers.

Demerol: A potent pain killer.

Dillberry: A clump of pubic hair and remnants of fecal matter at the entrance to the rectum.

Dopamine blockade: The hypothesized action of drugs used to treat schizophrenia. The drugs are thought to blockade neural receptors so that the neurotransmitter dopamine cannot reach the sites to which it normally binds.

Dybbuk: A demon who takes possession of someone and renders the mortal mad, irrational, vicious, sinful, corrupt.

Dystonic: Pertaining to a state of abnormal tonicity in any of the tissues.

E.E.G.: Electroencephalogram. A record of electric potentials of the brain derived from electrodes attached to the scalp.

Endorphin: One of a family of opioid-like polypeptides.

Epididymis: An elongated structure connected to the posterior surface of the testis.

Excrescence: Any outgrowth from the surface.

Fascia: A sheet of fibrous tissue that envelops the body beneath the skin; it also encloses muscles and groups of muscles, and separates their several layers or groups.

Fibrin: An elastic filamentous protein.

Flagellate: Possessing one or more whiplike locomotory organelles, indicative of spermatazoa.

Free radical: A highly reactive molecule carrying an unpaired electron and no charge.

Fundus: The bottom or lowest part of a sac or hollow organ; that part farthest removed from the opening or exit.

Gallop: A triple cadence to the heart sounds at rates of 100 beats per minute or more; usually indicative of a serious disease.

Gastric lavage: The washing out of the stomach by copious injections and rejections of fluid.

Genome: The total gene complement of an organism.

Gingival: Relating to the gums.

Glat kosher: Completely kosher. See Kosher.

Gluconeongenic: Related to the formation of glycogen, a carbohydrate storage molecule, from noncarbohydrates such as protein or fat, by conversion of the latter to glucose, a sugar.

Goyische: Pertaining to non-Jewish people. Used semidisparagingly in describing traits which are untypical of Jews and characteristic of mentally-deficient individuals.

Grave's disease: Toxic goiter characterized by diffuse hypertrophy of the thyroid gland; a form of hyperthyroidism.

Hashem: One of the words used in referring to the Jewish God.

Hemisphere: One of the functionally different halves of the cerebrum, a section of the brain controlling higher brain processes.

Hepatic: Relating to the liver.

Hippocampus: A brain structure forming part of the liver.

Hora: A Jewish dance of celebration.

Huntington's Chorea: A chronic hereditary disorder characterized by uncontrolled movements of the face and extremities, accompanied by a gradual loss of the mental faculties ending in dementia.

Hymeneal: Relating to the hymen (the membranous fold which occludes the external orifice of the vagina—the vaginal membrane).

Hyperadrenergic: Overly activated by adrenaline.

Hyperthyroidism: An abnormality of the thyroid gland in which thyroid secretion is usually increased and no longer under regulatory control of hypothalamic-pituitary centers.

Hypoglycemic: Pertaining to hypoglycemia, a condition in which there is an abnormally small concentration of glucose in the circulating blood.

Hypothalamus: A structure of the brain prominently involved in the functions of the autonomic nervous system and in endocrine mechanisms; it also appears to play a role in the nervous mechanisms underlying moods and motivational states.

Iatrogenic: Denoting an unfavorable response to therapy. In extreme cases, disease caused by a physician.

Icosahedral: Having twenty equal triangular surfaces (e.g. most viruses with cubic symmetry).

Inguinal: Relating to the groin.

Jendrassik's maneuver: A method of emphasizing the patellar reflex: the subject hooks his hands together by the flexed fingers and pulls against them with all his strength.

Inner labyrinth: The internal or inner ear, composed of the semicircular ducts, vestibule, and cochlea.

Internuncial: Acting as a medium of communication between two organs.

Kabbalah: The complex and esoteric body of Jewish mystical tradition, literature and thought.

Kashrut: Kosher-ness. Pertaining to Jewish dietary restrictions.

Kiddush: The prayer and ceremony that sanctifies the Sabbath and Jewish holy days.

Kinesthesia: The sense perception of movement. An illusion of moving in space.

Kipah: A yarmulke, or head-covering worn by observant Jewish males.

Kishke: The intestines: sweetbreads, often added to soups.

Kol Nidre: The holiest service in the Jewish calendar, falling on Yom Kippur, the Day of Atonement.

Kopf: Head.

Kugel: Pudding of noodles or potatoes.

Kvetch: To complain, fret, gripe. Also, one who does.

K-Y Jelly: A vaginal and rectal lubricant.

Lactiferous ducts: The milk-yielding ducts of the breasts.

Latkes: Potato pancakes, usually seasoned with chopped onions and spices.

L'Chayim: To Life!

Leukocyte: White blood cell.

Laryngeal: Relating in any way to the larynx, the organ of voice.

Lumbrosacral: Relating to the sacrum (tail-bone) and the lumbar vertebrae above.

Maccabean: Courageous Jewish fighters who held off the Syrians in 160-140 B.C.

Major tranquilizer: Antipsychotic agent usually prescribed to schizophrenics.

Masada: The site near the Dead Sea, where Jewish warriors immolated themselves rather than surrender to the Romans.

Mellaril: A major tranquilizer belonging to the family of phenothiazines, used for psychotic people.

Meningeal: Relating to the meninges, the membranous coverings of the brain and spinal cord.

Mensch: A human being; an upright, honorable, decent person; someone of consequence. The term "mensch" also reflects a social ideal of traditional culture, representing decency, generosity, kindness and above all else—integrity.

Methaqualone: A sedative and hypnotic, also a drug of abuse.

Midrash: The very highly developed analysis, exposition, and exegesis of the Holy Scriptures.

Minyan: Quorum, specifically the ten male Jews required for religious services.

Mikvah: The bath, prescribed by ritual, which a Jewish bride took before her wedding, and which religious Jewish women took (a) at the end of their menstrual period, (b) after bearing a child.

Mitzvah: A meritorious act, one that expresses God's will.

Mogen David: Star of David. A symbol of Jewish identity.

Mohel: The man who circumcises the male baby.

Molecular sieve: A gel-like material with pore sizes of such ranges as to exclude molecules above certain sizes.

Motzie: The blessing over bread.

Myocardial Infarction: A violent heart attack.

Nebish: An innocuous, ineffectual, weak, hapless unfortunate.

Neoembryogenic: Neologism for rebirthing. (Embryogenic: relating to the formation of an embryo.)

Oculogyric: Referring to rotation of the eyeballs.

Oma: Grandmother.

Oophorectomy: Removal of the ovaries.

Opa: Grandfather.

Ordeal Bean of Calabar: The dried deed of a vine of western Africa This ceremonial drug induces hallucinations. In toxic doses it causes vomiting, colic, salivation, sweating, dyspnea, vertigo, slow pulse and extreme prostration.

Orthomolecular: Designating the normal chemical constituents of the body. Physicians practicing orthomolecular medicine routinely use vitamins and other natural therapies.

Oy vay is mir: Oh, what a misfortune for me!

Pach: A spanking.

Papilla Mammae: Anatomical name for nipple.

Paroxysmal Priapism: A spasmodic and persistent erection of the penis.

Patellar reflex: The knee-jerk response.

Payess: The long, unshorn ear-ringlet hair and sideburn-locks worn by very Orthodox Jewish men.

Percussion: A diagnostic procedure designed to determine the density of a part by means of tapping the surface with a finger or specialized hammer.

Peripheral nervous system: The nerves and ganglia, as opposed to the central nervous system, which consists of the brain and spinal cord.

Peristalsis: The movement of the intestine to dispel its contents.

Pharmacognosy: A branch of pharmacology concerned with the physical characteristics and botanical sources of crude drugs.

Phenothiazines: A class of antipsychotic drugs.

Pheremones: Substance secreted to the outside by an individual and perceived by a second individual of the same species thereby producing a change in the sexual or social behavior of that individual. Usually attributed to insects.

Plantar: Relating to the sole of the foot.

Popess: The anus.

Procrustean sin: A tendency among second year medical students to feel that they are afflicted with every disease they read about in their textbook of pathology.

Prothrombin: A substance involved in the coagulation of blood.

Prostaglandins: A class of physiologically active substances with a wide variety of effects which were first found in genital fluids and accessory glands.

Pseudoparkinsonian tremors: Tremors resembling those of Parkinsons's disease.

Putz: An inept nincompoop. Also, penis.

Quadriceps: Denoting a muscle of the thigh and one of the calf.

Rachmones: Pity, compassion.

Rebbitsin: A rabbi's wife.

Retinal fundus (fundus oculi): The portion of the interior of the eyeball around the posterior pole, visible through an ophthalmoscope.

Sacculated: Pouched; sac-shaped.

Sacrovertebral articulation: The joining of the sacrum to the vertebrae above.

Scanning microscope: A microscope in which the object being viewed is examined by point directly by an electron beam and the image is formed on a television screen. The surface image has a three-dimensional quality.

Scapula: The shoulder blade.

Schlemiel: A simpleton; an unlucky or unfortunate person; a clumsy type; social misfit; a pipsqueak; a naive, trusting, gullible customer.

Schmaltz: Grease or fat. To sweet talk with excessive praise.

Schwartzes: Negroes.

Sciatic nerve: The nerve running from the hip region through the thigh.

Sclera: The white of the eye.

Scoliosis: Lateral curvature of the spine.

Sedative-hypnotic: A minor tranquilizer intended to induce sleep.

Shabbes: Sabbath.

Schnor (Schnorren): To beg, grub, panhandle or borrow.

Shnuppel: Neologism from German "schnuppern"—to sniff and lick simultaneously as in a hungry, curious animal.

Shuckle: To bow up and down in the midst of prayer.

Shul: Synagogue.

Shikse: A non-Jewish woman.

Schnipse: An endearing pinch to the leg.

Shomer Shabbas: One who observes the laws and customs of the Sabbath.

Spermatozoa: The generative element of semen which serves to impregnate the ovum.

Sphincter: The muscle fibers closing an opening, e.g. the anus.

Spinal ganglia: Aggregations of nerve cell bodies along the spinal cord.

Spinocortical tract: Pertaining to the cortex of the brain and the spinal cord.

Sternum: The breast bone.

Stellazine: A major tranquilizer belonging to the family of phenothizines. It often produces unpleasant side-effects.

Striated: A muscle marked by bands or stripes.

Subdural hematoma: A localized mass of blood, resulting from a hemorrhage, beneath the outer membrane enveloping the brain.

Synapse: The junction between two nerve cells across the electrochemical impulses pass.

Synergy: Coordinated or correlated action by two or more structures or drugs.

Synesthesia: A condition in which a stimulus, in addition to exciting the usual and normally located sensation, gives rise to a subjective sensation of different character or localization.

Systole: The contraction of the heart.

Tardive dyskinesia: A syndrome marked by involuntary movement of the lips and jaw. A side effect of certain anti-psychotic drugs.

Testicular feminization syndrome: A type of male pseudohermaphroditism characterized when complete by female genitalia.

Thorazine: An antipsychotic medication.

Thyroid cartilage: The largest of the cartilages of the larynx, it forms the Adam's apple.

Toches: Rectum.

Toches ahfen tish: (Literally, buttocks on the table.) Put up or shut up. Let's conclude this.

Torticollis: A contraction, often spasmodic, of the muscles of the neck; the head is drawn to one side and usually rotated so that the chin points to the other side.

Transplacental: Crossing the placenta.

Tumescent: Turgid; swollen.

Tzitzis: Fringes attached to the four corners of a prayer shawl.

Tzores: Troubles, misery.

Ulnar nerve: A nerve of the arm which supplies the forearm and hand.

Urethra: The canal leading from the bladder which discharges the urine.

Urodynamics: The study of the storage of urine within and the flow of urine through and from the urinary tract.

Urogenital: Relating to the organs of reproduction and urination.

Vas deferens: The secretory duct of the testicle.

Vescicle: A small sac containing liquid or gas.

Yarmulke: Traditional Jewish skullcap worn at all times by observant Orthodox Jews to indicate that God is above them.

Yekische: Pertaining to subservient German Jews.

Yenta: A talkative woman; female blabbermouth.

Yeshiva: A rabbinical college or secondary; a secondary Hebrew school.

Yid: A Jew.

Yiddeschemamma: A real Jewish mother.

Yiddlach: Jews refer to themselves as a group as Yiddlach.

Yom Kippur: The last of the annual Ten Days of Penitence; one of the two high holy days of the Jewish calendar.

Zion: Penis (slang).